Clinical Audit in Radiology

100+ RECIPES

Editors

Ray Godwin, MA, FRCP, FRCR
Consultant Radiologist, West Suffolk Hospital, Bury St Edmunds

Gerald de Lacey, MA, FRCR
Consultant Radiologist, Northwick Park and St Mark's Hospitals, Harrow

Adrian Manhire, MRCP, FRCR
Consultant Radiologist, City Hospital, Nottingham

EX RADIIS SALUTAS

Published by The Royal College of Radiologists

Clinical Audit in Radiology: 100+ Recipes

Editors: R Godwin FRCR, G de Lacey FRCR, A Manhire FRCR
Published by: The Royal College of Radiologists
38 Portland Place
London W1N 4JQ
United Kingdom
Fax: (+44(0)171) 323 3100

Publication of this book has been supported by a grant from the Clinical Audit Unit of the Executive of the National Health Service for England.

ISBN 1 872599 19 2

Associate editor: Claire Gilman of Grok Ltd, 30 Christ Church Road, East Sheen, London SW14 7AA.

Designed and printed in Great Britain by Intertype, 307 Aberdeen House, 22 Highbury Grove, London N5 2EA.

Line drawings (recipes 7 and 37) by Dr Laurence Berman of the Department of Clinical Radiology, Cambridge University and Addenbrooke's Hospital, using MacDraw Pro on Apple Macintosh.

How to order: *Clinical Audit in Radiology: 100+ Recipes* is available direct from the College at £25.00 post paid (surface mail). All orders must be prepaid and should be addressed to the Publications Secretary.

Contents

Foreword   *vii*

Acknowledgements   *ix*

Introduction   *xi*

Glossary of terms used in Clinical Audit   *xv*

Abbreviations used in this book   *xxi*

How to use this book – and other information   *xxiii*

Recipes

1	Accepting Recommendations for Change	*2*
2	Adequate Completion of Radiology Request Forms	*4*
3	Air Quality in the Process Area	*6*
4	Attendance at Audit Meetings	*8*
5	Barium Enema Fluoroscopy Times and Doses	*10*
6	Barium Meal Reports	*12*
7	Barium Meal Training	*14*
8	Bladder Cancer CT	*16*
9	Bone Scintigraphy Images	*18*
10	Cancer Staging	*20*
11	Cardiac Catheterisation	*22*
12	Chest Radiographs: Skin Dose and Film Quality	*24*
13	Clinical Information from A&E	*26*
14	Consent for a Radiological Examination	*28*
15	Contrast and Drug Recording	*30*
16	Coronary Angiography	*32*
17	Courtesy	*34*
18	CT Guided Biopsies	*36*
19	CT – Ward Staff Knowledge	*38*
20	Dark Room Safety	*40*
21	Department Opening Hours	*42*
22	Do the Reports Address the Questions?	*44*
23	Doppler in DVT	*46*
24	Double Reading of Mammograms	*48*
25	Emergency Skull Radiography	*50*
26	Employee Satisfaction	*52*
27	Fetal Abdominal Circumference Measurements	*54*
28	Fetal Anomaly Scan	*56*
29	Film Envelope Availability	*58*
30	Finger Doses	*60*
31	Fire Training	*62*
32	Foreign Body Radiography	*64*
33	Gall Bladder Ultrasound	*66*
34	Gonad Protection I	*68*
35	Gonad Protection II	*70*
36	GP Abdominal Ultrasound	*72*
37	GP Chest Radiography	*74*
38	Head CT – Lens Exclusion	*76*
39	Iliac Angioplasty Outcome	*78*

CONTENTS

Recipes (continued)

40   Image Labelling and Identification   *80*

41   In-Patient Information Letters   *82*

42   In-Patient Reporting I   *84*

43   In-Patient Reporting II   *86*

44   Insertion of Oesophageal Stents   *88*

45   Interventional Radiology – Care of the Patient   *90*

46   Interventional Radiology Packs   *92*

47   Investigation of Prostatism   *94*

48   ITU and CCU Chest Radiographs   *96*

49   IVC Filter Outcome   *98*

50   IVU Examination Times   *100*

51   IVU Radiograph Series   *102*

52   Journal Use   *104*

53   Leg Venograms and Patient Management   *106*

54   Low Osmolar Contrast Media   *108*

55   Lumbar Spine   *110*

56   Lumbar Spine Radiation Dose   *112*

57   Lung Scan Reports   *114*

58   Lung Scintigraphy   *116*

59   Majax Call-In   *118*

60   Mammography   *120*

61   Missing Films   *122*

62   MRI Patients and Metal   *124*

63   Neural Tube Defect   *126*

64   Out-of-Hours Imaging   *128*

65   Painful Hip   *130*

66   Patient Arrival Times   *132*

67   Patient Privacy   *134*

68   Patient Satisfaction I   *136*

69   Patient Satisfaction II   *138*

70   Patient Satisfaction in the Over 60s   *140*

71   Patient's Charter   *142*

72   Pelvimetry   *144*

73   Percutaneous Biopsy Procedures   *146*

74   Pneumothoraces Post Lung Biopsy   *148*

75   Portering   *150*

76   Pregnancy Questioning   *152*

77   Pre-Op Chest X Rays for Elective Surgery   *154*

78   Private Hospital Examinations   *156*

79   Private Patient Satisfaction   *158*

80   Radiation Dose to Radiologists during CT Injections   *160*

81   Radiography in Acute Back Pain   *162*

82   Radiography Referral Rate from A&E   *164*

83   Radiological Errors   *166*

84   Radiologist Response Time   *168*

85   Radiologists' Availability   *170*

86   Radiology Reporting by Other Doctors   *172*

87   Radiology Workload   *174*

Recipes (continued)

88	RCR Guideline Distribution	*176*
89	Reject Analysis of Radiographs	*178*
90	Reporting Skills	*180*
91	Resuscitation Equipment	*182*
92	Resuscitation Skills	*184*
93	Return of ICU Radiographs	*186*
94	Second Trimester Screening	*188*
95	Security – Staff ID	*190*
96	Speaker's Technique	*192*
97	Staff Dosimetry	*194*
98	Staff Radiation Dose in Angiography	*196*
99	Study Leave for Consultants	*198*
100	Study Time for Trainees	*200*
101	Swimmer's Views	*202*
102	Teaching Course Assesssment	*204*
103	Trainee Assessment	*206*
104	Trainees and Audit	*208*
105	Trainees and Research	*210*
106	Transvaginal Ultrasound	*212*
107	Ultrasound Organisation	*214*
108	Ultrasound Scanning in Obstructive Jaundice	*216*
109	Urgent CT Brain Scans and LPs	*218*
110	Urography in Renal Colic	*220*
111	Ventilation and Perfusion Scintigraphy	*222*
112	Vetting Nuclear Medicine Requests	*224*
113	Waiting and Appointment Times	*226*
114	Ward Nurses and X Ray Procedures	*228*
115	Your Use of this Book	*230*

Appendix

Recipe 1	Departmental record	*234*
Recipe 7	The local protocol for barium meal examinations	*236*
Recipe 9	Checklist for assessing bone scan images	*237*
Recipe 17	Questionnaire	*238*
Recipe 19	CT Scanner Suite – hospital staff questionnaire	*240*
Recipe 21	Questionnaire	*243*
Recipe 25	Head injury discharge card A	*244*
Recipe 25	Head injury discharge card B	*245*
Recipe 26	Further information	*246*
Recipe 33	Further information	*248*
Recipe 37	Guidelines	*249*
Recipe 37	Example of appropriate (bespoke) request form	*250*
Recipe 45	Pre-procedure questionnaire	*251*
Recipe 48	A: Audit form for each patient	*253*
Recipe 48	B: Radiologist assessment form	*254*
Recipe 48	C: Independent radiographer's evaluation	*255*
Recipe 50	Protocol for radiographers/nurses injecting IVUs	*256*
Recipe 52	Design of the audit	*257*

Appendix (continued)

Recipe 52   Covers   *258*
Recipe 55   Elements of the standard   *259*
Recipe 57   Questionnaire   *260*
Recipe 57   Alternative phrases for lung scan reports   *261*
Recipe 62   Questionnaire   *262*
Recipe 65   Protocol   *263*
Recipe 67   Questionnaire   *264*
Recipe 68   Questionnaire   *266*
Recipe 69   Questionnaire   *268*
Recipe 70   Questionnaire   *270*
Recipe 77   Further information   *272*
Recipe 87   Notes and norms   *273*
Recipe 87   Table   *274*
Recipe 87   Notes on table   *275*
Recipe 87   Resources   *276*
Recipe 87   References   *277*
Recipe 90   Proforma   *279*
Recipe 92   Levels of competence   *280*
Recipe 96   Further information   *281*
Recipe 96   Evaluation sheet   *283*
Recipe 102   Questionnaire   *284*
Recipe 103   Information   *286*
Recipe 103   Questionnaire   *287*
Recipe 104   Questionnaire   *288*
Recipe 105   Questionnaire   *290*
Recipe 110   Protocol   *291*
Recipe 114   X ray procedures questionnaire   *292*

Standard recipe proforma to assist with the planning and construction of a new audit project   *296*

Proforma for recording the results of a completed audit project   *298*

Proforma for recording use of this book (on-going data collection for Recipe 115)   *302*

Index by topic   *306*

Index by authors and hospitals or address   *310*

Index by type of audit   *312*

Foreword

The Royal College of Radiologists has been active in promoting the development and use of medical and clinical audit for many years, recognising it as an essential and valuable part of routine medical practice. This innovative and practical publication represents a further initiative designed to carry these processes forward, specifically aiming to improve the understanding of the nuts and bolts of the audit process and to stimulate the design of manageable forward programmes in audit within departments of clinical radiology.

Audit should be multi-disciplinary, involving all staff groups and patients, as well as wide-ranging within both the national and private health care systems. The wide range of authors invited to contribute to this book illustrates and emphasises this well. The variety of subjects addressed indicates just how extensively the audit process can be applied when trying to improve services and the care delivered to patients.

The College is indebted to all the members of its Clinical Radiology Audit Sub-Committee and to the Working Group for developing this book, as well as to the many individual authors involved in its production.

Dr Iain Watt MRCP FRCR
Dean of the Faculty of Clinical Radiology
The Royal College of Radiologists

It gives me great pleasure to see this project come to fruition. The advent of formal medical audit in 1990 was a landmark in the development of our Health Services. The obligation placed on all doctors to participate in these exercises has started to change the culture in which we practice medicine.

In the event many radiologists have found that it is easier to audit the use made of radiological resources by referring doctors than it is to audit our own contribution to the radiological service.

This book will help radiologists to bridge that gap by describing in detail methods of undertaking such audit. The approach is original and effective. It complements the latest edition of the College Guidelines, published in 1995, and brings great credit to its authors.

The College is pleased to have been associated with the production of this excellent book and is grateful to all the authors and to the editors for their hard work.

Dr Michael J Brindle MD MRad PRCR
President
The Royal College of Radiologists

Acknowledgements

The Editors are greatly indebted to all those who have influenced their understanding of the role, the scope and the value of clinical audit in medical practice. The following have been particularly influential: Professor Colin Roberts, Department of Epidemiology, University of Wales College of Medicine, Cardiff; Dr Charles Shaw, Caspe Research, 76 Borough High Street, London SE1; and Dr John Mitchell, previously of the King's Fund College and now at Mitchell Damon, 212 Bedford Chambers, London WC2.

The non-editorial members of The Royal College of Radiologists Working Group, who were responsible for planning and steering this book through to publication, have made major contributions. The Editors are thankful to Dr Maureen Gowland of Bolton General Hospital, to Dr Julian Tawn of the Royal Bournemouth Hospital and Dr Alan Cook of Dundee Royal Infirmary who between them constructed the Glossary, and to Chris Squire who provided the indexes.

The members of the Faculty Board of Clinical Radiology (RCR) provided support and encouragement at all stages of production. Particular thanks are due to Professor Judy Adams of Manchester University who was until recently Dean (Clinical Radiology) of the Royal College of Radiologists and who helped to steer the project through some early hiccups and was at all times a reliable and important source of support.

A particular debt of gratitude is due to Claire Gilman of Grok Ltd. Claire was brought into the project to oversee the copy-editing but she extended her remit way beyond those duties. Before applying her professional skills in regard to organisation, design and layout, Claire made herself fully conversant with all the concepts of medical and clinical audit. As a consequence, and time and time again, she set the standard for clarity, accuracy and consistency as applied to each audit project.

The Editors are very grateful to Martyn Partridge of Intertype. His patience, hard work and especially his design skills have been invaluable.

Special thanks are also due to Dr Denis Remedios and to Dr Elspeth Elson of Northwick Park and St Mark's Hospitals for proof reading the final drafts, and to Shelley Brier and Kathy Howes of the same hospitals for their uncomplaining stoicism as they were repeatedly asked to give additional proof of their patience and word processing skills.

Financial assistance and support have been essential: publication of this book has been made possible by a grant from the Clinical Audit Unit of the Executive of the National Health Service for England.

Finally, and most importantly, the Editors are thankful to each individual author. Those who have contributed to the book come from disparate medical and non-medical backgrounds but each and every one exhibited an unconditional enthusiasm when agreeing to provide a recipe. All the authors subsequently met the various deadlines efficiently and uncomplainingly. Without them this book would not exist.

Introduction

In 1989 the British Government announced the arrival of medical audit for all those working in the National Health Service (Ref. 1). In future all doctors were to adopt medical audit into their routine clinical practice, thereby formalising for many what had been a long standing custom of informal clinical review. The change from informal custom to a formal requirement was made explicit within the definition of medical audit as the systematic, critical analysis of the quality of medical care including the procedures used for diagnosis and treatment, the use of resources and the resulting outcome and quality of life for the patient (Ref. 1). The announcement was underpinned by considerable financial support (Ref. 2) as well as other measures including the stipulation that audit was a duty to be taken into account when drawing up consultant job plans (Ref. 3).

In 1993 the limited compass implied by medical audit was properly widened by a change in terminology. Medical audit became obsolete and clinical audit was the new requirement. Clinical audit is defined as the audit activities of all health care professionals, including nurses and other staff as well as doctors (Ref. 4).

Education in Audit

Despite numerous educational initiatives (Refs 5–7) there is evidence that many doctors remain confused by the audit process (Refs 6–12) and this includes a number of clinical radiologists (Refs 13 and 14). In order to address this confusion the Clinical Radiology Audit Sub-Committee (CRASC) of the Royal College of Radiologists has compiled this collection of audit topics with three principal objectives in mind: to act primarily as an educational tool, to illustrate through a step by step format how to plan a project and follow it through to completion, and to demonstrate the diverse range of topics, areas and subjects which can be addressed. Several opportunities result from this collection: it provides a menu of topics which can be used by a department when planning the annual forward programme in clinical audit (Refs 15 and 16), it creates the opening for identical regional or national audits to be carried out by different centres, and it will assist individuals who wish to evaluate a particular area of local practice but are uncertain how best to set about it, to seek a suitable methodology from amongst these projects.

None of the recipes is fully comprehensive. The limitations of the two page format, even with the use of appendices, does not allow every detail of the audit cycle (see page xxiii) to be spelt out. For example, all recipes move swiftly from stage (2) of the cycle (assessment of local practice) to stage (3) (comparison of findings with the standard) to stage (4) (listing the changes which might be indicated) without mentioning data analysis which will need to occur between each of these stages. This requirement for data analysis needs to be assumed within all the recipes.

Auditing others

Two important elements which underpin audit in clinical medicine will appear to have been breached in several recipes. Firstly, it is a widely accepted point of principle that the practice to be audited should involve our own work and not the work of others. But it is impossible for clinical radiologists to adhere unfailingly to this principle when we provide guidelines to others as to whether or not to request imaging investigations (Refs 17 and 18). Plainly, there can be no inhibition in carrying out audits of the effectiveness of guidelines (e.g. Recipes 37, 77 and 81), but it is mandatory that planning is carried out with thoughtfulness and care so that those who use our services and whose activities are being assessed are willing to co-operate fully in the audit. Secondly, it is axiomatic that audit must not be a witch hunt; yet some recipes explicitly address individual performance (e.g. Recipes 5, 17 and 87). Again, thoughtfulness and care are required during the planning of these audits and this includes an appropriate and proper anonymisation of individuals. There is no reason why such audits when sensitively constructed should be construed as threatening let alone as a form of medical McCarthyism.

Confidentiality

Proper construction of an audit of the work of others – indeed of all audits – necessitates rigorous attention to confidentiality. The main objective behind the formal introduction of regular and systematic audit (Ref. 12) is to determine whether local practice is good practice and thus to utilise the audit process as a tool for improving clinical care. But if audit findings are to be valid and accurate then there must be full co-operation by all those whose work or clinical activity is being assessed. If there is any suggestion that identifiable personal data might become freely available within the public domain than it is inevitable that doctors and other clinical professionals will shy away from providing this co-operation. Though it is entirely proper – essential even – for the general results of audit to be available to those who have a legitimate interest in promoting or ensuring high clinical standards (e.g. patients, the Royal Colleges, managers, purchasers), it is the specific results of audit in relation to identifiable individuals which need to be protected by careful anonymisation and guarantees of confidentiality. Of course, the information relating to any one individual or department needs to be known to a responsible individual or group who can ensure that change does occur; but this intelligence must be very carefully protected.

How to use this book

All readers are strongly advised to read the section entitled *How to Use this Book* (pages xxiii–xxxi). The layout, headings and subheadings used in each Recipe need to be fully understood. It is also important that attention is paid to the definitions within the Glossary and this is particularly relevant in relation to the use of the terms Structure, Process and Outcome.

This book has been designed primarily as an educational aid. Will it succeed in this aim? What will constitute success? It is intended that those radiologists who are presently confused or uncertain about audit will use this book to develop their understanding of the audit process. After a while they will feel confident enough to embark upon audits of their own design. If such audits are planned carefully, carried out simply but systematically and provide accurate and valid data then the main objectives behind the construction of this book will have been achieved.

The role of The Royal College of Radiologists

Each Recipe provides a standard against which local practice will be measured and in many instances that standard will be accepted by most Fellows and members of the College. But these are not College Recipes. Even though this collection has been supplied by individuals who are in the main either members or Fellows there are many important contributions from radiographers and other staff within Departments of Clinical Radiology. The role of the College has been solely to act as a publisher of an educational aid. As a consequence the choice of projects and the standards selected should not be seen as those which the College is necessarily choosing to underwrite or to promulgate unless it is clearly identified as a College standard. Furthermore, it should be noted that each standard includes a target (see page xxiv) which local practice is expected to have met on completion of the audit. In practice, the precise target that will be set will frequently differ between different departments carrying out exactly the same project because local circumstances vary. The target set in any one Recipe should not necessarily be regarded as the one which should be applied to all departments. Similarly, the changes in practice which are listed are simply some suggestions made by the authors; the College does not necessarily endorse their ranking nor does it regard them as being all inclusive. Each topic, each standard, each target, and each suggestion for change should be judged on its merits and the individual author be recognised as the advocate.

The Recipes

The commissioning of this volume of recipes was pragmatic. The Clinical Radiology Audit Sub-Committee (CRASC) of The Royal College of Radiologists asked a small working group to seek out and provide outlines for 100 audit projects and to design the layout of each Recipe so as to fit into a basic format similar to that which can be found in a standard and more orthodox cookery book. Each submission was edited by three members of the working group.

The Working Group

Dr Ray Godwin (Chairman), West Suffolk Hospital, Bury St Edmunds;
Dr Alan Cook, Dundee Royal Infirmary;
Dr Gerald de Lacey, Northwick Park and St Mark's Hospitals, Harrow;
Dr Maureen Gowland, Bolton General Hospital;
Dr Adrian Manhire, City Hospital, Nottingham;
Christopher Squire, MA, MSc, Clinical Audit Adviser, The Royal College of Radiologists;
Dr Julian Tawn, The Royal Bournemouth Hospital.

The Editors

Dr Ray Godwin
Dr Gerald de Lacey
Dr Adrian Manhire

References

1 Department of Health. Working for Patients. Working Paper 6, London: HMSO, 1989.

2 Department of Health. *Clinical Audit*. London: Department of Health, 1993.

3 Department of Health. *Terms and Conditions of Service of Hospital Medical and Dental Staff.* HC(90)16. London: DoH, 1990.

4 Calman KC. Quality: a view from the centre. *Quality in Health Care* 1992; 1 Supplement(s). (S)28–(S)33.

5 IK Crombie, HTO Davies, SCS Abraham, C du V Florey. *The Audit Handbook: Improving Health Care through Clinical Audit.* Chichester: Wiley, 1993.

6 Brunel University Health Economics Research Group. *Medical Audit: Taking Stock.* London: King's Fund Centre, 1993.

7 de Lacey G. What is Audit? Why should we be doing it? *Hospital Update* 1992;**18**:458–66.

8 Jacyna MR, de Lacey G, Chapman EJ. How does medical audit differ from research? How necessary are computers? *Hospital Update* 1992;**18**:592–6.

9 McKee M. Is money wasted on audit? *Journal of the Royal Society of Medicine* 1994;**87**:52–5.

10 Houghton G. Audit, peer review, and intellectual conformity. *Lancet* 1991;**338**:882–3.

11 Hancock C. Multidisciplinary clinical audit. *Nursing Standard* 1991;**338**:822-3.

12 de Lacey G. Clinical Audit: Don't Look a Gift Horse in the Mouth. *Clin Rad* 1995;**50**:815–17.

13 Lawrence M. Medicine and Books. *BMJ* 1995;**310**:812.

14 Hopkins A, ed. *Professional and Managerial Aspects of Clinical Audit.* London: Royal College of Physicians, 1994.

15 Godwin R. Nothing Succeeds Like Success – Some do's and dont's in Clinical Audit. *Clin Rad* 1995;**50**:818–20.

16 de Lacey G., Jacyna M., Chapman J. Setting up hospital audit – one model. *Hospital Update* 1992;**18**:670–676.

17 The Royal College of Radiologists. *Making the best use of a Department of Clinical Radiology. Guidelines for Doctors.* Third Edition. London: RCR, 1995.

18 McNally E., de Lacey G., Lovell P., Welch T. Posters for accident departments: simple method of sustaining reduction in x-ray examinations. *BMJ* 1995;**310**:640–42.

Glossary of Audit Terms

ALGORITHM

A fixed process containing a number of steps, which, when followed systematically, should produce a desired result (Ref. 1).

An algorithm is often illustrated as a flow chart, e.g. illustrating the steps which should be taken when investigating a patient who presents with a particular set of symptoms.

AUDIT

The systematic, critical analysis of the quality of medical or clinical care, including the procedures used for diagnosis and treatment, the use of resources, and the resulting outcome and quality of life for the patient (Ref. 2).

Medical Audit – looks at the work of doctors.

Clinical Audit – looks at the work of all health care professionals, which can include doctors (Ref. 3).

To review topics for audit it is useful to arrange them into categories. In 1966 Alevis Donabedian suggested that there are three types of question which can be asked about the quality of an episode of health care: what facilities were available? what was done? and what was the result for the patient? (Ref. 4). His terms for these three questions, structure, process and patient health outcome (usually abbreviated to 'outcome'), are now in general use; unfortunately this does not mean that they are always used in a rigorous and consistent way by all those carrying out clinical audit. In this book the Editors have adopted the Donabedian approach, using the following definitions.

• **Structure:** the availability and organisation of resources (human and material) required for the delivery of a service: For example, Recipe 34, Gonad Protection I, measures the % of rooms with a complete set of gonad protection equipment and with purpose-specified gonad shields: it is therefore a structure audit.

• **Process:** the activity undertaken (what was done? how well was it done? what should have been done?). For example, Recipe 35, Gonad Protection II, measures the % of examinations which comply with the departmental protocol for gonad protection: it is therefore a process audit.

• **(Patient Health) Outcome:** the alteration in the health status of an individual patient, directly attributable to clinical action or (inaction). It is customarily abbreviated to "outcome" and this has caused considerable confusion as it blurs the distinction between patient-based measures and other measures of "results". In this book the Editors have adopted the usage recommended by the UK Clearing House for Information on the Assessment of Health Services Outcomes (Ref. 5): this is based on the World Health Organisation's wide ranging definition of "health" as a complete state of physical, mental and social wellbeing and classifies outcome measures under four heads:

1 quantity of life (e.g. 5 year survival);

2 process-based measures (e.g. complication and readmission rates);

3 quality of life (e.g. measures of pain, handicap, depression);

4 satisfaction, entitlement to privacy, courtesy, etc. (e.g. score on a satisfaction survey).

All these measures are patient-based, which is the essence of what is meant by an outcome; satisfaction is included because it is an aspect of mental wellbeing. The Editors are aware that this definition may seem unnecessarily tight to those who use the term "outcome" as a loose synonym of "result".

Some examples will show where the Editors have drawn the line between outcome and process: Recipe 18, CT Guided Biopsies, is not an outcome audit. It is a process audit; the indicator (% of CT guided biopsies which have a diagnostic yield) is a measure of the practice of biopsy operators not of the state of health of a patient. Recipe 108, Ultrasound Scanning of Obstructive Jaundice, is an outcome audit; the indicator (% of cases where the ultrasound diagnosis matches the final clinical diagnosis) is a process-based measure of patient outcome. This reflects the commonsense view that a patient with a correct diagnosis is in a better state than without it, whether or not they can be offered any effective treatment. Recipe 67, Patient Privacy, is also an outcome audit; the indicator (% of patients who feel that they have their need for privacy met) is a measure of their mental wellbeing.

Outcome audits look at what is done as a whole, from the patient's point of view; the problems that such an audit may reveal (e.g. there's a 25% chance that a diagnosis is not correct) may prompt audits of each link in the whole diagnostic chain: these would be process audits.

AUDIT ASSISTANT   One of several possible titles used to describe a member of staff employed to provide support for audit activities. Responsibilities include advising on methodology, collection and analysis of data, the preparation of results for presentation at audit meetings, as well as the provision of technical and computer assistance. Other titles include Audit Officer, Audit Facilitator and Audit Co-ordinator.

AUDIT CYCLE   The audit cycle (or loop) has been identified as the basic framework upon which all audit projects are based (Fig. 1). The topic for audit is chosen, and the standard to be met is defined. Data is collected to identify what is really happening, and this is compared with the standard. If the required standard is not achieved, changes are introduced to improve performance. The cycle is then repeated to assess whether these changes have led to the standard's now being met.

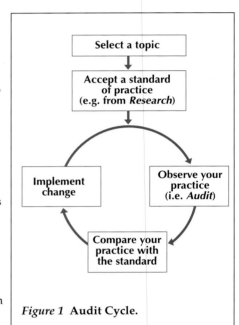

Figure 1 Audit Cycle.

AUDIT LEAD   Royal College of Radiologists' term used to describe the Radiologist co-ordinating audit within a Radiology Department.

AUDIT SPIRAL   This is a graphic illustration which is preferred to the Audit Cycle (Fig. 1), and emphasises that the audit process is a spiral of repeating cycles (see *How to Use this Book*, page xxiii).

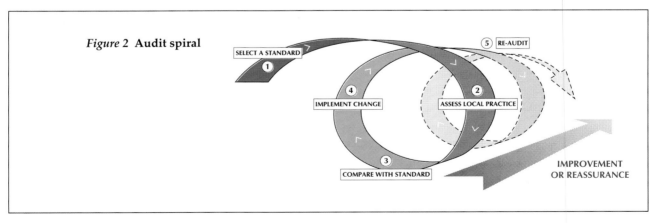

Figure 2 Audit spiral

BLITZ AUDIT   A simple audit carried out, usually without warning, to examine a single aspect of practice. Often this is an audit of structure or one aspect of process. It should be possible to complete the first stages of such an audit in a very short time. For example: a department can be checked for the quantity, placement and suitability of items of resuscitation equipment.

CLINICAL AUDIT   See **Audit**.

CLINICAL GUIDELINES (see also GUIDELINES)	Statements of principle which have been developed in order to assist practitioner and patient decisions about appropriate health care in specific clinical circumstances (Ref. 6). Guidelines are concepts of good practice against which the needs of the individual must also be considered. Guidelines are not rigid constraints upon clinical practice (Ref. 7). They are usually produced and agreed by a national body, for example, *Making the best use of a Department of Clinical Radiology: Guidelines for Doctors*, Royal College of Radiologists, 1995 (see **Royal College of Radiologists Guidelines**).
	Local Guidelines – Guidelines can be developed and introduced locally. They are usually adaptations of national guidelines, and are designed to meet local conditions and constraints. The process of developing a local guideline involves the consensus of all the relevant clinicians; this is essential if the guideline is to be implemented effectively. (See **Protocol**).
CLOSING THE LOOP	This is the completion of the full audit cycle. Practice is changed following the initial audit and the audit process is repeated to ensure that the changes introduced have been effective. (See **Audit Cycle**).
CRITERIA	Plural of Criterion, see below.
CRITERION (also known as REVIEW CRITERION)	A single variable which is selected to allow an element of care to be measured. A criterion may be qualitative or quantitative. It should be possible to define it, measure it and determine whether it is present or not (Ref. 8). For example: the drugs used for treating an IV contrast medium reaction should be available in all rooms where IV contrast medium is given. The Criterion being measured is the presence of these drugs. (See **Indicator** in *How to Use this Book*, page xxv).
CRITICAL INCIDENT AUDIT	This is an audit arising from a particular problem or error. For example: a carcinoma is found on colonoscopy, but it had been overlooked on a recent barium enema. This critical incident might lead to an audit of all barium enemas performed around that time.
DATA	Items of information, collected as a series of observations or measurements, and organised for analysis. The process of collection should aim to ensure that the data are complete, representative, relevant and valid. For audit studies, data may be collected prospectively over an agreed period of time, or for a predetermined number of cases, or retrospectively from existing information sources. Prospective collection can ensure that all the required information is obtained, but the process of collection may influence the behaviour of participants. Retrospective collection from existing records may often find those records to be incomplete.
EFFECTIVENESS	The extent to which application of an efficacious technology or intervention brings about the desired effects, e.g. change in diagnosis, altered management plans, improvement in health. It is a measure of the degree of conformity between the actual result and the desired outcome (Ref. 9). NB This term is not synonymous with efficacy. See the example under **Efficacy**, below.
EFFICACY	The technical relationship between a technology or intervention and its effects, i.e. whether it actually works (Ref. 9). NB This term is not synonymous with effectiveness. In the context of Radiology, an intervention is usually a diagnostic procedure. For example: a barium enema can be expected to identify colonic carcinomas when the whole colon has been outlined in double contrast, i.e. it is efficacious. However, in patients with a very tortuous colon some tumours may be missed as optimal visualisation cannot be achieved, i.e. this efficacious technology is not always effective under sub-optimal conditions (Ref. 10).
EFFICIENCY	The quality of being efficient. Assessment of efficiency is concerned with determining whether acceptable levels of efficacy and effectiveness are achieved when using the most prudent or optimal mix of resources. For example: in a barium enema, when all the colon has been adequately shown in double contrast, further radiographs will yield no additional diagnostic information, but will increase the cost of the procedure and thus decrease its efficiency.

ELEMENTS OF CARE	The basic items which together describe all the significant aspects of an episode of care. For example: adequate bowel preparation and a foam mattress on the fluoroscopy table are two elements of care during a barium enema examination.
EVALUATION	The systematic and scientific process of determining the extent to which a planned intervention or programme of interventions achieves the predetermined objectives. For example: in the barium enema audit, barium enemas are the planned interventions, demonstrating colonic carcinomas is the objective, and determining the percentage of proven lesions which have been demonstrated and reported is the evaluation (Ref. 10).
GUIDELINES (See also CLINICAL GUIDELINES)	A guideline is not a rigid constraint on practice, but is a concept of good practice against which the needs of the individual can be considered (Ref. 11).
INDICATOR	A quantitative criterion. It should be a measurable element of care amenable to change. An indicator, or series of indicators, should be identified within an audit project to clarify and simplify the process of data collection. See the example under Criterion, above. See also *How to Use this Book*, page xxv.
LOOP	See **Audit Cycle** and **Closing the Loop**.
MEDICAL AUDIT	See **Audit**.
NRPB	The National Radiological Protection Board was created by the Radiological Protection Act in 1970. Its functions are to give advice, conduct research and provide technical services in the field of radiation protection. A document on patient dose reduction was produced in association with the Royal College of Radiologists in 1990 to investigate the potential for reducing radiation dose to patients, without adversely affecting patient care (Ref. 12).
OUTCOME	See **Audit**.
PEER REVIEW	Refers to a process in which a group of doctors or other health care professionals discuss together patients they have managed, and give a judgement, by consensus, as to whether or not the management of each individual patient was appropriate. Discussion must be full, frank, open and honest (Ref. 13).
PERFORMANCE	The quality of care achieved, judged by both the process and outcome of that care.
PROCESS	See **Audit**.
PROTOCOL	(1) A system of rules about the correct way to act in formal situations (Ref 14). (2) An adaptation of a clinical guideline designed to meet local conditions and constraints (Scotland). This is the same as a local guideline. (See **Clinical Guidelines**).
QUALITY	The level of excellence. Many attempts have been made to define the quality of medical and health care (Ref. 15). In general, six aspects are usually emphasised (Ref. 16): access to services; relevance to need; effectiveness; equity; social acceptability; efficiency / economy.
QUALITY ASSURANCE	The managed process whereby the comparison of care against predetermined standards is guaranteed to lead to action to implement changes, and ensuring that these have produced the desired improvements (Ref. 17). For example: a Quality Assurance programme for double contrast barium enemas would include such parameters as radiographs obtained, image quality, adequacy of bowel preparation and radiation dose to the skin.
RANDOM CASE ANALYSIS	The detailed review of the care of a particular patient, who has been chosen at random from a list of cases. If any problems are identified, then this can be the starting point for a more detailed audit project. For example: an individual patient's radiological care may be followed from the time of receipt of the request card to the provision of the final report. This analysis may identify problem areas which warrant further investigation.

RESEARCH

A systematic investigation to establish facts or principles, and collect valid information on a subject. Research explores new ideas with the aim of defining and setting the standards of care for best clinical practice (Ref. 18).

This can be contrasted with audit, which aims to establish whether the actual care given to patients meets set standards.

Research identifies what can and should be done, whilst audit identifies whether it is actually being done.

For example, a study to determine whether endoscopic stent insertion or open surgical by-pass provides the better palliation for malignant biliary obstruction, is research. However, a study to determine whether the palliation of malignant biliary obstruction at a given hospital is carried out in accordance with the Association of Hepato-biliary Surgeons' guidelines, is audit (Ref. 19). See also *How to Use this Book*, page xxv.

RISK MANAGEMENT

Programmes or activities developed in order to anticipate and thus prevent injury or misadventure to patients, staff and the public, and thereby minimise the effects of such episodes should they occur (Ref. 20). For example: Radiologist staffing levels should be adequate so as to allow the prompt reporting and performance of radiological examinations.

ROYAL COLLEGE OF RADIOLOGISTS GUIDELINES

The booklet, *Making the best use of a Department of Clinical Radiology: Guidelines for Doctors*, is now in its third edition (Ref. 11). Its primary objective is to improve clinical practice, and it works best when used with a clinico-radiological dialogue, and when subjected to regular audit.

The guidelines carry substantial multi-disciplinary approval and have been endorsed by the Executive of the NHS for England (Ref. 21).

SAMPLE

A subgroup of a population selected for audit in such a way as to allow inferences to be made about the whole population, i.e. a representative subgroup. The method of choosing the sample is crucial to the validity of the audit. See: How to Use this Book, page xxv.

STANDARD

A conceptual model against which the quality or excellence of a particular activity may be assessed. It is the specification of process and/or outcome against which performance can be measured. In the context of health care, a standard indicates the best practice of clinical care to which all patients should be entitled (Ref. 22). This may be determined by research, consensus statements, local agreement or recommendations from learned societies.

For example, in an audit of barium enemas for colonic carcinoma, the standard may be that *100% of colonic carcinomas should be demonstrated on double contrast barium enema when present at the time of examination* (Ref. 10).

STRUCTURE

See **Audit**.

TARGET

Specification of the expected level of achievement which performance should meet or exceed. See: *How to Use this Book*, page xxiv and Ref. 22.

References

1   Sadler DJ, Parrish F, Coulthard A. Intravenous Contrast Media Reactions: How do Radiologists React? *Clin Radiol*, 1994;**49**:879–82.

2   Secretaries of State for Health, Wales, Northern Ireland and Scotland. *Working for Patients. Working Paper No. 6. Medical Audit*. London: HMSO, 1989.

3   Department of Health. *Clinical Audit*. London: Department of Health, 1993.

4   Donabedian A. Evaluating the Quality of Medical Care. *Milbank Memorial Fund Quarterly* 1966;**44**:166–206.

5   Long AF, Dixon P *et al.* The outcomes agenda: contribution of the UK clearing house on health outcomes. *Quality in Health Care* 1993;**2**:49–52.

6   Field MJ, Lohr KN. *Guidelines for Clinical Practice*. Washington DC: National Academy Press (USA), 1992.

7   The Royal College of Radiologists. *Medical Audit in Radiodiagnosis.* London: The Royal College of Radiologists, 1990.

8   Donabedian A. Explorations in Quality Assessment and Monitoring. In: *The Criteria and Standards of Quality, Vol. 2.* Ann Arbor, Michigan: Health Administration Press, 1982.

9   Mackenzie R, Dixon AK. Measuring the Effects of Imaging: an Evaluation Framework. *Clin Radiol* 1995;**50**:513–18.

10   Thomas RD, Fairhurst JJ, Frost RA. Wessex Regional Radiology Audit: Barium Enema in Colo-rectal Carcinoma. *Clin Radiol* 1995;**50**:647–50.

11   The Royal College of Radiologists. *Making the best use of a Department of Clinical Radiology: Guidelines for Doctors (Third Edition).* London: RCR, 1995.

12   National Radiological Protection Board and The Royal College of Radiologists. *Patient Dose Reduction in Diagnostic Radiology.* London: HMSO, 1990.

13   Jacyna MR. Pros and Cons of Medical Audit … a Conversation with a Sceptic. *Hospital Update* 1992;**18**: 512–18.

14   British Broadcasting Corporation. *English Dictionary.* London: BBC English and Harper Collins Ltd., 1993.

15   Jacyna MR. Audit Assesses Quality: But What is Quality? A Clinician's View. *Hospital Update* 1992;**18**:822–4.

16   Maxwell RJ. Quality Assessment in Health. *BMJ* 1984;**288**:1470–73.

17   Donabedian A. Reflections on the Effectiveness of Quality Assurance. In: Eds. Palmer RH, Donabedian A. Povar GJ. *Striving for Quality in Health Care.* Ann Arbor, Michigan: Health Administration Press, 1991.

18   Bull A. Audit and Research. *BMJ*, 1992;**305**:905–906.

19   Jacyna MR, de Lacey G, Chapman EJ. How does Medical Audit Differ from Research? How Necessary are Computers? *Hospital Update* 1992;**18**:592–6.

20   The Royal College of Radiologists. *Risk Management in Clinical Radiology.* London: The Royal College of Radiologists, 1995.

21   NHS Executive. Promoting Clinical Effectiveness. Leeds: NHSE, 1996.

22   Sellu D. Time to audit audit. BMJ 1996;**312**:128–9.

Further Reading

The following three publications have provided a rich source of inspiration. We strongly recommend that these references be read in full.

1   de Lacey G *et al.* Audit: an Instrument for Change. *Hospital Update*, 1992; June – November (six articles on aspects of audit).

2   Samuel O, Grant J, Irvine D. *Quality and Audit in General Practice. Meanings and Definitions.* London: Royal College of General Practitioners, 1994.

3   Scottish Office. *Clinical Guidelines: A report by a Working Group set up by the Clinical Resource and Audit Group.* Scottish Office, 1993.

Abbreviations

A&E	Accident and Emergency, as in A&E Department (Casualty).
AP	Antero-Posterior, a radiographic projection, in which the x ray beam passes through the patient from front to back.
BME	Barium Meal Examination, a radiographic investigation to outline the oesophagus, stomach and duodenum. The patient swallows barium sulphate suspension and effervescent granules or tablets.
BMJ	British Medical Journal.
CCU	Coronary Care Unit.
CEC	Council of European Communities.
CEO	Chief Executive Officer.
CME	Continuing Medical Education. These are schemes introduced by the various Medical Royal Colleges, to ensure that all consultant medical staff keep up to date with current medical developments.
COAD	Chronic Obstructive Airways Disease.
CRASC	Clinical Radiology Audit Sub-Committee of The Royal College of Radiologists.
CT	Computed Tomography. A radiographic examination which produces cross-sectional images through the patient, using an x ray tube which rotates around the patient in a special gantry.
CXR	Chest Radiograph, colloquially Chest X Ray.
D	Unit of Optical Density, which equals the logarithm of the ratio of the incident to the transmitted light intensities.
DCBE	Double Contrast Barium Enema, a radiographic examination to outline the colon using barium sulphate suspension and air (or carbon dioxide) introduced via the rectum.
DH, DoH	Department of Health.
DPA	Data Protection Act.
DVT	Deep Venous (or Vein) Thrombosis.
ERCP	Endoscopic Retrograde Cholangiopancreatogram. A radiographic examination to outline the common bile duct and the pancreatic duct, introducing contrast medium through the Ampulla of Vater using a side-viewing endoscope.
ESR	Erythrocyte Sedimentation Rate.
FHSA	Family Health Services Authority.
FRCR	Fellowship of The Royal College of Radiologists. The British professional examination in Clinical Radiology or in Clinical Oncology. Successful candidates become Fellows.
FSD	Film Source Distance, the distance between the focus of the anode of the x ray tube and the radiographic film.
GP	General Practitioner, i.e. family doctor.
Gy	Gray, the SI unit of absorbed dose of radiation. 1 gray = 1 joule per kilogram May be prefixed e.g. cGy = centigray = 1/100 gray mGy = milligray = 1/1000 gray
Gy/cm^2	Dose Area Product Measurement. Dose area product meters, e.g. the Diamentor (PTW, Freiberg), fit to the diaphragm housing of x ray sets. Provide a useful guide to the performance of both the equipment and the radiologist in keeping patient dose to a minimum.
HSE	Health and Safety Executive.
IPEMB	Institution of Physics and Engineering in Medicine and Biology (this is the current name of the merged IPSM (see below) and Biological Engineering Society).
ICRP	International Commission on Radiation Protection.
ICU	Intensive Care Unit (also known as ITU, see below).
ID	Identity or Identification, as in ID card.
IP	In-Patient.
IPSM	Institute of Physical Sciences in Medicine.
IPT	Image Processing Technician (Dark Room Technician).
ITU	Intensive Therapy Unit (also known as ICU, see above).
IUCD	Intra-Uterine Contraceptive Device.

IV	Intravenous, as in IV injection.
IVC	Inferior Vena Cava.
IVU	Intravenous Urography. A radiographic examination to outline the urinary tract using an intravenous injection of a water soluble radiographic contrast medium. Also known as Intravenous Pyelography (IVP) or Excretion Urography (EU).
kVp	A radiographic exposure factor, indicating the peak kilovoltage between the anode and cathode of the x ray tube.
LOCM	Low Osmolar Contrast Medium. A type of water soluble contrast agent used in radiography.
LP	Lumbar Puncture.
LPO	Left Posterior Oblique (Position).
MAAG	Medical Audit Advisory Group. A committee responsible for the organisation of audit in primary care, consisting of General Practitioners, Practice Nurses, and hospital representatives.
Majax	Major Accident.
mAs	Radiographic exposure factor.
MRI	Magnetic Resonance Imaging, a technique that produces sectional images through a patient, using a strong magnetic field and pulses of radiofrequency energy.
NHD	Notional Half Day (3.5 hours of consultant time).
NHS	National Health Service.
NM	Nuclear Medicine.
NRPB	National Radiological Protection Board.
NTD	Neural Tube Defect.
OP	Out-Patient.
PE	Pulmonary Embolism.
PGME	Post-Graduate Medical Education.
PIOPED	Prospective Investigation of Pulmonary Embolism Diagnosis. Set of criteria used for assessment of V/Q scans, based on an American study (*J Am Med Assoc* 1990;**263**:2753–9).
POPUMET	Protection of Persons Undergoing Medical Examination or Treatment. Popular name for the Ionising Radiation Regulations of 1985 and 1988.
RAO	Right Anterior Oblique (position).
RCA	Royal College of Anaesthetists.
RCR	Royal College of Radiologists.
RPA	Radiation Protection Advisor.
RPO	Radiation Protection Officer.
RT LAT	Right Lateral.
RTO	Resuscitation Training Officer.
SAE	Stamped, Addressed Envelope.
SCOPME	Standing Committee on Postgraduate Medical Education.
Sv	Sievert, the SI unit of dose equivalent. Not all ionising radiation has the same biological effect, so the absorbed dose is multiplied by a Quality Factor (QF) to give the dose equivalent: Dose equivalent (Sv) = absorbed dose (Gy) × QF The QF of x rays and gamma rays is 1.
SXR	Skull radiograph. Colloquially Skull X Ray.
TLD	Thermoluminescent Dosemeter, device to measure absorbed dose of radiation.
UK	United Kingdom.
US	Ultrasound, a technique that produces images using pulses of high frequency sound.
V/Q Scan, VQ	Ventilation and Perfusion Lung Scan, a Nuclear Medicine technique that compares the ventilation and perfusion of the lungs. Usually used for the diagnosis of pulmonary embolism.
WTE	Whole Time Equivalents (referring to the number of staff members).
XR	Radiograph, colloquially X Ray.

How to use this book – and other information

recipe n. 1 a statement of the ingredients and procedure required for preparing cooked food;

2 an expedient; a device for achieving something;

3 a medical prescription.

ingredient n. a component part or element in a recipe.

–The Concise Oxford Dictionary. Eighth edition 1990.

There are 115 recipes for clinical audit projects in this book. Each Recipe is laid out in an identical manner so that the essential ingredients are contained within a standard format on two pages. The ingredients are itemised under the following headings:

- Background

- The Audit Cycle
  - the standard
  - assessment of local practice
  - comparison of findings against the standard
  - change
  - when to repeat the audit

- Resources required
  - data collection
  - assistance required
  - estimate of costs
  - time needed (from the Radiologists and/or Radiographers)

- References

- Authors

Background

An explicit statement as to why the author considers that the audit is worth carrying out. An audit project has to be justified. Audit for audit's sake has neither point nor value.

The Audit Cycle is really a spiral

It is accepted practice to use the terms loop or cycle when describing the audit process. Conventionally this cycle is illustrated by using a circle (Fig. 1) but this graphic presentation of audit can be dispiriting as it gives an appearance of going round and round on a treadmill – it is more encouraging, as well as accurate (Ref. 1), to show that the process has a linear component and is more properly depicted as a spiral of repeating cycles (Fig. 2).

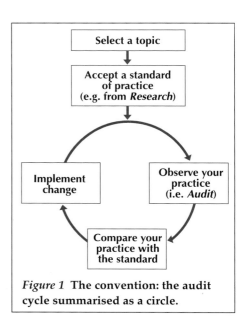

Figure 1 **The convention: the audit cycle summarised as a circle.**

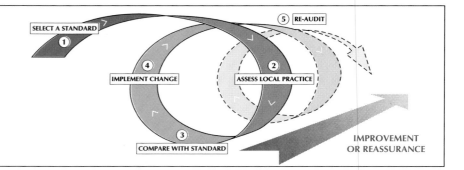

Figure 2 **Preferred: the audit cycle summarised as a spiral of repeating cycles.**

- **Continuous improvement … or reassurance?**

  It is customary to emphasise that continuous improvement is the *raison d'être* for completing the audit cycle. This implies that whatever we achieve is not good enough. When accompanied by an undue emphasis on an unremitting need for change this can also be dispiriting to those who find that many of their audits indicate that no change is necessary. For this reason the spiral illustration used throughout this book places as much emphasis on the word reassurance as on the words continuous improvement.

The standard to be measured against

A standard is stated for each Recipe. Many of the standards are derived from research (Ref. 2) or based on accepted guidelines (Ref. 3). Research based evidence is not always available and in these instances the best practice against which local practice will be compared can be agreed locally between colleagues using the best information currently available and simple common sense. Wherever this occurs the Recipe states that a local standard has been adopted.

- **The Target**

  All Recipes state the target to be reached – i.e. the expected level of achievement. The target is made explicit when defining the standard. For example in Recipe 84 the target has been set as follows: All (i.e. 100%) of paging calls for a radiologist to attend the Nuclear Medicine Department will result in a 5-minute (or less) response time. In this Recipe the target is 100%. This particular target has been set very high, whereas some departments may be a little less ambitious in Recipe 84 and choose to set a target of 90% or even 80%. Local circumstances (e.g. the Nuclear Medicine Department might be some distance from the Department of Clinical Radiology, or the lack of a paging system) will affect the precise target to be reached.

Assessment of local practice

This has three elements within each Recipe. Firstly, there is a statement regarding the indicator or indicators (i.e. the criteria) which will be measured. These indicators will eventually enable an assessment to be made as to whether the standard has been met. Secondly, there is a list of the data items which need to be collected so as to obtain these indicators. Thirdly, there is a suggestion as to how many patients, cases or episodes are needed for the audit (Refs 4–7).

• The Indicator

It is common for there to be confusion and misunderstanding in relation to the word indicator. The indicator relates directly to the standard which has been set and it represents the particular variable (or item of information) which needs to be measured. For example, in Recipe 84 the local standard has been defined as follows: All paging calls for a radiologist to attend the Nuclear Medicine Department will result in a 5-minute (or less) response time. The indicator which needs to be measured is the % of paging calls responded to within 5 minutes. Defining the indicator to be measured, and stating the target to be reached are two essential elements which must be included in the planning and design of all audit projects.

• Number of patients or cases: statistical considerations

The distinction between research and audit and their relationship to each other have been explained very clearly (Refs 2 and 8) but confusions still occur (Refs 2, 7 and 8). One confusion relates to the number of cases necessary for an audit project vis-à-vis a research project. Bull (Ref. 7) has addressed this and reminds us that clinical research examines what difference a particular clinical intervention will make in which patients. The essence of research is that it tests the links between the processes and the outcomes of care and establishes facts that are transferable to other patient samples. Consequently, the results of research must be statistically valid as facts that apply to a particular area of clinical practice in all circumstances. Research treats the study population as sample and the number of patients included is therefore crucial to the statistical analysis of the expected variation between one sample and the next. On the other hand, clinical audit reveals facts that apply only to the group of patients being studied. Hence the audit study population need not be a statistically representative sample and the number of patients included is in most instances not statistically important. Bull emphasises that clinical audit can legitimately be carried out on one patient alone. Of course this needs to be qualified as the number of patients audited should broadly reflect the number that are seen in local clinical practice. For example, if 100 cases were to be seen during a week then more cases should be included in the audit than if only one case was to be seen per year. All the same, in the latter circumstance an audit of that one solitary case would be valid (Ref. 7).

Comparing the audit findings against the standard

This comparison will indicate whether or not local practice falls below the standard and consequently whether changes need to be implemented.

- **Data Analysis**

  The limitations imposed by the Recipe format and space available have precluded any description of the way in which these comparisons will be made. The data collected will always require analysis – often at two levels. Firstly, to make a direct comparison against the standard. Secondly, in those instances where the standard has not been met there will have to be a further analysis as to why this is so. The precise changes which need to be introduced will depend on this second analysis. In each Recipe the necessity for data analysis needs to be taken as read.

Change

The results of some audits will show that local practice does meet and sometimes exceeds the agreed standard and no important changes need to be made. These audits are well worth carrying out because they provide evidence and reassurance to the auditors, and to others, that local standards are high. On the other hand, if the standard is not being met then change – sometimes simple and occasionally radical – needs to be introduced. Each Recipe includes suggestions regarding the changes which might be necessary in order to achieve an improvement, or suggestions as to how the changes might be introduced.

The suggested changes will depend on the author's own experience and imagination. If the audit has already been carried out then the changes specified will usually be those which were implemented when setting about improving local performance. On the other hand, some Recipes may not have been carried out and thus the changes that are listed are essentially conceptual. Naturally, the recommendations which are made in relation to change in any individual Recipe will not represent the only available options.

- **Responsibility for introducing change**

  It is important that all recommended changes resulting from an audit are addressed by those who have the authority to introduce change (e.g. a named individual, the Clinical Director, the Medical Director, sometimes the Chief Executive Officer). If those who carry out an audit see that their recommendations are forgotten or ignored then there will be very little enthusiasm for carrying out any other audits. For this reason an audit of the action taken on proposals for change made during the preceding 12 months has been included as **Recipe 1**. If this particular audit is carried out each year it will ensure that all suggestions for change will have been considered by those who can bring about change. This annual audit is crucial. If changes are not introduced when it has been shown that a particular standard is not being met then there is little point in carrying out audit.

Re-audit

Once change has been introduced a period of time needs to elapse before local practice is again re-assessed. The time interval before the re-audit is carried out is dependent on the need for, as well as the extent of, the changes. If a repeat audit reveals that the standard is still not being met then further steps need to be taken so as to obtain an improvement. Thereafter re-audit is again necessary as the spiral of continuous improvement continues. Re-audit is also necessary in those instances where the standard has been met. The standard might be raised either as a result of new research or through a change in local circumstances (e.g. an increase in staff, acquisition of a MRI scanner). Re-audit is then necessary to determine whether this new standard is being reached. Finally, regular re-audit is also necessary even when a standard has not been changed in order to provide continuing reassurance that previously high local standards are being maintained and have not been allowed to slip.

The Resources required

Collecting the data, the assistance needed, and likely costs. There are various methods by which any individual audit can be carried out and the data can usually be collected in several different ways. Similarly, the precise assistance that will be needed will vary between hospitals. In some centres the hospital audit office and the audit co-ordinators will do much of the work, whereas in other centres most of the data collection and analysis will be carried out by the radiologists and/or other staff within the department. Frequently, the use of computers will be of considerable help (Ref. 9). The methodology specified in each recipe is simply the one chosen by the author and the one considered to be best suited to the author's local circumstances.

• Costs

Each author has indicated the likely range of costs which will need to be met so as to complete all of the steps up to and including the comparison of the findings against the standard. Costing a project is an important aspect of audit planning because it may be necessary to make an approach for funds from the Hospital Clinical Audit Committee or elsewhere. On the other hand it is easy to overestimate the cost of audit, and careful planning will often show that the data can be collected very simply and cheaply during normal every day clinical practice.

For each Recipe an estimate has been made of the financial costs of completing the first three stages in the audit cycle (stages 1, 2, and 3 in Fig. 2) and the estimate is indicated by a £ symbol. These costs do not include the salaries of those clinical professionals and audit officers employed by the hospital. The costs refer solely to outside professional skills, or equipment, which will be needed in order to carry out these stages of the first cycle of the audit. The approximate costs are illustrated as shown in Fig. 3.

Figure 3 **Audit costs.**
In each recipe the
costs of carrying out
the audit are indicated
using a £ sign

First cycle	£0 – £50	=	low	=	£
First cycle	£51 – £500	=	modest	=	££
First cycle	£500+	=	high	=	£££

- **Time for audit**

  Audit requires time for planning, collecting and analysing the data, presenting the results, and preparing and implementing strategies to achieve change (Refs 10 and 11). For each Recipe the author has indicated the likely amount of Radiologist or Radiographer (and sometimes Audit Officer) time that will be necessary. The cost of this professional time has not been included in the financial cost (i.e. as indicated by the symbols £, ££, or £££) provided with each Recipe – time for audit should be an integral part of the normal work programme of all clinical professionals including doctors.

- **Alternative methods of data collection**

  Users may wish to alter the design of an individual Recipe, or utilise alternative ways in which to collect the data, or seek alternative assistance. Some alternative options are shown in Fig. 4. These options are also reproduced on Page 297 as part of a blank proforma which can be used when planning and designing all aspects of an entirely new audit project.

References and enquiries

All references are numbered, but their precise connotation does vary between Recipes. Most authors have followed the usual convention of indicating or acknowledging an original source by positioning the corresponding number in the text. Other authors have provided a list of references without positioning a number in the text, the intention being that the list of references represents some suggestions for further reading. A few authors have used a combination of these two approaches. The references provided with each Recipe are limited by the space available. Any enquiries for additional references or any other information can be directed to the author whose name and address is included at the end of each Recipe. In some instances the Recipe has been supplied by a doctor in training and he or she may have moved to another hospital. If an enquiry fails to elicit a prompt reply then correspondents are advised to address a further enquiry for the attention of the lead consultant in Clinical Audit in the Department of Diagnostic Radiology at the hospital.

Figure 4 **Planning an audit. Some of the options which need to be considered: deciding how to collect the data, assessing the assistance that will be needed, and estimating the likely costs.**

THE DATA will be collected by ...

☐ Computer records   ☐ Review of requests   ☐ Other (specify)

☐ Review of images   ☐ Ongoing data recording   _____

☐ Review of reports   ☐ Questionnaire   _____

ASSISTANCE from ...

☐ None   ☐ Data analysis   ☐ Other (specify)

☐ Secretarial   ☐ Software (off shelf)   _____

☐ Audit office   ☐ Software (customised)   _____

☐ Medical records   ☐ Clinical professionals   _____

ESTIMATED TIME to help complete stages 1–3 of the first cycle

RADIOLOGIST	RADIOGRAPHER	OTHER (specify)
Approx _____ hrs per week	Approx _____ hrs per week	Approx _____ hrs per week
for _____ weeks	for _____ weeks	for _____ weeks
= total _____ hours	= total _____ hours	= total _____ hours

ESTIMATED COSTS (stages 1–3 of the cycle) apart from radiologists' / radiographers' time

☐ None/minimal   ☐ Other (specify)   Stages 1–3 of the first cycle

☐ Temporary staff   _____

☐ Information technology   _____   £ _____

Authors

Each Recipe includes the names of the individuals who have provided the outline for the audit project. The following convention has been adopted: the prefix Dr on its own and without any further explanation indicates that the individual is a Clinical Radiologist (either a consultant or a specialist registrar). Where an author is a doctor from another discipline then the author's specialty is included in brackets.

The Appendix

Some of the Recipes require additional details which will not fit into the limited space provided by the basic two page proforma. In these instances the additional information is included in the Appendix. The Appendix is situated on pages 233–293 and each Appendix number corresponds to its Recipe number.

Constructing and planning other audits

The basic Recipe proforma is shown on page 296. This blank proforma has been provided in order to assist with the planning of any new audit project. Completion of the proforma is also very useful in helping to ensure that a new project really does represent audit and is not being confused with research (Refs 2,7,10–12).

Auditing audit – *your help required*

Audit asks two very simple questions: How well are you doing? and Where is your evidence? This collection of Recipes has been designed primarily to act as an educational tool to assist with the design and completion of projects which will supply that evidence. Will it be used for this purpose? The final Recipe (Recipe 115) has been included so as to enable The Royal College of Radiologists to carry out an audit of this book in 12–24 months time. Two pages (302–303) have been set aside for recording how and when the book has been used by radiologists, other clinicians, radiographers and hospital audit co-ordinators. Audit leads and hospital audit officers are asked to make a note on these pages each time the book is used; these notes will assist with the ongoing collection of data for Recipe 115.

Glossary

The terms used in audit need to be clearly understood. Audit will only achieve its main purpose of providing reassurance or improving clinical standards if there is rigorous adherence to precise definitions (Ref. 13). Loose and vague use of language inevitably leads to confusion (Ref. 14). A glossary explaining the terms and synonyms is included on pages xv–xx. In particular, users are asked to note that each Recipe is classified as being an audit of structure or process or outcome and it is important that the meanings of these three terms (page xv) as used in this book are fully understood.

Abbreviations

Many of the Recipes contain abbreviations and some readers, including audit assistants, may not be familiar with all of them. A list of all of the abbreviations used in the book is included on pages xxi–xxii.

The Index

The Recipes are printed in alphabetical order (1–115) – i.e. the order is dependent on the first letter of the short title. Thus, Recipe number 1 is Accepting Recommendations for Change, and Recipe number 115 is Your Use of this Book. There are three separate indexes arranged by audit topic, by author, and by type of audit. The Index by topic groups the recipes by more than 80 key phrases which reflect the wide variety of topics. Audits which address several topics have multiple entries (e.g. Recipe 37, GP Chest Radiography is indexed under Chest, GP issues and Requests). Some topics which are addressed implicitly rather than explicitly (e.g. Health and Safety) have been included in order to assist those working in these fields who might wish to use this book as a source of ideas. The Index by author and hospital or address lists all the Recipes credited to each author. The Index by type of audit lists the Recipes that are Structure audits and those that are Outcome audits.

Further Information on Clinical Audit

- For advice on audit in clinical radiology, or to discuss any matters arising from the audits in this book, please contact the Clinical Audit Adviser at:

  The Royal College of Radiologists
  38, Portland Place
  London W1N 4JQ
  Telephone: (0171) 436 4251
  Fax: (0171) 323 3100
  Email: coin@rcrad.ac.uk

- Advice on audit is also available from the National Centre for Clinical Audit at:

  BMA House
  Tavistock Square
  London WC1H 9JP
  Telephone: (0171) 383 6451
  Fax: (0171) 383 6373

- A learning pack, *Making Medical Audit Effective*, has been published by the Joint Centre for Education in Medicine. The authors are nationally acknowledged audit experts. The pack includes a set of self study modules, a bibliography, a list of contact names and example forms. It is available from:

  JCER Publications
  33 Millman Street
  London WC1N 3EJ

- Two supplements to the learning pack published by the JCER (on audit in clinical radiology and nuclear medicine) and a bibliography of other relevant papers are available from the Clinical Audit Adviser at The Royal College of Radiologists.

References

1   Vasanthakumar V, Brown PM. Audit spiral. Quality in Health Care 1992;**1**:142–3.

2   Jacyna MR, de Lacey G, Chapman EJ. How does medical audit differ from research? How necessary are computers? *Hospital Update* 1992;**18**:592–6.

3   The Royal College of Radiologists. *Making the best use of a Department of Clinical Radiology. Guidelines for Doctors.* Third edition. London: RCR, 1995.

4   Hamlyn AN. Computers in audit: servants or sirens. *BMJ* 1991;**303**:649.

5   Fowkes FGR. Medical audit cycle. A review of methods and research in clinical practice. *Med Ed* 1982;**16**:228–38.

6   Dixon N. Practical principles of medical audit. *Postgrad Med J* 1990;**66 (Suppl 3)**:17–20.

7   Bull A. Audit and research. *BMJ* 1993;**306**:67.

8   Proctor SJ. Why clinical research needs medical audit. *Quality in Health Care.* 1993;**2**:1–2.

9   Kinn S, Lee N, Millman A. Using computers in clinical audit. *BMJ* 1995;**311**:739–42.

10 Godwin R. Nothing succeeds like success – some do's and dont's in Clinical Audit. *Clin Rad* 1995;**50**:818–20.

11 de Lacey G. in: Is money wasted on audit? *Journal of the Royal Society of Medicine* 1994;**87**:52–5.

12 de Lacey G. Clinical audit: Don't look a gift horse in the mouth. *Clin Rad* 1995;**50**:815–17.

13 Houghton G. Audit, peer review, and intellectual conformity. *Lancet* 1991; 338: 822–3.

14 de Lacey G. What is audit? Why should we be doing it? *Hospital Update* 1992;**18**:458–66.

Recipes

<table>
<tr><td>

1

</td><td>

Accepting Recommendations for Change

</td><td>

☐ Structure
■ Process
☐ Outcome

</td></tr>
</table>

THE AUDIT

Whether the changes recommended as a result of audit have been acted upon.

(See Appendix, page 234)

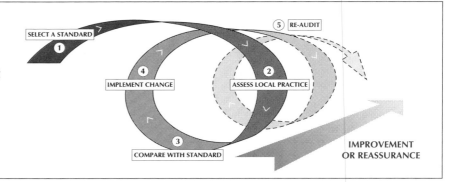

BACKGROUND

● **Why this audit is worth doing**

Audit projects which show that a standard has not been met require that changes be introduced into local practice so that improvement may occur (Ref. 1). Those who hold managerial responsibility within the Hospital, whether the Clinical Director, the Chief Executive Officer (CEO), or the Operational Board need to ensure that all recommended changes are addressed (Refs 2–4). If recommendations for change are ignored then the time spent carrying out an audit is wasted (Refs 1 and 3–5), and those carrying out the audit will not allow their time to be wasted in a similar manner again.

THE CYCLE

1 THE STANDARD

All changes recommended as a result of the Department's annual programme of audit activity should have been addressed (i.e. considered, where possible implemented, when not implemented then prioritised and reasons given for non-implementation) by the appropriate body – e.g. a named individual, or the Clinical Director, or the CEO, or the Operational Board.

2 ASSESS LOCAL PRACTICE

● **The indicator**

% of recommendations addressed by the appropriate body.

● **Data items to be collected**

In each audit meeting, every recommendation for action or change which is made, and the appropriate body to address it, should be recorded on a simple departmental proforma (see Appendix). Action taken since the last meeting should also be recorded on the same form.

Each year, on an agreed date, the Clinical Director and the Audit Lead in the Department of Clinical Radiology will present the results of a comparison between the recommendations of the previous 24 months with the actions subsequently taken.

● **Suggested number**

The recommendations made at 24 consecutive monthly audit meetings.

THE CYCLE (continued)

3 COMPARE FINDINGS WITH THE STANDARD

4 CHANGE

● **Some suggestions**

The Clinical Director and/or the CEO should meet with the audit group to explain in detail why specific recommendations had not been addressed or had not been implemented. Discuss the results at the same audit meeting.

Make sure the published audit meeting minutes state clearly and unambiguously the agreed decisions and required action. Clarify and explain how to complete the proforma used to record the results (Appendix, page 234).

Re-define the precise responsibilities and the precise communication pathways between the lead Consultant (Radiology) in clinical audit, the Clinical Director, the Chairman of the Hospital Clinical Audit Committee and the CEO.

5 RE-AUDIT every 3–6 months if standard has not been met, otherwise every 12 months.

RESOURCES
FIRST CYCLE £

● **Data collection**

Retrospective review.

● **Assistance required**

None.

● **Estimated radiologists' and radiographers' time to complete stages 1–3 of the first cycle**

The lead consultant in audit and the Clinical Director: 4 hours each.

● **Other estimated costs**

None.

REFERENCES

1 Shaw CD, Constain DW. Guidelines for medical audit: seven principles. *BMJ* 1989;**299**:498–9.

2 Lester E. A meeting too far. *BMJ* 1995;**310**:1014.

3 de Lacey G *et al.* Setting up hospital audit – one model. *Hospital Update* 1992;**8**:670–76.

4 Stocking B. How do we change systems of care in response to the findings in clinical audit? In: *Professional and Managerial Aspects of Clinical Audit.* London: Royal College of Physicians of London, 1994:131–8.

5 Godwin R. Nothing succeeds like success – Do's and don'ts in Clinical Audit. *Clin Radiol* 1995;**50**:818–20.

6 The Audit Commission. *Improving your Image. How to Manage Radiology Services More Effectively.* London: HMSO, 1995.

7 Baker R et al. Factors influencing participation in audit. *BMJ* 1995;**311**:1168

8 de Lacey G. Clinical audit: don't look a gift horse in the mouth. *Clin Radiol* 1995;**50**:815–17

9 Handy C. Understanding organizations. Fourth edition. Harmondsworth: Penguin, 1993:chapter 10.

SUBMITTED BY

The Clinical Radiology Audit Sub-Committee (CRASC) of the Royal College of Radiologists.

<table>
<tr><td>

2

</td><td>

Adequate Completion of Radiology Request Forms

</td><td>

☐ Structure
■ Process
☐ Outcome

</td></tr>
</table>

THE AUDIT

Adequacy of completion of radiology request forms.

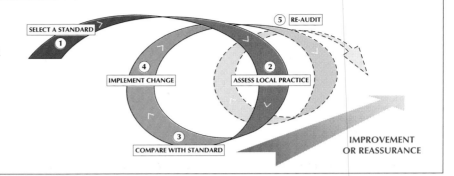

BACKGROUND

● **Why this audit is worth doing**

The usefulness of a radiological examination can be reduced if the clinical background and the specific problem to be answered is not provided with the request. Inadequate information can also lead to mistakes in patient identification and delay in returning reports to the correct destination, and can reduce the value of the report (Ref. 1).

THE CYCLE

1 THE STANDARD

● **A locally agreed standard**

All radiology request forms should contain adequate clinical and demographic information which identifies the patient and the destination for the report. All forms should include the following:

* the clinical background;

* the question to be answered;

* the patient's name, age, address and number;

* the ward;

* the name of the requesting doctor, and the name of the consultant looking after the patient.

2 ASSESS LOCAL PRACTICE

● **The indicator**

% of request forms with adequate information.

● **Data items to be collected**

For each request form, record the presence or otherwise of each of the items in the standard.

● **Suggested number**

200 randomly selected request forms.

THE CYCLE (continued)

3 COMPARE FINDINGS WITH THE STANDARD

4 CHANGE

● **Some suggestions**

Hold meetings with individual clinical firms to discuss the findings of this audit, and the requirements of the Department of Clinical Radiology. Include the basic principles at induction of new staff.

In specific cases:

- Send back individual forms which are incomplete.
- Check the patient's notes to confirm the reason for the request.

5 RE-AUDIT Continuous re-audit – every 6 months.

RESOURCES   FIRST CYCLE £

● **Data collection**

Review of request cards.

● **Assistance required**

Card and note pulling by audit staff.

● **Estimated radiologists' and radiographers' time to complete stages 1–3 of the first cycle**

Radiologist: 4–6 hours.

● **Other estimated costs**

None.

REFERENCES

1 Royal College of Radiologists. *Making the Best Use of a Department of Clinical Radiology: Guidelines for Doctors.* Third edition. London: RCR, 1995.

2 Royal College of Radiologists. *Clinical Radiology Quality Specification for Purchasers.* London: RCR, 1995.

SUBMITTED BY

Dr A Manhire and Mrs C Soar (Radiology Audit Officer), Nottingham City Hospital.

<table>
<tr><td>

3

</td><td>

Air Quality in the Process Area

</td><td>

☐ Structure

■ Process

☐ Outcome

</td></tr>
</table>

THE AUDIT

Measurement of air quality and toxic substances in the film processing areas.

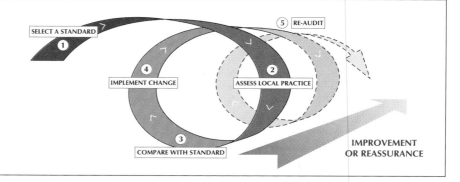

BACKGROUND

● **Why this audit is worth doing**

Health and Safety requirements are statutory, and the quality of air in and around film processing areas should be monitored for levels of toxic substances according to published guidance (Ref. 1). Levels above these values are a potential hazard to the health of those working near processors, and may cause symptoms such as headache, sore throat, fatigue and aggravation of asthma (Refs 2–4).

THE CYCLE

1 THE STANDARD

● **From Health and Safety Executive (Ref. 1)**

Measured levels should not exceed the following at any time:

Acetic acid, 10 parts/million (long term exposure);
Sulphur dioxide, 2 parts/million (long term exposure);
Odour threshold, 1 part/million.

2 ASSESS LOCAL PRACTICE

● **The indicator**

% of occasions when any of the levels stated in the standard are exceeded in any process area.

● **Data items to be collected**

Take readings for the above levels using a manual air pump (Accuro hand pump, Draga) with disposable measurement tubes. Such a pump may be purchased or the task of measurement can be performed by an external company. Information on who can perform this task can be obtained from the Occupational Health Department of the hospital. Record the date of each reading.

● **Suggested number**

The frequency of testing and number of tests are up to local management. One suggested policy is to make an assessment each week in each processing area. Another is to carry out a measurement after each routine service on processing equipment or after replacement or breakdown.

THE CYCLE (continued)

3 COMPARE FINDINGS WITH THE STANDARD

4 CHANGE

● **Suggested change**

Change is required by the Health and Safety Executive if levels are found to be in excess of the published maxima and may include the following:

- Improve the ventilation in the process areas.
- Service the processor, and check for faults.
- Install extraction fans.
- Use gluteraldehyde-free chemistry.

5 RE-AUDIT Every 12–24 months.

RESOURCES   FIRST CYCLE £(££)

● **Data collection**

Measurement of gas levels using a manual air pump and sample measurement tubes.

● **Assistance required**

Dark room staff.

Hygienist.

● **Estimated radiologists' and radiographers' time to complete stages 1–3 of the first cycle**

Radiographer: 10 mins per measurement in each processing area.

● **Other estimated costs**

The manual air pump costs approximately £150. Disposable tubes cost £35 for a pack of 10.

REFERENCES

1 Health and Safety Executive. *Occupational Exposure Limits 1994*. London: HSE, 1994.

2 Society of Radiographers. *Occupational Health Problems in Processing X-ray Photographic Films*. London: SoR, 1993.

3 Society of Radiographers. *Preventing the Darkroom Disease: Health Effects of Toxic Fumes Produced in X-ray Film Processing*. London: SoR, 1991.

4 Gordon M. Reactions to chemical fumes in radiology departments. *Radiography* 1987;**52**:85–9.

SUBMITTED BY

Mr G Ramsey (Superintendent Radiographer) and Dr A Manhire, Nottingham City Hospital.

<table>
<tr><td>

4

</td><td>

Attendance at Audit Meetings

</td><td>

☐ Structure
■ Process
☐ Outcome

</td></tr>
</table>

THE AUDIT

Doctor attendance at departmental audit meetings.

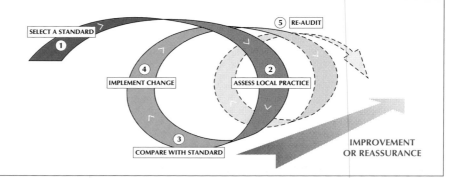

BACKGROUND

● **Why this audit is worth doing**

It is a Department of Health requirement that all doctors working in the NHS carry out regular and systematic clinical audit (Refs 1 and 2). Audit meetings act as a forum where departmental weaknesses and problems can be identified and addressed. There are often good reasons why doctors fail to attend. This audit may lead to the identification of changes which will help to make doctors able and willing to attend.

THE CYCLE

1   THE STANDARD

● **A locally agreed standard with two parts**

Of doctors (consultants and specialist registrars) timetabled to be in the Department of Clinical Radiology on the day of the monthly audit meeting, at least 80% should attend the meeting.

Each individual doctor should attend at least 80% of the monthly audit meetings.

2   ASSESS LOCAL PRACTICE

● **The indicators**

% of meetings attended by at least 80% of the doctors who are timetabled to be in the Department of Clinical Radiology.

% of doctors attending at least 80% of meetings.

● **Data items to be collected**

For each monthly meeting, record:

• the name of each doctor attending;

• any apologies;

• the names of all doctors timetabled to be in the Department of Clinical Radiology;

• % of doctors timetabled that attended.

For each doctor, calculate % of meetings attended

● **Suggested number**

12 consecutive monthly audit meetings.

THE CYCLE (continued)

3 COMPARE FINDINGS WITH THE STANDARD

4 CHANGE

● **Some suggestions**

The reasons given for failure to attend should give an indication as to whether the problem is timetabling, or doctors' perception of quality and value of meetings.

If the problem is timetabling:

- adjust rotas / patient lists;
- develop a forward plan with tasks set well in advance (e.g. 6–12 months);
- identify one doctor to deal with clinical problems at the time of the meeting.

If the problem is doctors' perception of meeting quality:

- elicit and then address the trainees' views on the educational value of the local audit arrangements (Ref. 3);
- provide lunch;
- alter the monthly meeting so as to include a regular research / clinical presentation (say, one hour) and the audit meeting to follow (one and a half hours). In this way the audit afternoon truly integrates education, research and audit (Ref. 4).

5 RE-AUDIT Continuous audit – i.e. every 12 months.

RESOURCES   FIRST CYCLE £

● **Data collection**

Ongoing data recording.

● **Assistance required**

None.

● **Estimated radiologists' and radiographers' time to complete stages 1–3 of the first cycle**

Radiologist: 4 hours.

● **Other costs**

None.

REFERENCES

1 Department of Health. *Working for Patients. Working Paper 6* London: HMSO Publications, 1989.

2. Royal College of Physicians of London. *Medical Audit Second Report*. London: RCP Publications, 1993:5.

3. Firth-Cozens J and Storer D. Registrars' and Senior Registrars' perceptions of their audit activities. *Quality in Health Care* 1992;**1**:161–4.

4. Jacyna MR, de Lacey G, Chapman EJ. How does medical audit differ from research? *Hospital Update* 1992;**18**:592–6.

5 Lough JRM *et al*. Factors influencing participation in audit. *BMJ* 1995;**311**:1168.

SUBMITTED BY

Dr D Johnson, Northwick Park and St. Mark's Hospitals, Harrow.

THE AUDIT

Fluoroscopy times and dose area products during barium enema examinations.

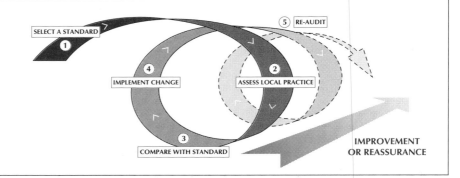

BACKGROUND

● **Why this audit is worth doing**

Radiation dose should be kept to a minimum in diagnostic imaging procedures. Fluoroscopy contributes a major proportion of radiation dose during barium enema examinations (Refs 1 and 2) so screening times should be as short as possible.

The regular measurement and audit of radiologists' screening times and dose area products can help to change practice and reduce radiation dose to the patient.

THE CYCLE

1 THE STANDARD

● **A locally agreed standard (Ref. 2)**

At least 90% of fluoroscopy times should be less than 2 minutes.

At least 90% of recorded fluoroscopy doses should be less than 6093 cGy/cm².

2 ASSESS LOCAL PRACTICE

● **The indicators**

% of fluoroscopy times less than 2 minutes.

% of fluoroscopy doses less than 6093 cGy/cm².

● **Data items to be collected**

For each patient, record:

- a patient identifier;
- patient size (all patients should be within the range 70 kg ± 10 kg, Ref. 3);
- the radiologist identified by code;
- fluoroscopy time;
- dose area product.

● **Suggested number**

25 patients per individual radiologist.

THE CYCLE (continued)

3 **COMPARE FINDINGS WITH THE STANDARD**

4 **CHANGE**

● **Some suggestions**

High-dose operators should observe low-dose operators, particularly considering:

- the use of coning;
- the use of intermittent screening;
- removal of the grid during the filling phase of the examination.

Consider installation of a persistent image system on the monitor.

Review the screen/film sensitivity used.

In some cases it may be necessary to review the age and efficiency of the equipment.

5 **RE-AUDIT** 6 months following implementation of changes.

RESOURCES   FIRST CYCLE £(££)

● **Data collection**

Ongoing data recording.

● **Assistance required**

Local Radiation Protection Advisor, to install measurement equipment, analyse results and discuss change.

● **Estimated radiologists' and radiographers' time to complete stages 1–3 of the first cycle**

Radiologist: 8 hours for data collection.

● **Other estimated costs**

None or minimal if only fluoroscopy timing is measured. If dose area product is also measured, appropriate equipment may need to be purchased.

REFERENCES

1 National Radiological Protection Board. *Patient Dose Reduction in Diagnostic Radiology.* Didcot: NRPB, 1990.

2 IPSM/NRPB/College of Radiographers. *National Protocol for Patient Dose Measurement in Diagnostic Radiology* Chilton: NRPB, 1992.

3 Royal College of Radiologists. *Making the Best Use of a Department of Clinical Radiology.* Third edition. London: RCR, 1995.

SUBMITTED BY

Dr J Tawn, Royal Bournemouth Hospital.

6 Barium Meal Reports

☐ Structure
■ Process
☐ Outcome

THE AUDIT

GP satisfaction with radiology reports on barium meals.

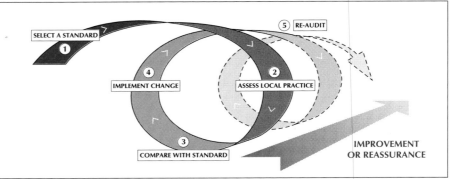

BACKGROUND

● **Why this audit is worth doing**

This audit will determine whether we have provided the GPs with the information that they required (i.e. whether the report addressed/referred to the specific clinical question being posed). It can help to improve communication between GPs and Radiologists (Refs 1 and 2). It can help identify other problems relating to reports (e.g. delay in reports being received).

THE CYCLE

1 THE STANDARD

● **A locally agreed standard with two elements**

All barium meal reports should be received by the requesting GP within 5 days of the examination being performed.

All barium meal reports should be deemed to be satisfactory by the GP to whom they are addressed.

2 ASSESS LOCAL PRACTICE

● **The indicators**

% of barium meal reports received by the requesting GP within 5 days of the examination being performed.

% of reports which are deemed to be satisfactory by the GP to whom they are addressed.

● **Data items to be collected**

Agree (locally) a standard design for a simple questionnaire to attach to each barium meal report when it is posted to the GP. It should address:

• GP satisfaction with the design/layout of the report;

• the appropriateness of the wording;

• the date of the examination and the date on which the report was received by the GP.

● **Suggested number**

100 consecutive reports to GPs.

THE CYCLE (continued)

3 COMPARE FINDINGS WITH THE STANDARD

4 CHANGE

● **Suggested change**

Obtain agreement of all Radiologists regarding a standard format for barium meal reports, i.e. reporting under agreed headings (e.g. clinical indication, drugs used, findings, summary). Inform trainees of this format.

The Clinical Director should address the cause(s) for delays in dispatching reports to GPs.

5 RE-AUDIT Every 6 months if the standard is not met, otherwise every 24 months.

RESOURCES   FIRST CYCLE £

● **Data collection**

Questionnaire.

● **Assistance required**

Secretarial.

● **Estimated radiologists' and radiographers' time to complete stages 1–3 of the first cycle**

Radiologist: 12 hours, to construct questionnaire and analyse responses.

● **Other costs**

Postage (including SAEs for return of the questionnaires).

REFERENCES

1 Fischer HW. Better communication between the referring physician and the radiologist. *Radiology.* 1983;**146**:845.

2 Clinger NJ *et al.* Radiology Reporting: Attitudes of Referring Physicians. *Radiology.* 1988;**167**:825–6.

3 The Royal College of Radiologists. *Making the Best Use of a Department of Clinical Radiology. Guidelines for Doctors.* 3rd Edition. London: RCR, 1995.

4 Rowland M, Shanks J. Broader definitions of clinical effectiveness needed. *BMJ* 1995;**311**:808.

5 Royal College of Radiologists. *Statement on Reporting in Departments of Clinical Radiology.* London: RCR, 1995.

6 Royal College of Radiologists. *Quality Specification for Purchasers.* London: RCR, 1995.

SUBMITTED BY

Dr N Ridley and Dr LS Wilkinson, Northwick Park and St Mark's Hospitals, Harrow; Dr LA Apthorp, Guys and St Thomas' Hospitals, London.

Barium Meal Training

☐ Structure
■ Process
☐ Outcome

THE AUDIT

Image quality of barium meal examinations in a training department.

(See Appendix, page 236).

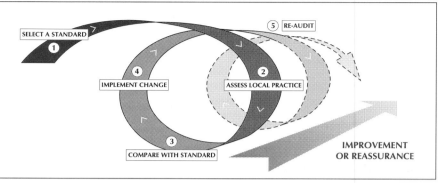

BACKGROUND

● **Why this audit is worth doing**

The detection of subtle mucosal lesions depends on high quality examinations. This requires that the entire mucosal surface of the stomach and the first and second parts of the duodenum are shown in double contrast. In order to achieve this trainees need to follow the local training protocol (see Appendix, page 236) regarding patient positioning and the films to be taken. Good habits are best ingrained in the early years of training.

THE CYCLE

1 THE STANDARD

● **A locally agreed standard**

All trainees should follow the local protocol each time they perform a barium meal examination (BME), and should demonstrate the entire mucosal surface of the stomach and the first and second parts of the duodenum.

2 ASSESS LOCAL PRACTICE

● **The indicator**

% of trainees who comply with the local protocol for all their BMEs.

● **Data items to be collected**

For each trainee, whether the protocol has been complied with in each of 10 randomly selected BMEs.

● **Suggested number**

All trainees in their first year of training.

THE CYCLE (continued)

3 COMPARE FINDINGS WITH THE STANDARD

4 CHANGE

● **Some suggestions**

Clarification of the local protocol.

A more coherent approach to BMEs by all the consultants.

The lead consultant (gastrointestinal radiology) to carry out more BMEs so as to provide adequate teaching/training.

Improved supervision of specialist registrars.

5 RE-AUDIT Every 6 months.

RESOURCES   FIRST CYCLE £

● **Data collection**

Review radiographs.

● **Assistance required**

Clerk (film pulling).

● **Estimated radiologists' and radiographers' time to complete stages 1–3 of the first cycle**

Radiologist: 12 hours.

● **Other estimated costs**

None.

REFERENCES

1 Op den orth JO. Use of barium in the evaluation of disorders of the upper gastrointestinal tract: current status. *Radiology* 1989;**173**:601–8.

2 Maruyama M. Comparison of radiology and endoscopy in the diagnosis of gastric cancer. In: Preece PE, Cuschieri A, Wellwod JM, eds. *Cancer of the Stomach*. London: Grune and Stratton, 1986: 124–44.

3 Shorvon PJ. Dyspepsia in general practice. *BMJ* 1990; **301**:46.

4 Simpkins KC. What use is barium? *Clin Radiol* 1988; **39**:469–73.

SUBMITTED BY

Dr P Gibson, Northwick Park & St. Mark's Hospitals, Harrow; Dr L Berman, Addenbrooke's Hospital, Cambridge.

8 Bladder Cancer CT

THE AUDIT

Adherence to the CT protocol in the initial assessment of bladder cancer.

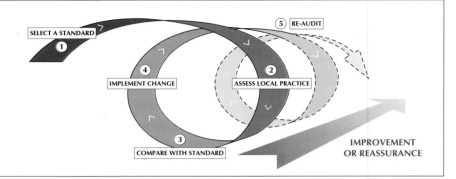

BACKGROUND

● **Why this audit is worth doing**

Failure to follow the optimum diagnostic and staging protocol can lead to a further and unnecessary repeat CT examination at the oncology centre. Adherence to an appropriate CT scanning protocol can therefore help to minimise patient radiation dose (Refs 1 and 2), costs, radiographers' and radiologists' time, and will not be a cause for delay in patient management.

THE CYCLE

1 THE STANDARD

● **A locally agreed standard**

All CT examinations performed for the initial assessment of all patients with bladder cancer should follow the protocol described by the 1994 Working Party of the Royal College of Radiologists (Ref. 1).

2 ASSESS LOCAL PRACTICE

● **The indicator**

% of examinations which adhered to the protocol described by the RCR Working Party (Ref. 1).

● **Data items to be collected**

For each examination:

- the scanning sequence;
- whether the protocol was adhered to;
- if not, how the examination varied from the protocol;
- a coded identifier for the radiologist;
- a coded identifier for the radiographer;
- any previous CT examinations carried out to date.

● **Suggested number**

15 consecutive cases of bladder cancer referred for a CT examination as part of the initial assessment.

THE CYCLE (continued)

3 COMPARE FINDINGS WITH THE STANDARD

4 CHANGE

● **Suggested change**

Present the results of the audit to the radiographers and radiologists. Discuss the causes of failure to meet the standard. Action can then be taken to improve adherence to the standard. Radiographers and radiologists must be aware of what the protocol is, and of how practice is falling short of the agreed standard. Keep the protocol readily available in the scanning suite.

5 RE-AUDIT Every 6 months if the standard is not met, otherwise every 12 months.

RESOURCES   FIRST CYCLE £

● **Data collection**

Patients identified from departmental computer records.

Review of hard copy images.

Review of radiologist's reports.

● **Assistance required**

None.

● **Estimated radiologists' and radiographers' time to complete stages 1–3 of the first cycle**

Radiologist: 9 hours.

● **Other estimated costs**

None.

REFERENCES

1 The Royal College of Radiologists. *The Use of Computed Tomography in the Initial Investigation of Common Malignancies*. London: RCR, 1994:23.

2 National Radiological Protection Board. *Protection of the Patient in X-ray Computed Tomography*. Didcot: NRPB, 1992:paragraph 35.

3 Davies HTO, Crombie IK. Assessing the quality of care: measuring well supported processes may be more enlightening than monitoring outcomes. *BMJ* 1995;**311**:755.

SUBMITTED BY

Dr P Gibson and Dr MI Shaikh, Northwick Park & St Mark's Hospitals, Harrow.

<table>
<tr><td>**9**</td><td># Bone Scintigraphy Images</td><td>☐ Structure
■ Process
☐ Outcome</td></tr>
</table>

THE AUDIT

Image quality of bone scintiscans.

(See Appendix, page 237).

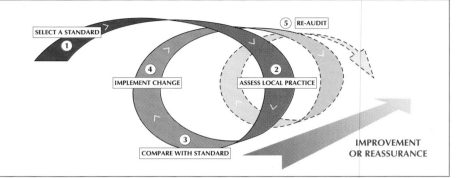

BACKGROUND

● **Data items to be collected**

Suboptimal images can affect the accuracy of a report and lead to errors. The regular use of an image quality checklist (Appendix, page 237), can bring to light image quality problems (technical or processing) which can then be addressed so as to improve the accuracy of reporting.

THE CYCLE

1   THE STANDARD

● **A locally agreed standard**

All bone scan images should meet all the relevant criteria for the particular patient examination (Appendix, page 237).

2   ASSESS LOCAL PRACTICE

● **The indicator**

% of images which meet all the criteria set out in the checklist for assessing bone scan images (see Appendix).

● **Data items to be collected**

Assess retrospectively a randomly selected sample of investigations. Record the percentage of bone scans which meet the standard. For each investigation, record whether or not it meets each of the criteria set out in the standard (see Appendix, page 237).

● **Suggested number**

50 examinations, randomly selected.

THE CYCLE (continued)

3 COMPARE FINDINGS WITH THE STANDARD

4 CHANGE

- **Some suggestions**

Present the results at the audit meeting. Discuss, to identify underlying problems.

Consider the need to seek technical advice on image quality. For example with:

- servicing of equipment;
- processing of images.

Consider the need for refresher courses or tutorials, particularly related to methods and positioning.

5 RE-AUDIT Every 12–24 months.

RESOURCES   FIRST CYCLE £

- **Data collection**

Image review.

Request forms.

- **Assistance required**

None.

- **Estimated radiologists' and radiographers' time to complete stages 1–3 of the first cycle**

Radiographer: 12 hours.

- **Other costs**

None.

REFERENCES

1 Clark S. *Specialty Supplement: Nuclear Medicine. Making Medical Audit Effective.* London: Joint Centre for Education in Medicine, 1993.

2 Collier BD *et al*. Bone. In: Early PJ, Sodee DB, eds. *Principles and Practice of Nuclear Medicine.* Second editon. St Louis: Mosby, 1995:339–69.

SUBMITTED BY

Dr D Remedios and Ms J Ryder (Superintendent Radiographer), Northwick Park and St. Mark's Hospitals, Harrow.

10 Cancer Staging

THE AUDIT

Staging of common cancers using CT.

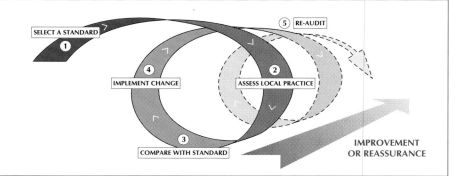

BACKGROUND

● **Why this audit is worth doing**

Adoption of standard procedures for CT staging will:

* improve the adequacy of initial CT examinations in cases of cancer;
* avoid the need to repeat the procedure in cases of tertiary referral;
* speed up patient examinations;
* standardise patient preparation prior to the examination.

THE CYCLE

1 THE STANDARD

● **A locally agreed standard**

All common cancers should be staged according to the guidelines (Ref. 1) of the Royal College of Radiologists (RCR).

2 ASSESS LOCAL PRACTICE

● **The indicator**

% of CT examinations for staging of common cancers that comply with the RCR guidelines.

● **Data items to be collected**

The number of CT examinations performed to stage the common cancers (Ref. 1). Record for each examination whether or not it complied with the RCR guidelines in respect of:

* the areas examined;
* the slice width;
* the use of intravenous contrast medium.

Record the total number of these examinations which complied with the RCR guidelines.

● **Suggested number**

50 consecutive CT staging examinations, reviewed retrospectively.

THE CYCLE (continued)

3 COMPARE FINDINGS WITH THE STANDARD

4 CHANGE

● **Some suggestions**

Make sure that it is fully agreed that the local policy is to stage all common cancers according to the RCR guidelines. Discuss this policy with:

• all consultant radiologists;

• all referring clinicians;

• local tertiary referral centres.

5 RE-AUDIT Every 12–24 months

RESOURCES   FIRST CYCLE £

● **Data collection**

Computer records.

Review of hard copy images.

● **Assistance required**

Film library clerks.

Data analysis.

● **Estimated radiologists' and radiographers' time to complete stages 1–3 of the first cycle**

Radiologist: 8 hours.

● **Other estimated costs**

None.

REFERENCES

1 Royal College of Radiologists. *The Use of Computed Tomography in the Initial Investigation of Common Malignancies.* London: RCR, 1994.

SUBMITTED BY

Dr RJ Godwin, West Suffolk Hospital, Bury St Edmunds.

<table>
<tr><td>

11 | Cardiac Catheterisation

</td><td>

☐ Structure
■ Process
☐ Outcome

</td></tr>
</table>

THE AUDIT

Radiation dose monitoring and dose limitation during cardiac catheterisation.

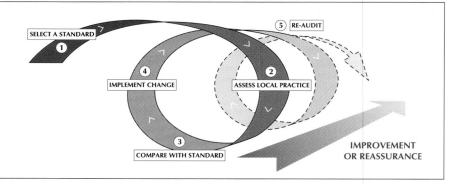

BACKGROUND

● **Why this audit is worth doing**

Cardiac catheterisation is a commonly performed investigation involving radiation exposure to the patient. The dose is comparable with that received during an IVP or barium enema examination. The examination is frequently performed by non-radiologists who may have had less training in radiation protection. This audit may help to reduce radiation dose to patients and staff.

THE CYCLE

1 THE STANDARD

● **A locally agreed standard**

During coronary arteriography, with or without left ventriculography, the mean dose for the department should be less than 3,200 cGy/cm² for cine angiography (2,100 cGy/cm² for digital angiography). In not less than 90% of cases, the dose should be less than 7,000 cGy/cm² for cine angiography (4,500 cGy/cm² for digital angiography).

2 ASSESS LOCAL PRACTICE

● **The indicators**

The mean dose to the patient for cine angiography.

% of cine angiograms where the dose is less than 7,000 cGy/cm².

The mean dose to the patient for digital angiography.

% of digital angiograms where the dose is less than 4,500 cGy/cm².

● **Data items to be collected**

For each examination record the following:

- the age, sex, height, weight and body mass index of the patient;
- the operator and radiographer;
- the procedure length;
- the radiation dose measured by dose area product meter (calibrated in air);
- the film length (cine);
- the number of frames (digital);
- the total number of runs;
- the number in which LV or aortograms were performed;
- the number of injections (runs) for each coronary artery;
- any complications during the procedure.

THE CYCLE (continued)

● **Suggested number**

200 consecutive cases in each catheter room.

3 COMPARE FINDINGS WITH THE STANDARD

4 CHANGE

● **Some suggestions**

The operators' attention should be drawn to the screening time, and further training will help to improve performance. Staff should attend a refresher course on radiation protection. Equipment manufacturers should be asked to service the equipment, and test output and image quality. Angiographic/catheter equipment should also be reviewed, especially catheter sizes and views taken.

5 RE-AUDIT Every 3 months if standard is not met, otherwise annually.

RESOURCES   FIRST CYCLE   £

● **Data collection**

Ongoing data recording on a proforma.

● **Assistance required**

None.

● **Estimated radiologists' and radiographers' time to complete stages 1–3 of the first cycle**

Radiographer: 5 minutes per case.

Radiologist: 2 hours.

● **Other estimated costs**

None.

REFERENCES

1   National Radiological Protection Board. *Patient Dose Reduction in Diagnostic Radiology*. Didcot: NRPB, 1990.

2   Coulden RA, Readman LP. Coronary angiography: an analysis of radiographic practice in the UK. *Br J Radiol*, 1993; **66:** 327–31.

SUBMITTED BY

Dr C Reek and Dr R Keal, Glenfield Hospital, Leicester.

12	# Chest Radiographs: Skin Dose and Film Quality	☐ Structure ■ Process ☐ Outcome

THE AUDIT

Skin dose and film quality of chest radiographs.

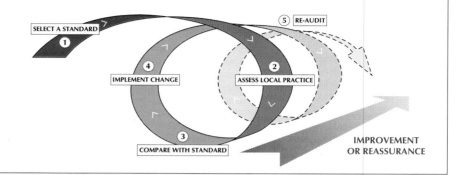

BACKGROUND

● **Why this audit is worth doing**

Chest radiography is one of the most frequently performed and repeated radiographic examinations (Ref. 1). Reduction of patient radiation exposure is desirable, and exposure factors should be set so as to minimise skin doses whilst maintaining adequate film quality (Ref. 2).

THE CYCLE

1 THE STANDARD

● **A locally agreed standard (based on Ref. 3)**

All chest radiographs should give:

• a skin dose of less than 0.3 mGy,

• films of diagnostic quality according to CEC Quality Criteria (Refs 3 and 4).

2 ASSESS LOCAL PRACTICE

● **The indicator**

% of chest radiographs which meet the criteria set out in the standard.

● **Data items to be collected**

For each radiograph record:

• a patient identifier;

• the size of the patient (large, medium or small);

• the radiation dose applied;

• whether an automatic exposure system was used;

• exposure factors (kVp, mAs, FSD (cm));

• the measured TLD dose (Ref. 4);

• film quality, assessed according to CEC Quality Criteria.

● **Suggested number**

100 consecutive chest radiographs.

THE CYCLE (continued)

3 COMPARE FINDINGS WITH THE STANDARD

4 CHANGE

● **Suggested change**

Present the results at a departmental audit meeting. Discuss alterations to technique/equipment. The dose can be reduced by increasing kVp up to the point at which image quality begins to deteriorate. kVp should be reviewed by reference to film-screen technical specification so as to use the optimal sensitivity of the system. Instruct radiographers to use the new optimum kVp rather than individual preference. Consider changes in film chemistry or temperature of processing, and consider using an anode filter.

5 RE-AUDIT Every 6 months.

RESOURCES   FIRST CYCLE £

● **Data collection**

Ongoing data recording.

Film review.

● **Assistance required**

Film library clerks to obtain review films.

Note pulling by audit staff.

Medical Physics Department for dose measurements (3 hours).

● **Estimated radiologists' and radiographers' time to complete stages 1–3 of the first cycle**

Radiologists: 5 hours to assess films.

● **Other estimated costs**

None.

REFERENCES

1 Royal College of Radiologists. *Making the Best Use of a Department of Clinical Radiology. Guidelines for Doctors.* Third edition. London: RCR, 1995.

2 National Radiation Protection Board. Vol IV no. 2 1993.

3 Council of European Communities Quality Criteria. XII/173/90 2nd ed June 1990.

4 IPSM/NRPB/College of Radiographers. *National Protocol for Patient Dose Measurement in Diagnostic Radiology.* Chilton: NRPB, 1992.

SUBMITTED BY

Dr B Barry, Dr N Broderick and Mr A Rogers (Medical Physicist), Nottingham City Hospital.

<table>
<tr><td>

13

</td><td>

Clinical Information from A&E

</td><td>

☐ Structure
■ Process
☐ Outcome

</td></tr>
</table>

THE AUDIT

Adequacy of clinical information from the Accident and Emergency (A&E) Department.

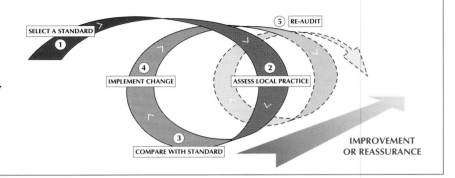

BACKGROUND

● **Why this audit is worth doing**

There is evidence that inadequate clinical information is associated with an increased level of inaccurate reports (Refs 1–3). Accurate clinical information is more likely to assist the radiologist in constructing a report which in turn will help the referring doctor with the management of the patient.

THE CYCLE

1 THE STANDARD

● **A locally agreed standard**

All request forms should contain adequate clinical information.

2 ASSESS LOCAL PRACTICE

● **The indicator**

% of request forms containing adequate clinical information.

● **Data items to be collected**

Assess request forms on a simple proforma completed at the time of reporting A&E films. For each request form, record the information provided as being adequate if there is included:

- a brief clinical history;
- the clinical signs;
- (trauma only) the precise site of injury;
- a coded identifier for the person signing the request form.

● **Suggested number**

200 consecutive request forms.

3 COMPARE FINDINGS WITH THE STANDARD

THE CYCLE (continued)

4 CHANGE

● **Some suggestions**

Hold meetings between the radiologists and the A&E officers to discuss the areas in which improvement is required. Provide formal instruction on how to complete request forms. Design and provide a request form which is specifically designed for A&E officers and nurse practitioners, with a view to obtaining excellent clinical information. Identify any referring doctor with a poor record of completing forms and discuss the benefits of good information.

5 RE-AUDIT Every 3 months if standard is not met, otherwise every 6 months.

RESOURCES   FIRST CYCLE £

● **Data collection**

Ongoing data recording.

● **Assistance required**

Data analysis assistance from the Audit Office: 3 hours.

● **Estimated radiologists' and radiographers' time to complete stages 1–3 of the first cycle**

Radiologists: a total of 3 hours.

● **Other estimated costs**

None.

REFERENCES

1 Rickett AB *et al*. The importance of clinical details when reporting accident and emergency radiographs. *Injury* 1992;**23**:458–60.

2 Berbaum KS *et al*. Impact of clinical history on fracture detection with radiography. *Radiology* 1988;**168**:507–511.

3 Berbaum KS *et al*. Influence of clinical history upon detection of nodules and other lesions. *Invest Rad* 1988; **23**:48–55.

4 de Lacey GJ *et al*. An assessment of the clinical effects of reporting accident and emergency radiographs. *Br J Radiol* 1980;**53**:304–309.

5 Berbaum KS *et al*. Impact of Clinical History on radiographic detection of fractures: a comparison of radiologists and orthopedists. *AJR* 1989;**153**:1221–4.

6 Seltzer SE *et al*. Resident film interpretation. A staff review. *AJR* 1981;**137**:129–33.

7 Vincent CA *et al*. Accuracy of detection of radiographic abnormalities by junior doctors. *Arch Emerg Med* 1988;**5**:101–109.

SUBMITTED BY

Dr G Kaplan and Dr D Remedios, Northwick Park & St. Mark's Hospitals, Harrow.

14	Consent for a Radiological Examination	☐ Structure ■ Process ☐ Outcome

THE AUDIT

Adequacy of consent for radiological procedures.

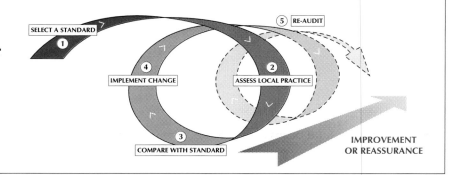

BACKGROUND

● **Why this audit is worth doing**

Adequate patient consent is not simply a matter of completing a consent form but involves discussing and explaining what the procedure entails with the patient, including benefits and possible complications. Recording the discussion in the patient's notes represents good practice. This audit can help to establish this good practice as routine practice within the department.

THE CYCLE

1 THE STANDARD

● **A locally agreed standard**

All procedures involving the use of either a local or a general anaesthetic should be preceded by:

• a discussion of the procedure, including an explanation of the benefits and possible complications;

• completion of a consent form;

• recording of this process in the patient's notes.

2 ASSESS LOCAL PRACTICE

● **Data items to be collected**

For each procedure record a coded identifier for the radiologist who carried out the procedure. Record whether the patient's notes contain:

• evidence of discussion of the procedure;

• evidence that the discussion included reference to the benefits and possible complications of the procedure;

• a completed consent form.

● **Suggested number**

30 consecutive radiological procedures using either a local or a general anaesthetic.

THE CYCLE (continued)

3 COMPARE FINDINGS WITH THE STANDARD

4 CHANGE

● **Suggested change**

Present the (anonymised) results to all the consultants, and follow up with full and frank discussions. Gain full agreement that in all examinations where patients require the use of a local or a general anaesthetic:

- the patient should be given written information on procedures, as an information pack;
- the radiologist performing the procedure is responsible for obtaining the patient's written consent.

5 RE-AUDIT Every 6 months.

RESOURCES   FIRST CYCLE   £

● **Data collection**

Computer records to identify cases.

Notes search.

● **Assistance required**

Note pulling by audit staff.

● **Estimated radiologists' and radiographers' time to complete stages 1–3 of the first cycle**

Radiologist: 5 hours for review of 30 case notes.

● **Other estimated costs**

None.

REFERENCES

1 DoH Health Service Management. *A Guide to Consent for Examination or Treatment.* London: HMSO, 1993.

2 Nuffield Working Party on Communications with Patients. *Talking With Patients. A Teaching Approach.* Oxford: The Nuffield Provincial Hospitals Trust.

3 Royal College of Radiologists. *Consent by Patients to Examination or Treatment.* London: RCR, 1991.

SUBMITTED BY

Dr RJ Godwin, West Suffolk Hospital, Bury St Edmunds.

15 Contrast and Drug Recording

THE AUDIT

Recording of dose, make, batch number and expiry date for contrast medium used for intravenous urograms (IVUs).

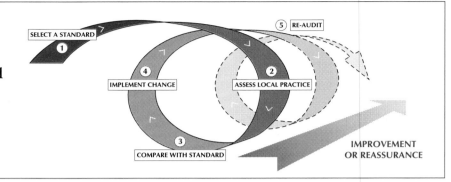

BACKGROUND

● **Why this audit is worth doing**

Reaction to intravenous contrast agents and side effects from drugs are uncommon but potentially serious occurrences. Maintaining a record of the batch and dose is therefore important for medico-legal reasons, and is a recommendation of the Royal College of Radiologists (Ref. 1). This audit can help to ensure that adequate records are kept.

THE CYCLE

1 THE STANDARD

● **A locally agreed standard**

Every request card for an IVU should record the dose, batch number, manufacturer and expiry date of any intravenous contrast agent or drug used in that procedure.

2 ASSESS LOCAL PRACTICE

● **The indicator**

% of request cards that record the information set out in the standard.

● **Data items to be collected**

For each request card, whether each of the data items set out in the standard is present or absent.

● **Suggested number**

50 consecutive IVUs.

THE CYCLE (continued)

3 COMPARE FINDINGS WITH THE STANDARD

4 CHANGE

● **Some suggestions**

If information is missing, meetings should be held with all the radiographers and x ray helpers to ensure that the standard is known and understood. Radiographers should be reminded to record all appropriate information on the request cards at the time of the examination. Consider also reprinting (i.e. redesigning) the request forms.

5 RE-AUDIT Every 12–24 months.

RESOURCES

FIRST CYCLE £

● **Data collection**

Review of request cards.

● **Assistance required**

Audit Assistant to review request cards (5 hours).

Clerical staff to identify and collect together the request cards (5 hours).

● **Estimated radiologists' and radiographers' time to complete stages 1–3 of the first cycle**

None.

● **Other estimated costs**

None.

REFERENCES

1 Royal College of Radiologists. *Consent by Patients to Examination or Treatment*. London: RCR, 1991.

SUBMITTED BY

Mrs C Soar (Radiology Audit Officer) and Dr K Dunn, Nottingham City Hospital.

THE AUDIT

Fluoroscopy times during coronary angiography.

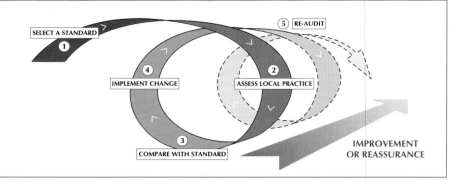

BACKGROUND

● **Why this audit is worth doing**

Prolonged fluoroscopy (screening) during coronary angiography leads to an increased radiation dose to the patient and to the staff. This audit can help to indicate whether changes in practice are necessary.

THE CYCLE

1 THE STANDARD

● **A locally agreed standard**

90% of coronary angiograms should have a total fluoroscopy time of 5 minutes or less.

2 ASSESS LOCAL PRACTICE

● **The indicator**

% of examinations with a fluoroscopy time of 5 minutes or less.

● **Data items to be collected**

For each examination:

• the date of the examination;

• the screening time in minutes;

• a coded operator identifier.

● **Suggested number**

All examinations during a 4-week period.

THE CYCLE (continued)

3 COMPARE FINDINGS WITH THE STANDARD

4 CHANGE

● **Some suggestions**

Present the results of the audit to all groups involved in coronary angiography.

Hold tutorials/seminars on radiation dose and protection – to supplement the core of knowledge course.

Hold a refresher course (for doctors), addressing the technical aspects of angiography.

Improve the supervision by the consultant(s) of specialist registrars in training.

An alternative method of audit which may gain additional information on patient dose is shown in recipe 11, page 22.

5 RE-AUDIT Every 3 months.

RESOURCES

FIRST CYCLE £

● **Data collection**

Ongoing data recording.

● **Assistance required**

Data analysis assistance from the Clinical Audit Office.

● **Estimated radiologists' and radiographers' time to complete stages 1–3 of the first cycle**

Radiographer: 2 hours.

● **Other estimated costs**

None.

REFERENCES

1 National Radiological Protection Board. *Dosimetry Working Party of the Institute of Physical Sciences in Medicine. National Protocol for Patient Dose Measurements in Diagnostic Radiology*. Didcot: NRPB, 1992.

2 Plaut S. *Radiation Protection in the X-ray Department*. London: Butterworth Heinemann, 1993.

3 Cosman M. Managing radiation safety in imaging departments. *RAD Magazine* 1995;**21**:32.

4 Wilson E and Ebdon-Jackson S. Secretary of State's POPUMET Inspectorate: The first six years. *Health Trends* 1994;**26**:67–9.

SUBMITTED BY

Dr G Kaplan and Mrs J Brown (Superintendent Radiographer), Northwick Park and St. Mark's Hospitals, Harrow.

17 | Courtesy

☐ Structure
■ Process
☐ Outcome

THE AUDIT

The doctor's attitude as perceived by the patient when a practical procedure or consultation commences late.

(See Appendix, pages 238–239)

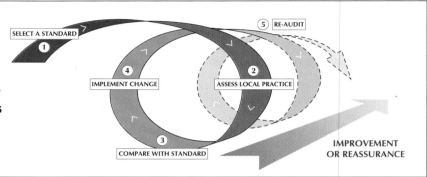

BACKGROUND

● **Why this audit is worth doing**

Efficient scheduling for out-patient examinations is to be expected and the Patient's Charter (Ref. 1) has properly reinforced this expectation. When a delay does occur some doctors do not apologise, nor do they always provide an explanation for the delay. Good manners are fundamental to all doctor-patient relationships and an assessment of courteous behaviour will identify those areas or circumstances where this may or may not be occurring in the Department of Clinical Radiology. Remember also that "there can be no defence like elaborate courtesy" (EV Lucas, 1868–1938).

THE CYCLE

1 THE STANDARD

● **A locally agreed standard**

On all occasions when a practical procedure is delayed beyond the scheduled appointment time, the radiologist should:

- apologise to the patient;

- give to the patient a brief but credible explanation as to the cause of the delay.

2 ASSESS LOCAL PRACTICE

● **The indicator**

% of occasions of delay in commencing the procedure, in which both an apology and a credible explanation are given.

● **Data items to be collected**

Patients should be asked to complete the simple questionnaire (Appendix, page 238). Record the number of patients who answer:

- *yes* to question 2;

- *yes* to question 6;

- *yes* to question 7.

● **Suggested number**

100 consecutive patients. Example: attending for a non-obstetric ultrasound (US) examination.

THE CYCLE (continued)

3 COMPARE FINDINGS WITH THE STANDARD

4 CHANGE

● **Suggested change**

Presentation of the results of the audit to all of the consultant radiologists. The results should be anonymised, and full and frank discussion should follow. If the standard has not been met then the consultants should be asked to agree that this courtesy be extended to all patients. If a subsequent repeat audit shows that the standard is still not being achieved then the Clinical Director should take appropriate action. This might include:

* limiting the number of cases scheduled during each session, to reduce the pressure on the consultants;

* re-organisation of individual doctors' work programme in order to minimise the number of delays and thus reduce the number of apologies required;

* counselling of doctor(s) in terms of communication skills and common courtesy.

5 RE-AUDIT Every 3 months if the standard is not met, otherwise every 12 months.

RESOURCES   FIRST CYCLE £

● **Data collection**

Questionnaire (Appendix, page 238).

● **Assistance required**

X ray helper to give the questionnaire to each patient on completion of the examination and to explain the reasons for the enquiry.

Audit officer to collect and analyse the questionnaire and tabulate the anonymised results.

● **Estimated radiologists' and radiographers' time to complete stages 1–3 of the first cycle**

None.

● **Other estimated costs**

None.

REFERENCES

1 National Charter Standards, Department of Health. Patients' Charter, 1995. London: DoH, 1995.

2 Rowland M, Shanks J. Broader definitions of clinical effectiveness are needed. *BMJ* 1995;**311**:808.

SUBMITTED BY

Mr R Glanville-Brown (Patient), c/o Alex Alagappa & Co., 4, Kingsend, Ruislip, Middlesex.

18 | CT Guided Biopsies

Structure
■ Process
Outcome

THE AUDIT

Success rate of CT guided biopsies.

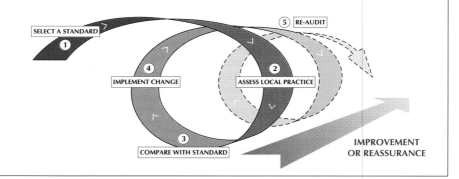

BACKGROUND

● **Why this audit is worth doing**

The adequacy of the specimen obtained has a direct bearing on patient management. A high success rate instills confidence in the procedure amongst the referring clinicians.

THE CYCLE

1 THE STANDARD

● **A locally agreed standard**

80% of CT guided biopsies should have a diagnostic yield (i.e. a cellular aspirate or core which is representative of the lesion, Refs 1–3).

2 ASSESS LOCAL PRACTICE

● **The indicator**

% of CT guided biopsies which have a diagnostic yield.

● **Data items to be collected**

For each biopsy record:

* CT biopsy (radiology) report – including details of the needle used. For each biopsy record:
* cytological and / or histopathological report;
* coded indicator for the operator.

● **Suggested number**

30 consecutive patients.

3 COMPARE FINDINGS WITH THE STANDARD

THE CYCLE (continued)

4 CHANGE

● **Some suggestions**

Discuss the results of the audit with the radiologists and pathologists involved.

Introduce a *biopsy book* to encourage follow-up of cases.

Ensure feedback to radiologists from pathologists and clinical colleagues.

The Cytology Technician should check fine needle aspirates (FNAs) for cellularity.

Use 18 G needles where feasible. Obtain as large a specimen as is safe and feasible.

5 RE-AUDIT Every 12 months.

RESOURCES   FIRST CYCLE   £

● **Data collection**

Computer records to identify patients.

Review radiology reports.

Review pathology reports.

● **Assistance required**

None.

● **Estimated radiologists' and radiographers' time to complete stages 1–3 of the first cycle**

Radiologist: 6 hours for reviewing the pathology reports and analysing the data.

● **Other costs**

None.

REFERENCES

1 Husband J E, Golding S J. The role of CT-guided needle biopsy in an oncological service. *Clin Radiol* 1983;**34**:255–60.

2 Ferrucci JT *et al.* Diagnosis of abdominal malignancy by radiologic fine needle biopsy. *AJR* 1980;**134**:323–30.

3 Bernardino M E. Percutaneous biopsy. *AJR* 1984;**142**:41–5.

4 Labadie M, Liaras A. Percutaneous biopsy: Cytology. In: Dondelinger R. eds. *Interventional Radiology* New York:Thieme Medical Publishers, 1990.

5 Burbank F *et al.* Image Guided automated core biopsies of the breast, chest, abdomen and pelvis. *Radiology* 1994;**191**:165–71.

6 Moulton, JS, Moore PT. Coaxial percutaneous biopsy technique with automated biopsy devices: value in improving accuracy and negative predictive value. *Radiology* 1993;**186**:515.

SUBMITTED BY

Dr D Remedios, Northwick Park and St Mark's Hospitals, Harrow.

RECIPES

19 | CT – Ward Staff Knowledge

THE AUDIT

Ward staff knowledge of the processs of CT scanning.

(See Appendix, pages 240–242)

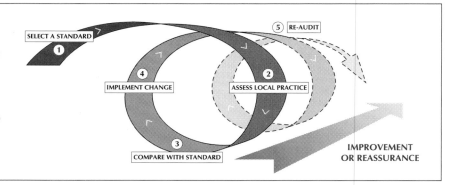

BACKGROUND

● **Why this audit is worth doing**

Patients benefit from and are reassured by advance information on procedures that they are to undergo. Better understanding of medical procedures by ward staff (Refs 1 and 2) can be of help to patients, and will assist in reducing anxiety and confusion (e.g. with preparation instructions). Improved staff knowledge can improve interdepartmental communication and avoid wasted appointments.

THE CYCLE

1 THE STANDARD

● **A locally agreed standard**

All nursing staff on the ward should have an adequate knowledge of CT scanning. All nursing staff should know that CT scanning involves the use of x rays.

2 ASSESS LOCAL PRACTICE

● **The indicators**

% of nursing staff who have an adequate knowledge of CT scanning.

% of nursing staff who know that CT scanning involves the use of x rays.

● **Data items to be collected**

Use the questionnaire in the Appendix (page 240) to collect the information from each member of staff. Record a member of staff as having adequate knowledge of CT scanning if they:

• can differentiate CT from other scans (e.g. nuclear medicine, ultrasound, MRI);

• know that oral or intravenous contrast media may be used;

• are aware of aspects of patient preparation.

Record also whether staff know that a CT scan involves x rays.

● **Suggested number**

50 members of (ward) staff.

THE CYCLE (continued)

3 COMPARE FINDINGS WITH THE STANDARD

4 CHANGE

● **Some suggestions**

Distribute an explanatory leaflet for ward staff. A number of commercial companies produce leaflets which are suitable.

Encourage nurses to observe CT scans when they accompany patients to the CT unit.

Arrange educational talks for nurses and nurses-in-training.

5 RE-AUDIT Every 12–24 months.

RESOURCES   FIRST CYCLE   £

● **Data collection**

Questionnaire.

● **Assistance required**

Audit assistant for data analysis.

● **Estimated radiologists' and radiographers' time to complete stages 1–3 of the first cycle**

Radiographer: 20 hours.

● **Other estimated costs**

None.

REFERENCES

1 Clark CR, Gregor FM. Developing a sensation information message for femoral arteriography. *J Adv Nursing* 1988;**13**:237–44.

2 Hjelm Karlesson K. Effects of information to patients undergoing intravenous pyelography. An intervention study. *J Adv Nursing* 1989;**14**:853–62.

3 Royal College of Radiologists. *Making the Best Use of a Department of Clinical Radiology*. Third edition. London: RCR, 1995:11–12.

SUBMITTED BY

Miss S Grundy (Superintendent Radiographer) and Dr J Tawn, Royal Bournemouth Hospital.

20 | Dark Room Safety

■ Structure
☐ Process
☐ Outcome

THE AUDIT

Protective equipment in the dark room and film processing areas.

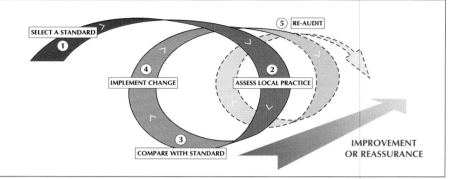

BACKGROUND

● **Why this audit is worth doing**

The chemicals used in the dark rooms and film processing areas represent a potential health risk to the image processing technician (IPT) and to the radiographers (Refs 1–3). The Clinical Director needs to confirm – through regular audit – that the IPTs are provided with and have available all the necessary safety equipment to meet Health and Safety requirements (Refs 3 and 4).

THE CYCLE

1 THE STANDARD

● **A locally agreed standard**

In all areas where x ray chemicals are used the following safety equipment (Refs 1–6) should be available and in good condition:

- a long sleeved protective coat (e.g. white coat or hospital gown);
- a disposable plastic apron;
- a pair of safety spectacles or goggles;
- a heavyweight 24-inch gauntlet glove;
- a facial mask as approved by Occupational Health (i.e. charcoal filter type specific for photographic chemicals);
- an eye bath and medically approved eye wash solution.

2 ASSESS LOCAL PRACTICE

● **The indicator**

Number of areas in which all the items listed in the standard are available and in good condition.

● **Data items to be collected**

For each area, list which items of safety equipment are:
- available;
- in good condition.

● **Suggested number**

All areas where x ray chemicals are used.

THE CYCLE (continued)

3 COMPARE FINDINGS WITH THE STANDARD

4 CHANGE

● **Some suggestions**

Bring any areas which do not meet the standard to the attention of the Clinical Director. Consider:

- purchase of new equipment;

- introduction of a system whereby faults in, or loss of, any item of safety equipment leads to rapid replacement;

- keeping a continuous record book, to record the results whenever the audit is carried out;

- keeping all equipment within a specified area or cupboard (safety cupboard). This will enable lost or misplaced material to be noted more easily as well as making it easily available for use.

5 RE-AUDIT every 3–6 months.

RESOURCES   FIRST CYCLE   £

● **Data collection**

Ongoing data recording.

Inspection of safety equipment by the Health and Safety (radiographer) representative.

● **Assistance required**

None.

● **Estimated radiologists' and radiographers' time to complete stages 1–3 of the first cycle**

Radiographer: 1 hour.

● **Other estimated costs**

None.

REFERENCES

1 Society of Radiographers. *Preventing the Darkroom Disease : Health Effects of Toxic Fumes Produced in X-ray Film Processing*. London: SoR, 1991.

2 Health and Safety Executive. *Glutaraldehyde and You*. Sudbury: HSE Books, 1992.

3 Health and Safety Executive. *The Requirements of the Control of Substances Hazardous to Health (COSHH)*. Sudbury: HSE Books, 1992

4 Management of Health and Safety at Work Regulations. London: HMSO, 1993.

5 Health and Safety Executive. *Occupational Exposure Limits*. Sudbury: HSE Books, 1995.

6 Environmental Protection Act (EPA). Duty of Care, Section 34. London: HMSO, 1990.

SUBMITTED BY

Mr R Douglas-Law (Senior Image Processing Technician) and Miss M Saint Leger (Radiographer), Northwick Park and St. Mark's Hospitals, Harrow.

<table>
<tr><td>

21

</td><td>

Department Opening Hours

</td><td>

☐ Structure
☐ Process
■ Outcome

</td></tr>
</table>

Opening hours of the
Department of Clinical
Radiology.

(See Appendix, page 243)

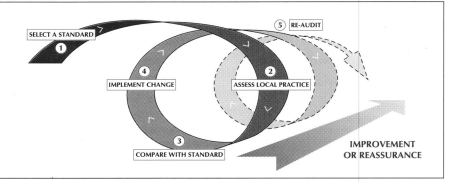

BACKGROUND

● **Why this audit is worth doing**

Many patients may need to take time off work in order to have a radiographic examination. The
opening hours for routine departmental work should be appropriate to the needs of most patients. This
audit was originally carried out in a department offering open access to GP patients between the hours
of 9.00 a.m. and 5.00 p.m. on a walk-in-and-wait basis. Patients are offered the alternative of an
appointment on another day, when they should have their examination within 30 minutes of their
appointment time (Refs 1 and 2). This audit is designed to show whether or not an extension of the
opening hours is necessary.

THE CYCLE

1 THE STANDARD

● **A locally agreed standard**

95% of patients should be satisfied with the current hours of opening.

2 ASSESS LOCAL PRACTICE

● **The indicators**

% of patients who are satisfied with the current Radiology department hours of opening.

● **Data items to be collected**

For each patient, record:

• a patient identifier;

• the age of the patient;

• whether the patient is employed, a student or retired;

• whether the patient is satisfied with the current hours of opening.

● **Suggested number**

Survey at least 100 consecutive patients referred for radiography by their General Practitioner.

THE CYCLE (continued)

3 COMPARE FINDINGS WITH THE STANDARD

4 CHANGE

- **Some suggestions**

If patients are not satisfied with the current opening hours, consideration should be given to the following:

- extension of the working day to 6.00 p.m.;
- opening the Department of Clinical Radiology on Saturday mornings;
- a modest increase in staffing levels so as to decrease waiting time during the current working day.

5 RE-AUDIT Repeat 6–12 months after implementation of changes.

RESOURCES   FIRST CYCLE £

- **Data collection**

Questionnaire (Appendix, page 243), using semi-interview technique.

- **Assistance required**

Helper to fill in questionnaire using semi-interview technique.

Audit Assistant for data analysis.

- **Estimated radiologists' and radiographers' time to complete stages 1–3 of the first cycle**

Radiologist: 2 hours.

- **Other estimated costs**

None.

REFERENCES

1 Department of Health. *The Patient's Charter*. London: DoH, 1991.

2 Department of Health. *The Patient's Charter and You*. London: DoH, 1995.

3 The Audit Commission. *Improving your Image. How to Manage Radiology Services More Effectively*. London: HMSO, 1995.

SUBMITTED BY

Mr G Horne (Radiographer) and Dr J Tawn, Royal Bournemouth Hospital.

22 Do the Reports Address the Questions?

THE AUDIT

Whether radiology reports address the questions posed by the requesting clinician.

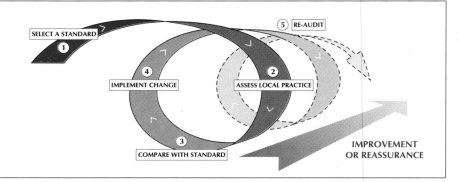

BACKGROUND

● **Why this audit is worth doing**

Most requests for radiological examinations pose a clinical question (e.g. any evidence of infection?). The subsequent phrasing of the report should attempt to anwer the question or suggest an investigation that may help to give an answer. *Question and answer based* reporting can improve communication.

THE CYCLE

1 THE STANDARD

● **A locally agreed standard**

Where request forms contain an identifiable question, explicit or implicit, the question should be explicitly addressed by the report in all cases.

2 ASSESS LOCAL PRACTICE

● **The indicator**

Of request forms containing an identifiable question, % where this question is explicitly addressed in the report.

● **Data items to be collected**

For each request:

* whether an identifiable question is asked in the report;

* what this question is;

* whether the question is explicit or implicit;

* whether the question is answered in the report;

* whether the question is addressed in the report.

● **Suggested number**

100 consecutive requests.

THE CYCLE (continued)

3 COMPARE FINDINGS WITH THE STANDARD

4 CHANGE

● **Some suggestions**

Develop an environment and an approach whereby each request poses an explicit clinical question and the corresponding report attempts to answer this question, or suggests an appropriate further investigation.

Give guidance to junior staff at induction.

Regularly discuss unclear requests and reports at the various clinical and audit meetings.

5 RE-AUDIT Every 12–24 months.

RESOURCES   FIRST CYCLE £

● **Data collection**

Computer records.

Review of requests and reports.

● **Assistance required**

Audit staff for examination of requests and reports.

● **Estimated radiologists' and radiographers' time to complete stages 1–3 of the first cycle**

Radiologist: 3 hours for reviewing the requests and reports.

● **Other costs**

None.

REFERENCES

1 Lafortune M *et al*. The radiological report. *J Can Assoc Rad* 1982;**33**:255–66.

2 Sierra AE *et al*. Readability of the radiologic reports. *Invest Rad* 1992;**27**:236–9.

3 Hessel SJ *et al*. The composition of the radiologic report. *Invest Rad* 1975;**10**:385–90.

4 Royal College of Radiologists. *Statement on Reporting in Departments of Clinical Radiology*. London: RCR, 1995.

5 Royal College of Radiologists. *Clinical Radiology Quality Specification for Purchasers*. London: RCR, 1995.

6 The Audit Commission. *Improving your Image. How to Manage Radiology Services More Effectively*. London: Audit Commission, 1995.

7 McLoughlin RF *et al*. Radiology reports: how much descriptive detail is enough? *Am J Radiol* 1995;**165**:803–806.

SUBMITTED BY

Dr RJ Godwin, West Suffolk Hospital, Bury St Edmunds.

23	# Doppler in DVT	☐ Structure ■ Process ☐ Outcome

Use of doppler
ultrasound to diagnose
deep vein thrombosis
(DVT)

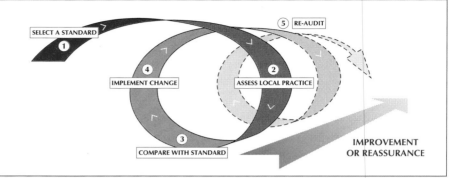

BACKGROUND

● **Why this audit is worth doing**

Doppler ultrasound when used as the first imaging investigation can assist in reducing the number of cases requiring venography.

THE CYCLE

1 THE STANDARD

● **A locally agreed standard**

All patients with suspected lower limb DVT should have duplex/colour flow doppler ultrasound as the first imaging investigation.

2 ASSESS LOCAL PRACTICE

● **The indicator**

% of patients suspected of a lower limb DVT who have duplex scans as the first investigation.

● **Data items to be collected**

Total number of requests for lower limb venography.

Number of requests which are for lower limb duplex scans.

Number of requests which are for lower limb venography without prior duplex.

● **Suggested number**

50 consecutive requests for investigation of suspected lower limb DVT, collected retrospectively.

3 COMPARE FINDINGS WITH THE STANDARD

THE CYCLE (continued)

4 CHANGE

● **Some suggestions**

Introduce a departmental protocol which will divert requests for venography to ultrasound.

Train existing staff in duplex scanning.

Increase staffing levels in ultrasound.

Provide education and information to the referring clinicians.

5 RE-AUDIT   Every 6–12 months.

RESOURCES   FIRST CYCLE   £

● **Data collection**

Computer records.

Review of case notes.

● **Assistance required**

Clerk (case note pulling).

● **Estimated radiologists' and radiographers' time to complete stages 1–3 of the first cycle**

Radiologist: 3 hours.

● **Other costs**

None.

REFERENCES

1 Verstraete M. The diagnosis and treatment of deep vein thrombosis. Editorial. *N Engl J Med* 1993;**329**:1418–20.

2 Lewis BD *et al*. Diagnosis of acute deep venous thrombosis of the lower extremities; prospective evaluation of colour Doppler flow imaging versus venography. *Radiology* 1994;**192**:651–5.

3 Keogan MT *et al*. Bilateral lower extremity evaluation of deep venous thrombosis with colour flow and compression sonography. *J Ultrasound Med* 1994;**13**:115–118.

4 Bradley MJ *et al*. Colour flow mapping in the diagnosis of calf deep vein thrombosis. *Clin Radiol* 1993;**47**:399–402.

5 Fletcher JP *et al*. Ultrasound diagnosis of lower limb deep venous thrombosis. (Review). *M J Austral* 1990:**153**:453–5.

6 Bradley M. Ultrasonography of lower limb deep vein thrombosis. *Reflections* 1995;**1**:2–4.

SUBMITTED BY

Dr LS Wilkinson and Dr N Ridley, Northwick Park and St. Mark's Hospitals, Harrow.

THE AUDIT

Double reading of mammograms in a breast screening unit.

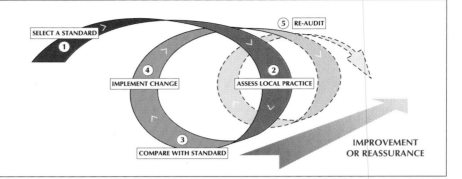

BACKGROUND

● **Why this audit is worth doing**

In an effective breast screening programme, small early tumours should be identified. The number of women recalled for further examination should not be too high, but as many tumours as possible should be identified by mammography. This balance is difficult to maintain. Double reading can increase sensitivity, but lower specificity (Ref. 1). Where double reading is followed by review and discussion, then it may be possible to decrease recall and maintain specificity (Ref. 2).

THE CYCLE

1 THE STANDARD

● **A locally agreed standard**

All mammograms should be read by at least two experienced radiologists.

2 ASSESS LOCAL PRACTICE

● **The indicators**

% of mammograms recorded as double read.

● **Data items to be collected**

For each mammogram film set, computer record of the number of readers (0, 1, 2, more than 2).

● **Suggested number**

200 mammograms.

THE CYCLE (continued)

3 COMPARE FINDINGS WITH THE STANDARD

4 CHANGE

● **Some suggestions**

Re-emphasise that no examination is considered to be complete until it has been double read. Leave mammograms on the roller viewer until they are double read.

Arrange for a minimum of three radiologists to be involved in breast screening. Review holiday arrangements to ensure that at least two radiologists are available at any one time.

5 RE-AUDIT every 12–24 months.

RESOURCES   FIRST CYCLE £

● **Data collection**
Computer records.

● **Assistance required**
Clerical assistant.

● **Estimated radiologists' and radiographers' time to complete stages 1–3 of the first cycle**
Radiologist: 1 hour.

● **Other estimated costs**
None.

REFERENCES

1 Anderson C et al. The efficiency of double reading mammograms in breast screening. *Clin Radiol* 1994;**49**:245–51.

2 Anttinen IP et al. Double reading of mammography screening films – one radiologist or two? *Clin Radiol* 1993;**48**:414–21

SUBMITTED BY

Dr M Creagh-Barry and Dr J Tawn, Royal Bournemouth Hospital.

25 Emergency Skull Radiography

THE AUDIT

Compliance with Accident and Emergency (A&E) Skull Radiography (SXR) guidelines.

(See Appendix, pages 244–245)

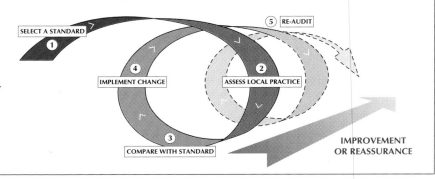

BACKGROUND

● **Why this audit is worth doing**

SXR constitutes 5–25% of all A&E examinations (Ref. 1). The application of guidelines can help reduce the number of patients unnecessarily referred for radiography (Refs 2 and 3). Locally designed strategies have been shown to reinforce guidelines (Ref. 4).

THE CYCLE

1 THE STANDARD

● **A locally agreed standard**

No more than 30% of all patients discharged from A&E following a minor head injury should have been referred for SXR (Ref. 4).

2 ASSESS LOCAL PRACTICE

● **The indicator**

% of patients with minor head injury who were referred for SXR before discharge.

● **Data items to be collected:**

Prepare two versions of the head injury discharge card:

- one for patients who have undergone SXR (Appendix, page 244);
- one for patients who have not undergone SXR (Appendix, page 245). This discharge card is constructed so as to explain to a patient and relatives why skull radiography was not performed.

Record how many of each type of card are given out. Cards are sequentially numbered in order to facilitate counting.

● **Suggested number**

200 consecutive patients given head injury discharge cards.

THE CYCLE (continued)

3 COMPARE FINDINGS WITH THE STANDARD

4 CHANGE

● **Some suggestions**

Local reinforcement of guidelines by use of posters (Ref. 4).

Educational meetings with A&E Officers.

5 RE-AUDIT Every 6–12 months.

RESOURCES   FIRST CYCLE £

● **Data collection**

Ongoing data recording.

● **Assistance required**

Cooperation of A&E medical and nursing staff.

● **Estimated radiologists' and radiographers' time to complete the first cycle (stages 1-3)**

Radiologist: 8 hours.

● **Other estimated costs**

None.

REFERENCES

1 Roberts CJ. The effective use of diagnostic radiology. *Journal of the Royal College of Physicians of London* 1984;**18**:62–5.

2 de Lacey G *et al*. Testing a policy for skull radiography (and admissions) following mild head injury. *Br J Radiol* 1990;**63**:14–18.

3 Royal College of Radiologists. *Making the Best Use of a Department of Clinical Radiology. Guidelines for Doctors*. 3rd Edition. London: RCR, 1995.

4 McNally E *et al*. Posters for accident departments: simple method of sustaining reduction in X-ray examinations. *Brit Med J* 1995;**310**:640–42.

SUBMITTED BY

Dr D Remedios, Northwick Park & St. Mark's Hospitals, Harrow; Dr E McNally, Nuffield Orthopaedic Centre, Oxford.

26 | Employee Satisfaction

THE AUDIT

Staff sickness rate as a measure of employee satisfaction.

(See Appendix, pages 246–247)

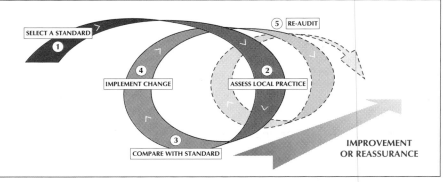

① SELECT A STANDARD

⑤ RE-AUDIT

④ IMPLEMENT CHANGE

② ASSESS LOCAL PRACTICE

③ COMPARE WITH STANDARD

IMPROVEMENT OR REASSURANCE

BACKGROUND

● **Why this audit is worth doing**

Absenteeism from work tends to be low when employment conditions are perceived as good (Ref. 1). Conversely, high levels of sickness absence may be a sign of employee dissatisfaction. Sickness absence can be an indicator of the employees' ability to cope with or maintain normal roles at work (Refs 2 and 3). There have been suggestions that NHS absenteeism rates are particularly high (Ref. 1). Monitoring absenteeism is an essential first step towards actively reducing it.

THE CYCLE

1 THE STANDARD

● **Two locally agreed standards**

The overall staff absence ratio (as defined in the Appendix) in the Department of Clinical Radiology should be below 30:1.

The absence ratio of each staff group in the Department of Clinical Radiology should be below 30:1.

2 ASSESS LOCAL PRACTICE

● **The indicators**

Overall staff absence ratio.

Number of staff groups in which the absence ratio is below 30:1.

● **Data items to be collected**

For each staff group, and for the whole department:

● the total number of working days available;

● the number of episodes of sickness;

For each episode of sickness:

● the number of days;

● the date and day(s) of the week;

● the reason for the sickness (See Appendix, page 247, item 5.5);

● certification (uncertified, self certified or certified by GP/Doctor). (See Appendix, page 247, item 5.6).

● **Suggested number**

Review data over a 1 year period.

3 COMPARE FINDINGS WITH THE STANDARD

4 CHANGE

● **Some suggestions**

There are several risk factors in relation to absenteeism. Nevertheless one factor – work characteristics – can be modified (Refs 2 and 4). When appropriate changes are made these may lead to a reduction in sickness absence. Inform the Chief Executive Officer, the Medical Director and departmental staff about the results of the audit and instigate full and frank discussions. Consider:

- re-evaluating the working conditions and / or workload of the Department;
- constructing guidelines on roles and tasks for individual staff members;
- improving the variety of responsibilities and support provided (Ref. 2);
- introducing a counselling service;
- re-assessment of individuals / roles of individuals who are in management positions within the department;
- training of managers in the management of absence;
- changing the number of staff;
- other possible courses of action (e.g. improving the quality of food in the canteen and providing access to sports facilities (Ref. 1)).

5 RE-AUDIT Every 6 months if standard is not met, otherwise every 12 months.

RESOURCES   **FIRST CYCLE**   **£**

● **Data collection**

Retrospective using computer records.

● **Assistance required**

Clerical assistance from the Personnel Department.

● **Estimated radiologists' and radiographers' time to complete stages 1–3 of the first cycle**

Clinical Director: 8 hours.

Superintendent Radiographer: 26 hours.

● **Other estimated costs**

None.

REFERENCES

1 Balcombe J. *Wish you Were Here.* Birmingham: The Industrial Society, 1993.

2 North F *et al.* Explaining Socioeconomic Differences in Sickness Absence: The Whitehall II Study. *BMJ* 1993;**306**:361–6.

3 Pines A. *et al.* Rates of Sickness Absenteeism Among Employees in a Modern Hospital: The Role of Demographic and Occupational Factors. *Br J Ind Med* 1985;**42**:326–35.

4 Absenteeism in Government: A Catalogue of Failure (1995). From: The Office of David Chidgey MP, House of Commons, London SW1A 0AA.

SUBMITTED BY

Dr G de Lacey, Dr A Brown, Ms A McQueen (Superintendent Radiographer) and Mrs K Rose (Workforce Planning Manager), Northwick Park & St. Mark's Hospitals, Harrow.

27 Fetal Abdominal Circumference Measurements

☐ Structure
■ Process
☐ Outcome

THE AUDIT

Accuracy of fetal abdominal circumference measurements using ultrasound (US).

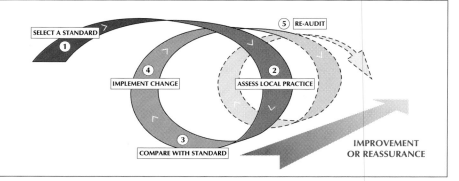

BACKGROUND

● **Why this audit is worth doing**

Abdominal circumference measurements are used for monitoring fetal growth in the detection of fetal growth retardation. Changes in equipment and staff, variations in work intensity and introduction of other parameters which need to be measured can easily lead to a fall-off in accuracy of abdominal circumference measurements; this fall-off may take some time to become apparent clinically.

THE CYCLE

1 THE STANDARD

● **A locally agreed standard with two parts**

In all cases where at least two sonographers measure fetal abdominal circumference on the same pregnancy on the same day, the difference between the measurements should not be greater than 5 mm.

The departmental mean of all such differences should not be greater than 2 mm.

2 ASSESS LOCAL PRACTICE

● **The indicators**

% of cases where two or more sonographers measure the same pregnancy on the same day, in which the difference between the measurements is greater than that in the standard.

The departmental mean of all differences.

● **Data items to be collected**

For each comparison between two sonographers, the following should occur. Each measures abdominal circumference on the same fetus on the same day. The difference between the two measurements is calculated. Analysis of the results of all the comparisons is made by the incomplete squares method (Ref. 3).

● **Suggested number of cases/patients**

All sonographers carrying out obstetric US. Each sonographer should be compared against each of the other sonographers in the department. A programme should be drawn up to enable this assessment to be made.

THE CYCLE (continued)

3 COMPARE FINDINGS WITH THE STANDARD

4 CHANGE

● **Suggested change**

Improved accuracy in measurement may be achieved by:

- identification of which staff are making inaccurate measurements, and therefore need retraining;
- review of the process which is in use for monitoring machine calibration.

5 RE-AUDIT Every six months if standard has been met.

RESOURCES

FIRST CYCLE £(££)

● **Data collection**

Ongoing data recording.

● **Assistance required**

Audit officer for data recording and analysis.

● **Estimated radiologists' and radiographers' time to complete stages 1–3 of the first cycle**

Radiologist: 1 hour per sonographer tested, for analysis of data.

● **Other estimated costs**

Statistician's time for incomplete squares analysis (Ref. 3).

REFERENCES

1 Sarmandal P, Grant JM. Effectiveness of ultrasound determination of fetal abdominal circumference and fetal ponderal index in the diagnosis of asymmetrical growth retardation. *Br J Obstet Gynaecol* 1990;**97**:118–23.

2 Richards B *et al.* Operator variation in ultrasound measurements. *Br J Radiol* 1985;**58**:279.

3 Richards B *et al.* Computer based quality assurance systems for assessment of ultrasound measurements. *Medical informatics*. Berlin: Springer-Verlag, 1985.

SUBMITTED BY

Dr M Gowland, Bolton General Hospital.

RECIPES

THE AUDIT

Patients awareness of why a scan is carried out.

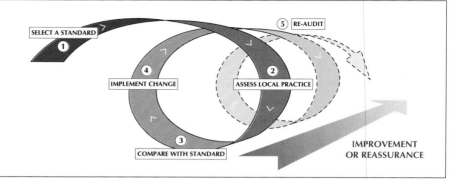

BACKGROUND

● **Why this audit is worth doing**

A second trimester anomaly scan should now be routinely offered to the majority of pregnant women who attend an antenatal clinic. Often, because the prospect of seeing the baby in the womb is pleasant, it is not appreciated that the primary purpose of the examination is the detection of fetal abnormality. This lack of awareness can intensify the distress which is inevitable if an abnormality is detected.

THE CYCLE

1 THE STANDARD

● **A locally agreed standard**

All patients should be aware before attending for an anomaly scan that one of the objectives of the examination is the detection of fetal abnormality.

2 ASSESS LOCAL PRACTICE

● **The indicator**

% of patients attending for an anomaly scan who are aware that one of the objectives of the examination is the detection of fetal abnormality.

● **Data items to be collected**

For each patient, record on a simple questionnaire whether they know that one of the objectives of this examination is the detection of fetal abnormality.

● **Suggested number**

100 consecutive women attending for a second trimester anomaly scan.

THE CYCLE (continued)

3 COMPARE FINDINGS WITH THE STANDARD

4 CHANGE

● **Some suggestions**

Review the written information given to women before they attend for a scan. Redesign of a patient information leaflet may be necessary.

Ensure that all women are sent the information.

Encourage referring doctors to inform patients and to give them the opportunity to choose not to have the scan.

5 RE-AUDIT Every 6–12 months.

RESOURCES

FIRST CYCLE £

● **Data collection**

Simple questionnaire.

● **Assistance required**

Midwife or sonographer to assist with questionnaire completion.

● **Estimated radiologists' and radiographers' time to complete stages 1–3 of the first cycle**

Radiologist: 2 hours.

● **Other estimated costs**

None.

REFERENCES

1 Green J, Statham H. Testing for fetal abnormality in routine antenatal care. *Midwifery* 1993;**9**:124–35

2 Tymstra TJ *et al*. Women's opinions on the offer and use of prenatal diagnosis. *Prenat Diagn* 1991;**11**:893–8.

3 Katz V *et al*. Role of ultrasound and informed consent in the evaluation of elevated maternal serum alpha-fetoprotein. *Am J Perinatol* 1991;**8**:73–6.

4 Rowland M, Shanks J. Broader definitions of clinical effectiveness are needed. *BMJ* 1995;**311**:808.

SUBMITTED BY

Dr M Gowland, Bolton General Hospital.

THE AUDIT

Availability of patient examination envelopes from the departmental filing system.

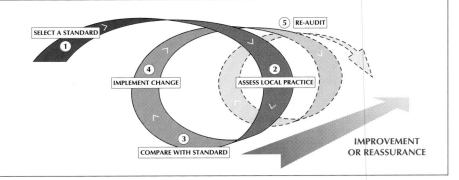

BACKGROUND

● **Why this audit is worth doing**

If patient examination envelopes are lost, examinations may have to be repeated, causing delays in patient care and affecting relations with other departments. Previous examinations must be kept for comparison with later examinations, particularly in orthopaedic patients. An efficient filing system must be maintained (Refs 1 and 2).

THE CYCLE

1 THE STANDARD

● **A locally agreed standard**

The whereabouts of all film envelopes should be known to the department at all times.

2 ASSESS LOCAL PRACTICE

● **The indicators**

% of film envelopes whose location is known.

● **Data items to be collected**

Number of envelopes in file.

Number of envelopes not in file but whereabouts known.

Number of envelopes not in file and whereabouts unknown (effectively lost).

● **Suggested number of cases/patients**

A random set of 50 film envelopes. In practice, choose clinics which require films to be pulled for the next week – this sample will be random and will cause no extra work for staff.

THE CYCLE (continued)

3 COMPARE FINDINGS WITH THE STANDARD

4 CHANGE

● **Some suggestions**

Publish film envelope availability figures regularly. Review the filing system to identify any need for change. Particularly:

- institute a *request for return of film envelope* system with other departments within the hospital;
- limit access to the filing area – especially out of hours;
- improve the booking in/out system of film envelopes;
- consider using a computerised bar code booking/tracking system.

5 RE-AUDIT every 3–6 months.

RESOURCES

FIRST CYCLE £

● **Data collection**

Ongoing data recording.

Computer records.

File film search.

● **Assistance required**

Film library clerks.

● **Estimated radiologists' and radiographers' time to complete stages 1–3 of the first cycle**

Radiologist: 3 hours.

● **Other estimated costs**

None.

REFERENCES

1 The Audit Commission. *Improving your Image. How to Manage Radiology Services More Effectively.* London: Audit Commission, 1995.

2 National Radiological Protection Board. *Patient Dose Reduction in Diagnostic Radiology.* Didcot: NRPB, 1990.

SUBMITTED BY

Dr RJ Godwin, West Suffolk Hospital, Bury St Edmunds.

RECIPES

<table>
<tr><td>**30**</td><td># Finger Doses</td><td>☐ Structure
■ Process
☐ Outcome</td></tr>
</table>

THE AUDIT

Radiation dose to the pulp of the index finger of staff handling syringes containing radionuclides.

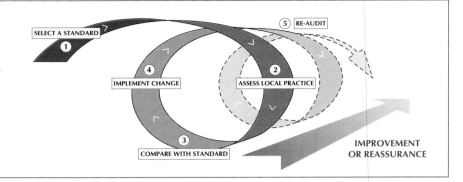

BACKGROUND

● **Why this audit is worth doing**

There can be variation in the radiation dose to the fingers from handling syringes in the isotope injection area (Refs 1 and 2). All finger doses should be within the International Commission on Radiation Protection (ICRP) recommended annual limit.

THE CYCLE

1 THE STANDARD

● **A locally agreed standard based on the ICRP recommended annual limit (Ref. 3).**

All finger doses should be less than 500 mSv per annum.

2 ASSESS LOCAL PRACTICE

● **The indicator**

% of workers who receive a finger dose less than 500mSv.

● **Data items to be collected**

Radiation dose to the fingers for each designated worker should be obtained using thermo-luminescent dosemeters (TLDs). Pro rata extension of these doses will give an estimate of the annual radiation dose to the fingers.

● **Suggested number**

Every designated worker handling syringes in the injection area during a one month period.

THE CYCLE (continued)

3 COMPARE FINDINGS WITH THE STANDARD

4 CHANGE

● **Suggested change**

Discuss the audit results with all designated staff. Organise an individual assessment of handling practices for staff members. Make the appropriate alterations to technique so as to improve the practice. Purchase lead syringe shields if not presently available.

5 RE-AUDIT Every 3 months if standard is not achieved, otherwise every 12 months.

RESOURCES

FIRST CYCLE £

● **Data collection**

Ongoing data recording.

● **Assistance required**

Hospital Physicist to calculate the doses received.

● **Estimated radiologists' and radiographers' time to complete stages 1–3 of the first cycle**

Radiologist: 1 hour.

Radiographer: 4 hours.

● **Other estimated costs**

None.

REFERENCES

1 Henson P W. Radiation dose to the skin in contact with unshielded syringes containing radioactive substances. *Br J Radiol* 1973;**46**:927–77.

2 Harding L K *et al*. The value of syringe shields in a nuclear medicine department. *Nuc Med Communications* 1985;**6**:449–54.

3 ICRP Publication. Recommendations of the International Commission on Radiation Protection. *Annals of the ICRP* 1977;**1**:3.

SUBMITTED BY

Ms J Ryder (Superintendent Radiographer) and Dr C Green (Principal Physicist), Northwick Park & St. Mark's Hospitals, Harrow.

31 | Fire Training

☐ Structure
■ Process
☐ Outcome

THE AUDIT

Attendance of staff at fire lectures.

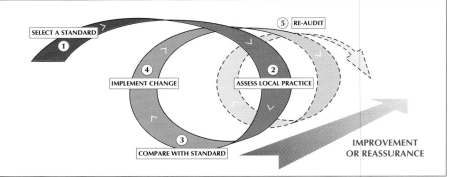

BACKGROUND

● **Why this audit is worth doing**

All staff and voluntary workers within a hospital are required to undergo regular training in how to respond to a fire. This is a statutory requirement linked to Health & Safety regulations (Ref. 1). It is essential that all staff in the Department of Clinical Radiology know the procedures for responding to a fire alarm and how to deal with the patients and the visitors in the department. Failure to comply can (in certain circumstances) lead to criminal prosecution.

THE CYCLE

1 THE STANDARD

● **A locally agreed standard**

All staff members should have attended a formal fire lecture during the previous twelve months.

2 ASSESS LOCAL PRACTICE

● **The indicator**

% of staff who have attended a fire lecture during the previous twelve months.

● **Data items to be collected**

The hospital fire officer should supply the names of all departmental members who have attended a course in the previous twelve months.

● **Suggested number**

All members of staff, including medical staff and all bank (i.e. reserve) staff.

THE CYCLE (continued)

3 COMPARE FINDINGS WITH THE STANDARD

4 CHANGE

● **Some suggestions**

Discuss the audit results and disseminate the percentage compliance. To ensure all staff attend a course annually (including medical and bank staff) it would be useful to:

• make staff aware of their statutory obligation;

• arrange a course of lectures devoted to radiology department staff;

• arrange that the departmental manager book the courses well in advance and at the same time reduce patient bookings in order to facilitate attendance.

5 RE-AUDIT every 12–24 months.

RESOURCES   FIRST CYCLE   £

● **Data collection**

List of staff.

Fire officer records.

● **Assistance required**

Hospital Fire Officer.

Clinical audit officer to collect data and analyse results (1 hour).

● **Estimated radiologist's and radiographer's time to complete stages 1–3 of the first cycle**

None.

● **Other estimated costs**

None.

REFERENCES

1 Health & Safety at Work Act 1974.

2 King's Fund. *Standards for an Acute Hospital* London: King's Fund, 1990.

SUBMITTED BY

Miss J Wright (Radiography Services Manager), West Suffolk Hospital, Bury St Edmunds.

THE AUDIT

Presence of a localising marker in radiography for presence of foreign bodies.

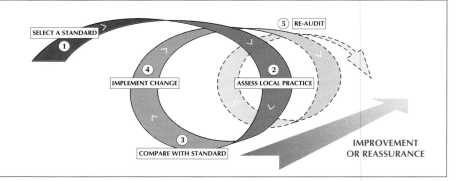

BACKGROUND

● **Why this audit is worth doing**

The correct identification and localisation of a foreign body in a soft tissue wound can be difficult (Refs 1 and 2). Several factors help with their identification on radiographs. One of these is the presence of an opaque localising marker placed adjacent to the site of injury, so as to be visible on the radiograph.

THE CYCLE

1 THE STANDARD

All radiographs that are obtained in order to identify a possible soft tissue foreign body should have a localising marker adjacent to the site of injury.

2 ASSESS LOCAL PRACTICE

● **The indicator**

% of radiographs which have a localising marker adjacent to the site of injury.

● **Data items to be collected**

For each radiograph, whether or not an opaque localising marker is visible.

● **Suggested number**

The last 100 radiographs for which the clinical request was for the identification of a possible soft tissue foreign body.

THE CYCLE (continued)

3 **COMPARE FINDINGS WITH THE STANDARD**

4 **CHANGE**

● **Some suggestions**

Present the audit results to radiographers and radiologists, discuss technique and circulate recommendations on methods. Make sure suitable opaque markers are available within the department. Carry out the subsequent audit with the assistance and involvement of the radiography staff and referring casualty doctors.

5 **RE-AUDIT** Every 12–24 months.

RESOURCES

FIRST CYCLE £

● **Data collection**

Radiograph request cards.

Film review.

● **Assistance required**

Film library clerks, radiographers and audit staff.

● **Estimated radiologists' and radiographers' time to complete stages 1–3 of the first cycle**

Radiologists (or radiographers): 4 hours total.

● **Estimated costs**

None.

REFERENCES

1 Remedios D *et al*. Imaging foreign bodies. *Imaging* 1993;**5**:171–9.

2 Raby N, Berman L, de Lacey G. *Accident and Emergency Radiology. A Survival Guide.* London: WB Saunders, 1995:208–15.

SUBMITTED BY

Dr AM Cook, Dundee Royal Infirmary; Dr MP O'Sullivan, Mrs V Benneson (Superintendent Radiographer) and Ms C Lowley (Audit Officer), Hull Royal Infirmary.

<table>
<tr><td>

33

</td><td>

Gall Bladder Ultrasound

</td><td>

☐ Structure
■ Process
☐ Outcome

</td></tr>
</table>

THE AUDIT

Adherence to a protocol during routine examination of the gall bladder by those in training.

(See Appendix, page 248)

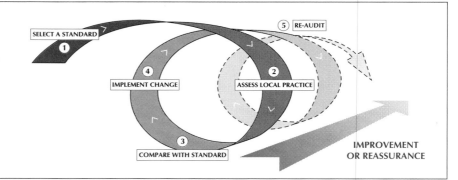

BACKGROUND

● **Why this audit is worth doing**

False positive and false negative reports occur following ultrasound (US) examination of the gall bladder (Ref. 1). Adherence to an examination protocol can assist in keeping errors to an absolute minimum. Good practice is best learnt during the early years of training.

THE CYCLE

1   THE STANDARD

● **A locally agreed standard**

All routine examinations of the gall bladder should follow the protocol in the Appendix, page 248 (Modified from Ref. 2).

2   ASSESS LOCAL PRACTICE

● **The indicator**

% of US examinations which follow the defined protocol.

● **Data items to be collected**

Review each examination, and its request form, and record whether the protocol was adhered to.

● **Suggested number**

50 consecutive requests for US examination of the gall bladder; the examinations having been performed by specialist registrars.

3   COMPARE FINDINGS WITH THE STANDARD

THE CYCLE (continued)

4 CHANGE

● **Some suggestions**

Present the results of the audit to all the trainees as a group and to the Head of Training.

Review the clarity and explicitness of the written protocol for examination of the gall bladder.

Make the protocol available in the US room in written form.

Improve the supervision of US examinations by the consultants.

5 RE-AUDIT Every 6 months if standard is not met, otherwise every 12 months.

RESOURCES   FIRST CYCLE £

● **Data collection**

Review of hard copy images.

● **Assistance required**

Clerk (film pulling).

● **Estimated radiologists' and radiographers' time to complete stages 1–3 of the first cycle**

Radiologist: 8 hours.

● **Other estimated costs**

None.

REFERENCES

1 Allen-Mersh TG et al. Does it matter who does ultrasound examination of the gall bladder? *BMJ 1985;* **291**:389–90.

2 Cosgrove D, Meire H, Dewbury K. *Clinical Ultrasound. Abdominal and General Ultrasound, Volume I.* Edinburgh: Churchill Livingstone, 1993:178–80.

3 de Lacey GJ et al. Should cholecystography or ultrasound be the primary investigation for gall bladder disease? *The Lancet* 1984;**1**:205–7.

4 Meire HB. Defensive ultrasound scanning. *RAD Magazine* 1995;**21**:15.

5 Davies HTO, Crombie IK. Assessing the quality of care: measuring well supported processes may be more enlightening than monitoring outcomes. *BMJ* 1995;**311**:766.

6 Hicks NR. Some observations on attempts to measure appropriateness of care. *BMJ* 1994;**309**:730–33

SUBMITTED BY

Dr MI Shaikh and Dr P Gibson of Northwick Park & St Mark's Hospitals, Harrow.

34 | Gonad Protection I

THE AUDIT

Availability of gonad protection.

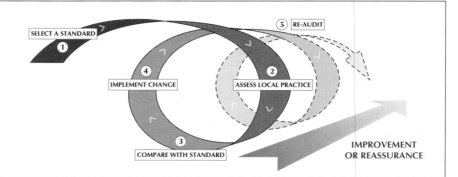

BACKGROUND

● **Why this audit is worth doing**

If gonad protection is not readily to hand it can lead either to examinations being performed without its use or to the regular use of inappropriate materials as an alternative. This audit will help to identify protection needs, and the appropriate allocation of gonad protection equipment within a department, and thereby promote best radiation protection practice.

THE CYCLE

1 THE STANDARD

● **A locally agreed standard with two components**

All x ray rooms where plain film radiography is carried out should have a complete and appropriate set of gonad protection equipment available in an agreed location.

All x ray rooms should have gonad shielding of an agreed quality and manufactured specifically for this purpose.

2 ASSESS LOCAL PRACTICE

● **The indicators**

% of rooms with a complete set of gonad protection.

% of rooms with purpose-specified gonad shields.

● **Data items to be collected**

Record for each x ray room:

- presence of gonad protection;
- place of storage;
- completeness of the gonad protection set;
- type of equipment available;
- whether purpose-specified gonad shields are present.

● **Suggested number**

All x ray rooms.

THE CYCLE (continued)

3 COMPARE FINDINGS WITH THE STANDARD

4 CHANGE

● **Some suggestions**

Ask for a protection safety survey from the local Radiation Safety Adviser in order to solve problems revealed by (repeatedly) unsatisfactory audit results.

Consider the purchase of purpose-manufactured protection kits such as the King's Lynn Gonad Protection System (Ref. 1). Provide each room with a kit.

Store gonad shields on purpose-built racks.

Remove and destroy all other lead protection alternatives (used for gonad protection) found in the rooms, which are not appropriate or purpose-produced.

5 RE-AUDIT Every 3–6 months.

RESOURCES   FIRST CYCLE £

● **Data collection**

Simple inspection proforma.

● **Assistance required**

None.

● **Estimated radiologists' and radiographers' time to complete stages 1–3 of the first cycle**

Radiographer: 10 minutes.

● **Other estimated costs**

None.

REFERENCES

1 White J. The King's Lynn Gonad Shield. *Radiography* 1977;**43**:137–8.

2 Plaut S. *Radiation Protection in the X Ray Department*. Oxford: Butterworth-Heinemann, 1993:113–4.

SUBMITTED BY

Mrs C Hepburn (Radiographer), West Suffolk Hospital, Bury St Edmunds.

35 | Gonad Protection II

THE AUDIT

Use of gonad protection.

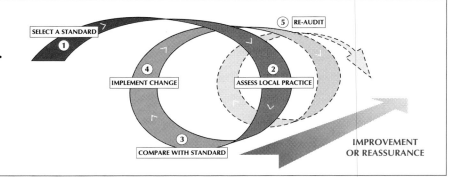

BACKGROUND

● **Why this audit is worth doing**

A written departmental protocol for the correct use of gonad protection, with regular audit, will:

• avoid confusion over when and where gonad protection is required;

• help new staff and locum staff to adapt readily and easily to local policy;

• reduce gonad dose without significant loss of radiographic information.

THE CYCLE

1 THE STANDARD

● **A locally agreed standard**

Gonad protection should be used according to the local policy stated in the Radiographic Index (Ref. 1) in all cases.

2 ASSESS LOCAL PRACTICE

● **The indicator**

% of examinations which comply with the departmental protocol for gonad protection.

● **Data items to be collected**

Assess each radiograph to determine:

• the presence or absence of gonad protection;

• whether the protection device was appropriate;

• whether the protection was placed correctly;

• whether the departmental protocol has been complied with;

• a coded identifier for the radiographer who carried out the procedure.

● **Suggested number**

100 radiographic examinations which would require gonad protection according to the departmental protocol, and where the protection should be visible on the radiograph.

THE CYCLE (continued)

3 COMPARE FINDINGS WITH THE STANDARD

4 CHANGE

● **Suggested change**

Discuss the results of the audit at a departmental audit meeting. By the use of confidential coding make individual staff members aware of their own rate of compliance with the departmental protocol.

5 RE-AUDIT every 12–24 months.

RESOURCES   FIRST CYCLE £

● **Data collection**

Computer records to identify patients and examinations which require gonad protection.

Review of radiographs.

● **Assistance required**

Film library clerks.

● **Estimated radiologists' and radiographers' time to complete stages 1–3 of the first cycle**

Radiographer: 3 hours for review of films.

● **Other estimated costs**

None.

REFERENCES

1 *The Ionising Radiations (Protection of Persons Undergoing Medical Examination or Treatment) Regulations 1988 (POPUMET)*. London: HMSO, 1988.

2 National Radiological Protection Board. *Occupational, public and medical exposure: guidance on the 1990 recommendations of the ICRP*. Didcot: NRPB, 1990.

SUBMITTED BY

Mrs S Peagram (Senior Radiographer) West Suffolk Hospital, Bury St Edmunds.

THE AUDIT

Abnormalities found on GP referrals for ultrasound (US) examination of the upper abdomen.

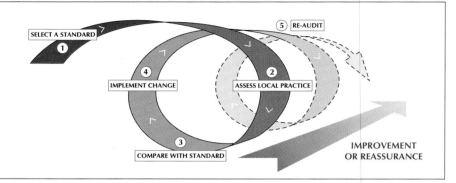

BACKGROUND

● **Why this audit is worth doing**

Waiting times for US exams are increasing as the number of requests goes up. Up to 45% of the requests come from GPs, who have open access. It is desirable to find out whether requests from GPs yield as many abnormal results as those from the hospital out-patient (OP) doctors. If they do not, it may be necessary to agree new guidelines.

THE CYCLE

1 THE STANDARD

● **A locally agreed standard**

% of GP patient requests for whom an abnormality is found (which is deemed to be clinically relevant to the signs/symptoms) should be no less than that from OP requests.

2 ASSESS LOCAL PRACTICE

● **The indicator**

% of GP patient requests and of OP requests, for whom an abnormality is found which is deemed to be clinically relevant to the signs/symptoms.

● **Data items to be collected**

For each patient, record:

• the source of the referral (GP/OP/other);

• whether a clinically relevant abnormality is found (yes/no/other).

From these results, calculate:

• the number of GP patient requests;

• the number of OP requests;

• % of GP patient requests for which a relevant abnormality is found;

• % of OP requests for which a relevant abnormality is found.

● **Suggested number**

100 consecutive GP referrals and 100 concurrent consecutive OP referrals.

THE CYCLE (continued)

3 COMPARE FINDINGS WITH THE STANDARD

4 CHANGE

● **Some suggestions**

If this audit shows a sizeable difference between the findings from GP referrals, and those from out-patient referrals, it may indicate that GP open access should be addressed by issuing guidelines for US requests. This could entail:

• organising hospital-based meetings for GPs to discuss the appropriate use and limitations of US;

• drafting guidelines for use by GPs, and circulating these to the GPs.

It may also be appropriate to vet GP requests for compliance and explain to them why certain requests are inappropriate.

5 RE-AUDIT Every 12–24 months.

RESOURCES   FIRST CYCLE £

● **Data collection**

Ongoing data recording.

● **Assistance required**

Secretarial support.

Goodwill and co-operation of the local GPs.

● **Estimated radiologists' and radiographers' time to complete stages 1–3 of the first cycle**

Radiologists: 2 hours per week for 8 weeks = 16 hours.

● **Other estimated costs**

None.

REFERENCES

1 Charlesworth CH, Sampson MA. How do General Practitioners Compare with the Outpatient Department when requesting upper abdominal ultrasound examination? *Clin Radiol*;1994,**49**:343–5.

2 Sorensen K, Hasch E. Ultrasonic Diagnosis in Patients Referrred from General Practice. *Ugeskrift für Laeger* 1985,**147**:121–3.

3 Colquhoun IR *et al*. An Analysis of Referrals for Primary Diagnostic Abdominal Ultrasound to a General X-Ray Department. *Br J Radiol* 1988,**61**:297–300.

SUBMITTED BY

Dr C Charlesworth, Wycombe General Hospital; Dr M Sampson, Southampton General Hospital.

THE AUDIT

Appropriateness of requests for chest radiography from GPs.

(See Appendix, pages 249–250)

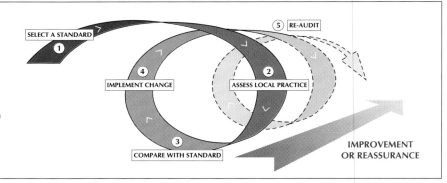

BACKGROUND

● **Why this audit is worth doing**

Chest radiography can be requested when it is not clinically necessary. This causes increased waiting times, unnecessary use of limited resources, and unnecessary radiation dose to the patient. There exist guidelines as to when a chest radiograph is inappropriate (Ref. 1). GPs work remote from hospitals, and thus the opportunity of reinforcement of the Guidelines is lessened, as compared with their hospital colleagues. This audit will show whether it is necessary to take steps to further reinforce the Guidelines.

THE CYCLE

1   THE STANDARD

● **A locally agreed standard**

95% of all requests from GPs for chest radiographs should contain clinical information which justifies the request, as indicated by the guidelines provided by the Royal College of Radiologists (Appendix, page 249, Ref. 1).

2   ASSESS LOCAL PRACTICE

● **The indicator**

% of chest radiograph requests that contain clinical information which justifies the request, as indicated by the guidelines provided by the Royal College of Radiologists (Appendix, page 249).

● **Data items to be collected**

For each request, record:

● whether the clinical information on the request justifies the examination;

● a coded GP identifier;

● the radiology report.

● **Suggested number**

100 consecutive chest radiograph requests by GPs.

THE CYCLE (continued)

3 COMPARE FINDINGS WITH THE STANDARD

4 CHANGE

● **Some suggestions**

Arrange meetings with GPs to discuss the audit results, and to enable them to air their views.

Make sure all GPs hold a current copy of the Royal College of Radiologists guidelines (Ref. 1); consider seeking funding for this from the FHSA or MAAG (Ref. 2).

Provide a revised request form for chest radiography (see Appendix, page 250).

Plan a prospective collaborative audit with individual GP practices.

5 RE-AUDIT every 12–24 months.

RESOURCES   FIRST CYCLE £

● **Data collection**

Review of request forms.

● **Assistance required**

Goodwill of the local GPs.

Audit assistants: 12 hours to pull forms and review – using a checklist based on the Royal College of Radiology guidelines (Appendix, page 249, Ref. 1).

● **Estimated radiologists' and radiographers' time to complete stages 1–3 of the first cycle**

Radiologist: 2 hours, for assessing appropriateness of requests.

● **Other costs**

None.

REFERENCES

1 Royal College of Radiologists. *Making the Best Use of a Department of Clinical Radiology. Guidelines for Doctors.* Third edition. London: RCR, 1995:42–4.

2 Royal College of Radiologists. *A protocol for the Effective Implementation of Guidelines to Good Radiological Practice.* London: RCR, 1992.

3 Timmis AD. Routine chest radiographs in admissions to coronary care. Lancet 1995;**345**:652–3.

4 Wosomm D *et al*. Routine chest radiographs in admissions to coronary care. Lancet 1995;**345**:62.

5 Eagle KA. Medical decision making in patients with chest pain. *New England Journal of Medicine* 1991;**324**:1282–3.

6 The Audit Commission. *Improving your image. How to Manage Radiology Services More Effectively.* London: Audit Commission, 1995.

7 Davies HTO, Crombie IK. Assessing the quality of care: measuring well supported processes may be more enlightening than monitoring outcomes. *BMJ* 1995; **311**: 755.

SUBMITTED BY

Dr G Kaplan, Northwick Park & St. Mark's Hospitals, Harrow.

38 | Head CT – Lens Exclusion

☐ Structure
■ Process
☐ Outcome

THE AUDIT

Exclusion of the lens of the eye in routine head CT examinations.

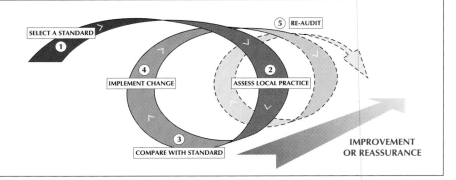

BACKGROUND

● **Why this audit is worth doing**

The exclusion of the lens from the standard brain CT examination will:

- reduce the radiation dose to the eye;
- reduce the likelihood of lens damage and cataract formation.

THE CYCLE

1 THE STANDARD

● **A locally agreed standard**

All brain scans should be performed with the base line set so as to exclude the lens of the eye.

2 ASSESS LOCAL PRACTICE

● **The indicator**

% of routine head CT scans performed with the lens excluded from the scan field.

● **Data items to be collected**

Record the number of brain scans in which:

- the lens of one or both eyes is/are included in the (field of) examination;
- the lenses of both eyes are not included.

● **Suggested number**

50 consecutive brain scans (where the examination of the orbits was not a requirement).

THE CYCLE (continued)

3   **COMPARE FINDINGS WITH THE STANDARD**

4   **CHANGE**

● **Suggested change**

Develop a protocol for brain CT in which the base line is set so as to exclude the eye lens. Identify exclusions to this protocol (e.g. examination for diplopia or exophthalmos). Emphasise to radiographers the importance of excluding the eye. Persuade supervising radiologists to avoid making exclusions to the protocol.

5   **RE-AUDIT**   Every 12–24 months.

RESOURCES   FIRST CYCLE   £

● **Data collection**

Computer records.

Film file review.

● **Assistance required**

Film library clerks.

● **Estimated radiologists' and radiographers' time to complete stages 1–3 of the first cycle**

Radiologist: 2 hours to examine 50 scans, 2 hours to discuss the findings with other parties.

● **Other estimated costs**

None.

REFERENCES

1   Spencer, D. *CT Scanning Angles Selected for Routine CT Brain Scanning. How does the Selected CT Scanning Angle Affect the Eye-Lens Dose?* MSc dissertation. London: City University, 1992.

2   NRPB ASP6 (1984). *Radiography* 1984;**595**:25–6.

3   National Radiological Protection Board. *Protection of the Patient in X-ray Computed Tomography.* Didcot: NRPB, 1992.

SUBMITTED BY

Ms D Spencer (Superintendent Radiographer) and Dr RJ Godwin, West Suffolk Hospital, Bury St Edmunds.

THE AUDIT

Patency of iliac arteries, 5 years after angioplasty.

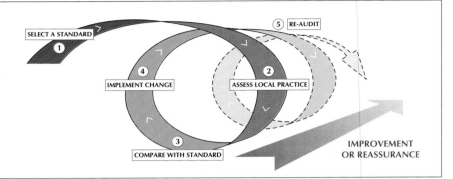

BACKGROUND

● Why this audit is worth doing

Iliac angioplasty is accepted as being a successful treatment for iliac arterial disease. It is important to ensure that the outcome from iliac angioplasty in individual centres meets the expected literature outcome figures (Ref. 1), so that the continued performance of iliac angioplasty in that centre can be justified.

THE CYCLE

1 THE STANDARD

● A locally agreed standard

72% of iliac arteries should remain clinically patent, 5 years after iliac angioplasty (Ref. 1).

2 ASSESS LOCAL PRACTICE

● The indicator

% of iliac arteries which remain clinically patent 5 years after iliac angioplasty.

● Data items to be collected

For each iliac angioplasty, at 5 year follow-up, record whether the iliac artery remains clinically patent.

● Suggested number

50 consecutive patients who have undergone iliac angioplasty and remain alive at 5 years.

THE CYCLE (continued)

3 COMPARE FINDINGS WITH THE STANDARD

4 CHANGE

● **Some suggestions**

All factors which may contribute to the outcome should be reviewed. Variables that are predictive of early and late success may be considered in the choice of patients for this procedure (Ref. 2). Technique and choice of equipment should also be considered.

Discussions between vascular surgeons and radiologists should result in recommendations which can be circulated and adopted as a local protocol.

5 RE-AUDIT   Every 3 years.

RESOURCES   FIRST CYCLE   £

● **Data collection**

Notes search.

Search of Department of Clinical Radiology case indexing system.

● **Assistance required**

Audit staff.

● **Estimated radiologists' and radiographers' time to complete stages 1–3 of the first cycle**

Radiologists: 30 hours.

● **Other estimated costs**

None.

REFERENCES

1 Becker GJ *et al*. Noncoronary angioplasty. *Radiology* 1989;**170**:921–40.

2 Wayne Johnston K. Iliac arteries: reanalysis of results of balloon angioplasty. *Radiology* 1993;**186**:207–12.

SUBMITTED BY

Dr AM Cook, Dundee Royal Infirmary; Dr JF Dyet and Dr AA Nicholson, Hull Royal Infirmary.

40 Image Labelling and Identification

THE AUDIT

Radiographic image labelling and identification.

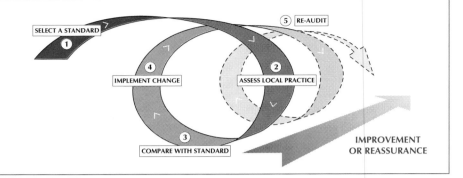

SELECT A STANDARD ①
⑤ RE-AUDIT
④ IMPLEMENT CHANGE
② ASSESS LOCAL PRACTICE
③ COMPARE WITH STANDARD
IMPROVEMENT OR REASSURANCE

BACKGROUND

● **Why this audit is worth doing**

Radiographic images must carry unambiguous patient identification. Medical images must include the correct date. Film side markers and information labels are also required in order to provide important examination information.

THE CYCLE

1 THE STANDARD

● **A locally agreed standard**

All hard copy images should contain (legibly) the following patient and procedure information:

* the patient's correct surname and forename;
* date of birth;
* hospital number;
* date of the examination;
* anatomical side marker.

2 ASSESS LOCAL PRACTICE

● **The indicator**

% of hard copy images which contain the required patient and procedure information.

● **Data items to be collected**

For each image record whether each of the items in the standard is present and legible.

● **Suggested number**

200 consecutive hard copy images (regard a sheet of multiformat images as one image).

THE CYCLE (continued)

3 COMPARE FINDINGS WITH THE STANDARD

4 CHANGE

● **Suggested change**

Identify the failures and the reasons for failures. Discuss the results at radiographer audit meetings. Some appropriate changes might include:

• introduction of a code for identification of staff so as to enable individuals to identify their own work;

• purchase of new equipment – labels or light markers.

5 RE-AUDIT Every 12 months.

RESOURCES   FIRST CYCLE   £

● **Data collection**

Film review.

● **Assistance required**

Film library clerks.

● **Estimated radiologists' and radiographers' time to complete stages 1–3 of the first cycle**

Radiographer: 10 hours.

● **Other estimated costs**

None or minimal.

REFERENCES

1 Jenkins, D. *Radiographic Photography & Imaging Processes.* Lancaster: MTP, 1986:157.

2 Chesney DN, Chesney MO. *Radiographic Photography.* Oxford: Blackwell, 1971:308–309.

SUBMITTED BY

Mr N Beeton (Deputy Superintendent Radiographer) and Dr RJ Godwin, West Suffolk Hospital, Bury St Edmunds.

In-Patient Information Letters

THE AUDIT

Whether in-patients receive an information letter prior to a special procedure.

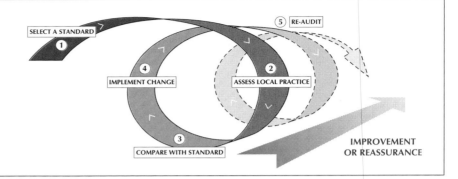

BACKGROUND

● **Why this audit is worth doing**

Letters are sent to all ward patients, via the ward sister, prior to special procedures. Information regarding the procedure, the appointment time, and duration of the examination are provided in order to prepare them for the procedure. This audit was carried out when it became apparent that some in-patients were not receiving these letters.

THE CYCLE

1 THE STANDARD

● **A locally agreed standard**

All patients should receive the letter.

2 ASSESS LOCAL PRACTICE

● **The indicator**

For each ward, % of patients in the ward who have received the letter prior to radiological investigation.

● **Data items to be collected**

For each patient:

• whether or not the patient received the letter;

• the name of the ward.

● **Suggested number**

50 consecutive special procedures.

THE CYCLE (continued)

3 COMPARE FINDINGS WITH THE STANDARD

4 CHANGE

● **Some suggestions**

Education sessions with staff should stress the importance of patient information. Meetings with ward sisters should be followed up with ward based information leaflets, giving details of radiology procedures.

5 RE-AUDIT Every 3 months.

RESOURCES

FIRST CYCLE £

● **Data collection**

Questionnaire.

● **Assistance required**

Audit Assistant (12 hours).

● **Estimated radiologists' and radiographers' time to complete stages 1–3 of the first cycle**

Radiographer: 18 hours.

● **Other estimated costs**

None.

REFERENCES

1 Jones L *et al. Consumer Feedback for the NHS*. London: King's Fund, 1987.

2 Fitzpatrick R. Surveys of patient satisfaction I. Important general considerations. *BMJ* 1991;**302**:887–9.

SUBMITTED BY

Dr M De Nunzio and Dr A Manhire, Nottingham City Hospital.

42 | In-Patient Reporting I

THE AUDIT

The time taken to report in-patient (IP) radiological examinations.

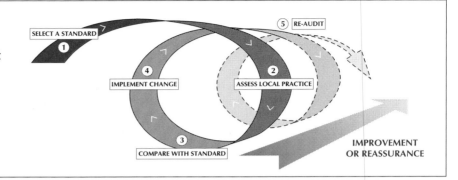

BACKGROUND

● **Why this audit is worth doing**

Delay in reporting IP radiographs may contribute to delay in making appropriate clinical decisions (Ref. 1). This may lead to wasted patient bed-days and associated resources, and also have effects on waiting lists. This audit will help to give a true assessment of the scale of the problem, and further analysis will indicate appropriate change.

THE CYCLE

1 THE STANDARD

● **A locally agreed standard**

Every IP radiograph should be reported within one working day of the examination being performed. (A working day excludes weekends, bank holidays and statutory days.)

2 ASSESS LOCAL PRACTICE

● **The indicator**

% of IP examinations reported within one working day of completion.

● **Data items to be collected**

For each consecutive IP examination listed from the radiology information system (or from a prospective study), record the time the examination was completed and the time when the corresponding report was printed.

● **Suggested number**

100 consecutive IP examinations.

THE CYCLE (continued)

3 COMPARE FINDINGS WITH THE STANDARD

4 CHANGE

● **Some suggestions**

Investigate the prioritisation and organisation of IP reporting. Particularly consider alternative processes for reporting (e.g. a continuously manned *hot* reporting system with immediate typing of reports (Ref. 2)). Make sure unreported films are returned quickly from the wards. Certain reports can be written directly into the patient's notes at the time of the examination.

5 RE-AUDIT

RESOURCES

FIRST CYCLE £

● **Data collection**

Computer records or prospective data recording.

● **Assistance required**

Audit staff for data analysis (16 hours).

● **Estimated radiologists' and radiographers' time to complete stages 1–3 of the first cycle**

Radiologist: 2 hours.

● **Other estimated costs**

None.

REFERENCES

1 Royal College of Radiologists. *Clinical Radiology Quality Specification for Purchasers*. London: RCR, 1995.

2 The Audit Commission. *Improving your Image. How to Manage Radiology Services More Effectively*. London: Audit Commission, 1995.

SUBMITTED BY

Dr MJ Brindle, The Queen Elizabeth Hospital, King's Lynn.

THE AUDIT

Reporting of in-patient (IP) procedure results in the patient's notes at the time of the examination.

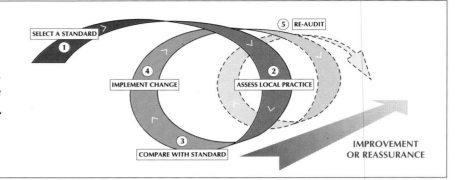

BACKGROUND

● **Why this audit is worth doing**

Writing the result into the notes immediately after the examination:

• speeds up the communication of results and assists the referring clinician;

• places the result in the main body of written information;

• decreases the opportunity for the result to be lost;

• encourages the practice of notes being present at the time of examination;

• provides timely information to enable alterations in patient management;

• is essential for all urgent out-of-hours examinations.

THE CYCLE

1 THE STANDARD

The result of all IP radiological procedures (excluding plain film examinations) should be written into the patient's notes at the time of completion of the examination.

2 ASSESS LOCAL PRACTICE

● **The indicator**

% of procedures for which the report was written into the patient's notes at the time of completion.

● **Data items to be collected**

For each request, record whether or not the patient's notes contain evidence of a report having been written in the notes at the time of the examination.

● **Suggested number**

50 consecutive examinations excluding plain film examinations.

THE CYCLE (continued)

3 COMPARE FINDINGS WITH THE STANDARD

4 CHANGE

● **Some suggestions**

Encourage all staff to adhere to the standard. Indicate that this is the agreed practice at the induction time of new junior medical staff. Arrange for all IPs to be accompanied by their clinical notes and previous films at the time of examination. Make sure that pens are available in all the appropriate examination rooms. Consider using a standard colour (e.g. green ink) to identify all the reports.

5 RE-AUDIT Every 6 months.

RESOURCES   FIRST CYCLE £

● **Data collection**

Computer records.

Notes search.

● **Assistance required**

Note pulling by audit staff.

● **Estimated radiologists' and radiographers' time to complete stages 1–3 of the first cycle**

Radiologist: 3 hours.

● **Other estimated costs**

None.

REFERENCES

1 Royal College of Radiologists. *Statement on Reporting in Departments of Clinical Radiology*. London: RCR, 1995.

2 The Audit Commission. *Improving your Image. How to Manage Radiology Services More Effectively*. London: Audit Commission, 1995.

3 Royal College of Radiologists. *Clinical Radiology Quality Specification for Purchasers*. London: RCR, 1995.

SUBMITTED BY

Dr RJ Godwin, West Suffolk Hospital, Bury St Edmunds.

44 Insertion of Oesophageal Stents

THE AUDIT

Patency following insertion of metal oesophageal stents compared with surgical insertion of Atkinson tubes.

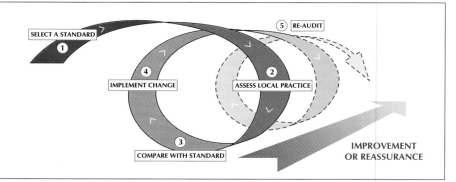

BACKGROUND

● **Why this audit is worth doing**

Radiological insertion of metallic stents is relatively easy but the stents are expensive. Is the (local) cost greater than that of (local) surgical insertion of Atkinson tubes?

THE CYCLE

1 THE STANDARD

● **A locally agreed standard**

In all cases, patency following insertion of oesophageal stents should equal that of surgical equivalents. Financial cost should be the same or less. Patient satisfaction should be equal to or greater than that with surgical stents.

2 ASSESS LOCAL PRACTICE

● **The indicators**

% of cases of insertion of oesophageal stents in which all of the following are at least as good as when surgical insertion of Atkinson tubes was used:

- patency;
- cost of the stent;
- cost of the procedure;
- length of stay in days in hospital;
- survival in days;
- patient satisfaction with swallowing.

● **Data items to be collected**

Record for each oesophageal stent:

- cost of the stent;
- cost of the procedure;
- patient's age;
- length of stay in hospital;
- survival in days;
- dietary limitations (solid/semi-solid/liquid);
- evidence of patency.

Compare each oesophageal stent against an equivalent case where surgical insertion of Atkinson tubes was used.

THE CYCLE (continued)

- **Suggested number**

30 consecutive metal oesophageal stents.

3 COMPARE FINDINGS WITH THE STANDARD

4 CHANGE

- **Some suggestions**

Consider total costs by looking at readmission rates and patent satisfaction with stents.

Negotiate with suppliers of stents to reduce price. Inform purchasers of health care of the benefits to patients of metallic stents.

5 RE-AUDIT Every 12 months.

RESOURCES   FIRST CYCLE £

- **Data collection**

Notes search.

- **Assistance required**

Audit staff: 6 hours, for note pulling.

- **Estimated radiologists' and radiographers' time to complete stages 1–3 of the first cycle**

None.

- **Other estimated costs**

None.

REFERENCES

1 Knyrim K *et al*. A controlled trial of an expansible metal stent for palliation of esophageal obstruction due to inoperable cancer. *New Engl J Med* 1993;**329**:1302–1307.

2 Cwikiel W. Esophageal stenting. In: Cope C ed. *Current Techniques in Interventional Radiology*. Second edition. Philadelphia: Current Medicine, 1995:133–42.

SUBMITTED BY

Dr K Stevens and Dr A Manhire, Nottingham City Hospital.

45

Interventional Radiology – Care of Patients

■ Structure
■ Process
□ Outcome

THE AUDIT

The standard of care of patients undergoing interventional radiology procedures.

(See Appendix, pages 251–252)

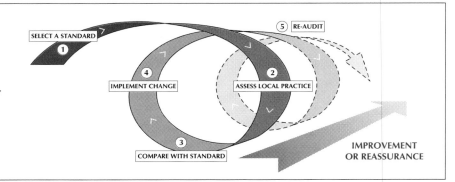

1 SELECT A STANDARD
2 ASSESS LOCAL PRACTICE
3 COMPARE WITH STANDARD
4 IMPLEMENT CHANGE
5 RE-AUDIT

IMPROVEMENT OR REASSURANCE

BACKGROUND

● **Why this audit is worth doing**

It is essential to assess the standard of patient care so that changes can be introduced if the agreed standards are not met.

THE CYCLE

1 THE STANDARD

● **A locally agreed standard with two parts, based on Ref. 1**

Whenever a radiological procedure is conducted under sedation or anaesthesia (except local anaesthesia):

- the patient should be medically assessed in advance of the appointment to identify whether he or she might be at risk (See Appendix, page 251);

- the anaesthesia should be given by an anaesthetist with help from a suitably trained nurse or Operating Department assistant (ODA);

- sedation should be carried out by someone suitably qualified, other than the radiologist carrying out the procedure.

Whenever a radiological procedure is conducted under sedation or anaesthesia (except local anaesthesia), the following should be available:

- clear written guidelines on drugs and doses used for sedation, as previously agreed between the Department of Clinical Radiology and the Department of Anaesthetics;

- anaesthetic help, if required, when patients are undergoing sedation;

- a clinical area for the procedure, fully equipped for resuscitation (Ref. 1).

- a recovery area for monitoring and observation.

2 ASSESS LOCAL PRACTICE

● **The indicators**

% of radiological procedures conducted under sedation or anaesthesia in which all of the following oocur:

- the patient is medically assessed in advance of the appointment;

- anaesthesia is given by an anaesthetist, with help from a suitably trained nurse or ODA;

- sedation is carried out by someone suitably qualified, other than the radiologist carrying out the procedure.

THE CYCLE (continued)

% of radiological procedures carried out, for which all of the following are available:

- clear written guidelines on drugs and doses used for sedation, as previously agreed between the Department of Clinical Radiology and the Department of Anaesthetics;
- anaesthetic help, if required, for patients undergoing sedation;
- a fully equipped clinical area;
- a recovery area for monitoring and observation.

● **Data items to be collected**

For each procedure use a simple proforma to record whether each of the points in the two parts of the standard are met.

● **Suggested number**

40 consecutive interventional procedures.

3 COMPARE FINDINGS WITH THE STANDARD

4 CHANGE

● **Some suggestions**

Action to be taken by the radiologist in overall charge of interventional procedures may include:

- establishment of written protocols for monitoring procedures;
- staff training;
- considering resources and appropriate staffing levels.

Involvement of the Clinical Director and/or the Chief Executive Officer may be necessary.

5 RE-AUDIT Every 4 months.

RESOURCES   FIRST CYCLE   £

● **Data collection**

Ongoing data collection.

● **Assistance required**

Hospital Resuscitation Officer.

● **Estimated radiologists' and radiographers' time to complete stages 1–3 of the first cycle**

Radiologist: 2 hours per week for 8 weeks = 16 hours.

Radiographer: 1 hour per week for 8 weeks = 8 hours.

● **Other estimated costs**

None.

REFERENCES

1 Royal College of Radiologists. *Sedation and Anaesthesia in Radiology. Report of a Joint working Party.* London: RCR, 1992.

2 McDermott VGM *et al*. Sedation and patient monitoring in vascular and interventional radiology. *Brit J Rad* 1993;**66**:667–71.

SUBMITTED BY

Dr L Wilkinson, Northwick Park and St Mark's Hospitals, Harrow.

46 Interventional Radiology Packs

Value for money of interventional radiology packs and of general disposables.

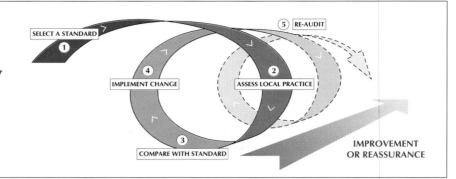

BACKGROUND

● **Why this audit is worth doing**

Introduction of cross-charging between directorates has meant that the Department of Clinical Radiology has to pay for sterilised packs for interventional procedures. Some items in the pack may be unnecessary and others may be obtainable at a lower cost.

THE CYCLE

1 THE STANDARD

● **A locally agreed standard**

All types of interventional radiology procedure pack used in the department should be judged to:

* contain only items necessary for the procedure;

* be the best value for money of the packs available for the procedure (in terms of keeping the cost to a minimum without sacrificing quality).

2 ASSESS LOCAL PRACTICE

● **The indicator**

% of types of packs used in the department which are judged to contain only the necessary items, and which are judged to be the best value pack.

● **Data items to be collected**

For each type of pack used:

* whether any items are identified as not required – by consensus of the radiologists performing the procedure;

* whether a pack of better value is available – by consensus of the radiologists performing the procedure.

● **Suggested number**

All types of procedure packs used in the department.

THE CYCLE (continued)

3 **COMPARE FINDINGS WITH THE STANDARD**

4 **CHANGE**

● **Some suggestions**

If cheaper packs than those currently used are of equivalent quality, they should be used instead.

If an item appears redundant, it should be removed, or replaced with a cheaper item.

Discuss purchasing policies with the commercial companies to identify cost savings – e.g. *call off* ordering, bulk purchase, joint purchasing with another directorate or unit.

5 **RE-AUDIT** Every 12–24 months.

RESOURCES   FIRST CYCLE   £

● **Data collection**

Review of pack items.

Review equipment catalogue.

Identification of users' requirements.

● **Assistance required**

Radiology nursing staff (4 hours).

● **Estimated radiologists' and radiographers' time to complete stages 1–3 of the first cycle**

Radiologist: 2 hours.

● **Other estimated costs**

None.

REFERENCES

1   The Audit Commission. *Improving your Image. How to Manage Radiology Services More Effectively.* London: Audit Commission, 1995.

SUBMITTED BY

Mrs H Brooks (Radiographer), Mrs C Simons (Radiology Nurse) and Dr A Manhire, Nottingham City Hospital.

Investigation of Prostatism

THE AUDIT

Imaging investigation chosen for prostatism.

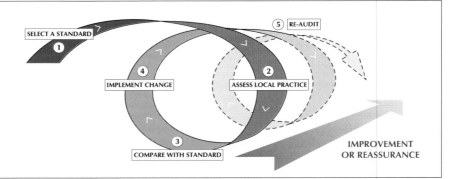

BACKGROUND

● **Why this audit is worth doing**

Prostatism is a common clinical problem. Ultrasound (US) should be the first line imaging examination as it can assess the kidneys and bladder with none of the risks associated with an IVU.

THE CYCLE

1 THE STANDARD

● **A locally agreed standard**

All patients with clinically suspected prostatism who require imaging should have US performed as the first line investigation (Ref. 1).

2 ASSESS LOCAL PRACTICE

● **The indicator**

% of patients with clinically suspected prostatism requiring imaging who have US performed as the first line investigation.

● **Data items to be collected**

For each patient, whether the first request was for US.

● **Suggested number**

100 consecutive patients referred for US or IVU, whose clinical details refer to prostatism.

THE CYCLE (continued)

3 COMPARE FINDINGS WITH THE STANDARD

4 CHANGE

● **Suggested changes**

Urologists are generally aware that US should be the first line imaging investigation, but some other clinicians are not as familiar with this practice. This change can be achieved by discussion between urologists/other clinicians and radiologists, or by circulation of recommendations. In individual cases, if US is not the first line imaging investigation, change the request from IVU to US.

5 RE-AUDIT Every 12 months.

RESOURCES

FIRST CYCLE £

● **Data collection**

Review of request cards and corresponding reports.

● **Assistance required**

Audit staff: 15 hours to review the cards and reports.

● **Estimated radiologists' and radiographers' time to complete stages 1–3 of the first cycle**

Radiologist: 4 hours.

● **Other estimated costs**

None.

REFERENCES

1   Wasserman N F *et al*. Assessment of Prostatism: Role of Intravenous Urography. *Radiology* 1987;**165**:831–5.

2   Dunnick N D *et al. Textbook of Uroradiology.* Baltimore: Williams & Wilkins, 1991:375–6.

3   Royal College of Radiologists. *Making the Best Use of a Department of Clinical Radiology.* Third edition. London: RCR, 1995.

SUBMITTED BY

Dr A M Cook, Dundee Royal Infirmary.

THE AUDIT

The quality of ITU and CCU chest radiographs.

(See Appendix, pages 253–255)

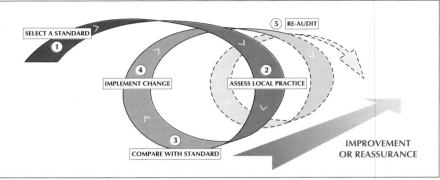

BACKGROUND

● **Why this audit is worth doing**

The received view is that these films are often of poor quality when compared to those obtained in the main department, even allowing for the difficult circumstances in which these examinations are performed. This audit can assist in maintaining, and providing reassurance on, film quality.

THE CYCLE

1 THE STANDARD

● **A locally agreed standard**

The quality of all chest films obtained in ITU and/or CCU should be deemed to be adequate by the clinicians, by the radiologists, and by the radiographers.

2 ASSESS LOCAL PRACTICE

● **The indicator**

% of chest films regarded as adequate to excellent by the ITU/CCU clinicians, by the radiologists, and by the radiographers.

● **Data items to be collected**

Evaluate each film as follows:

● the radiographer who took the film should complete Questionnaire A, part 1 (Appendix, page 253).

● ITU/CCU clinician should complete Questionnaire A, part 2 (Appendix, page 253).

● the reporting radiologist should complete Questionnaire B (Appendix, page 254).

● two independent radiographers should complete Questionnaire C (Appendix, page 255).

Record the number of films passed as adequate to excellent by all groups.

● **Suggested number**

100 consecutive chest films.

3 COMPARE FINDINGS WITH THE STANDARD

THE CYCLE (continued)

4 CHANGE

● **Some suggestions**

Present the audit results to all staff, and follow up with full and frank discussion. The Superintendent Radiographer and Clinical Director should address any problem areas revealed by the audit. It may be necessary to:

● improve the equipment;

● re-train in mobile radiography.

Reporting radiologists should bring unsatisfactory films to the attention of the radiographer on an individual case basis.

5 RE-AUDIT Every 12–24 months.

RESOURCES   FIRST CYCLE   £

● **Data collection**

Ongoing data recording via questionnaires (Questionnaires A and B).

Review radiographs (Questionnaire C).

● **Assistance required**

Audit Officer for data analysis.

● **Estimated radiologists' and radiographers' time to complete stages 1–3 of the first cycle**

Radiologist: 4 hours.

Radiographers: 20 hours total.

● **Other costs**

None.

REFERENCES

1   Winer-Muram HT *et al*. Guidelines for reading and interpreting chest radiographs in patients receiving mechanical ventilation. *Chest* 1992;**102(supplement)**:5655–705.

2   Goodman LR. Cardiopulmonary disorders in the critically ill. In: Goodman LR, Putnam CE, eds. *Intensive Care Radiology: Imaging of the Critically Ill*. Second edition. Philadelphia: WB Saunders, 1983: 61–113.

3   Goodman LR, Putnam CE. Diagnostic imaging in acute cardiopulmonary disease. *Clin Chest Med* 1984;**5**:247–64.

4   Wiener MD *et al*. Imaging of the intensive care unit patient. *Clin Chest Med* 1991;**12**:169–98.

5   Turner AF. Interpretation of the conventional chest x-ray in the critically ill and injured. In: Shoemaker WC *et al*. eds. *Textbook of Critical Care*. Second edition. Philadelphia: WB Saunders, 1984: 230–41.

6   Watkins PR. *A Practical Guide to Chest Imaging*. Edinburgh: Churchill Livingstone, 1984.

7   Wandtke JC. Bedside chest radiography. *Radiology* 1994;**190**:1–10.

8   Paulin S. Bedside chest radiography. *Radiology* 1994;**192**:282–4.

9   Glazer HS *et al*. New techniques in chest radiography. *Radiol Clin North Am* 1994;**32**:711–29.

SUBMITTED BY

Dr G Kaplan and Mrs S Taylor (Superintendent Radiographer), Northwick Park & St Mark's Hospitals, Harrow.

THE AUDIT

The effectiveness of permanent IVC filters in the prevention of pulmonary embolism (PE).

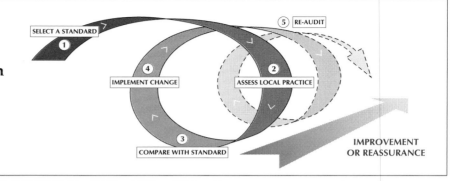

BACKGROUND

● **Why this audit is worth doing**

The percutaneous insertion of an IVC filter is an accepted method for reducing the incidence of recurrent PE in specific clinical situations. This audit can ensure that the outcome from IVC filtration meets the expected outcome figures quoted in the medical literature, so that the local practice of percutaneous insertion of IVC filters is seen to be satisfactory.

THE CYCLE

1 THE STANDARD

● **A locally agreed standard**

Clinically apparent recurrent PE should occur in no more than 2.7% of patients in the first six months following insertion of a permanent IVC filter (Refs 1 and 2).

2 ASSESS LOCAL PRACTICE

● **The indicator**

% of patients with IVC filters who suffer a clinically apparent pulmonary embolus occurring within 6 months of insertion.

● **Data items to be collected**

For each patient in whom an IVC filter has been inserted:

• the date of insertion;

• the date of any episode of clinically apparent PE.

● **Suggested number**

All patients with IVC filters inserted during the last 3 years.

THE CYCLE (continued)

3 COMPARE FINDINGS WITH THE STANDARD

4 CHANGE

● **Some suggestions**

If the standard is not achieved, then all factors contributing to outcome (such as case selection, risk factors, technique and type of filter) should be further investigated. Consideration should be given to:

- type of filter used;
- size of filter used;
- position of the filter;
- orientation of the filter;
- any evidence of movement or degradation of the filter.

5 RE-AUDIT   Every 3 years.

RESOURCES   FIRST CYCLE   £

● **Data collection**

Notes search, identification of IVC filter patients.

● **Assistance required**

Note pulling by audit staff.

● **Estimated radiologists' and radiographers' time to complete stages 1–3 of the first cycle**

Radiologist: 30 hours.

● **Other estimated costs**

None.

REFERENCES

1   Roehm JO *et al.* The bird's nest inferior vena cava filter: progress report. *Radiology* 1988;**168**:745–9.

2   Wells I. Inferior vena cava filters and when to use them. *Clin Radiol* 1989;**40**:11–12.

3   Perry JN, Wells IP. A long term follow-up of Gunther vena caval filters. *Clin Radiol* 1993;**48**:35–7.

4   Perry JN, Wells IP. Case report: structural failure of a bird's nest inferior vena cava filter. *Clin Radiol* 1994;**49**:431–2.

SUBMITTED BY

Dr AM Cook, Dundee Royal Infirmary; Dr JF Dyet and Dr AA Nicholson, Hull Royal Infirmary.

THE AUDIT

Examination times for
intravenous urography
(IVU).

(See Appendix, page 256).

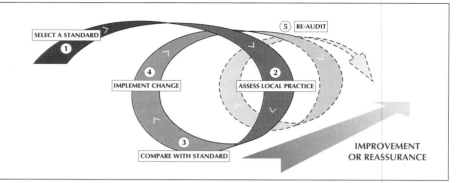

BACKGROUND

● **Why this audit is worth doing**

The total time taken for an IVU examination may be unnecessarily protracted. This audit can help to determine and minimise the causes of delay.

THE CYCLE

1   THE STANDARD

● **A locally agreed standard**

In 90% of examinations, all of the following should occur:

• the examination should commence within 10 minutes of the appointment time;

• the waiting time for injection should be less than 5 minutes;

• the waiting time to show the film to the radiologist should be less than 2 minutes.

2   ASSESS LOCAL PRACTICE

● **The indicator**

% of IVUs in which:

• the examination commences within 10 minutes of the appointment time;

• the waiting time for contrast injection is less than 5 minutes;

• the waiting time to show films to the radiologist is less than 2 minutes.

● **Data items to be collected**

For each IVU record:

• a patient identifier;

• the appointment time;

• the start time (when patient actually enters the examination room);

• the time spent waiting to show control films to radiologist;

• the time spent waiting for doctor to arrive to inject contrast medium;

• the time spent waiting to show final series of films to radiologist;

• the time the patient goes to the changing room.

● **Suggested number**

50 consecutive out-patient IVUs.

THE CYCLE (continued)

3 COMPARE FINDINGS WITH THE STANDARD

4 CHANGE

● **Some suggestions**

Radiology nurses and / or senior radiographers (following training) could perform IV contrast medium injections (Ref. 1). See Appendix, page 256 for protocol.

A supervising radiologist to be nominated for each session.

5 RE-AUDIT 6 months after full implementation of changes.

RESOURCES

FIRST CYCLE £

● **Data collection**

 Ongoing data recording.

● **Assistance required**

None.

● **Estimated radiologists' and radiographers' time to complete stages 1–3 of the first cycle**

Radiographer: 10 hours.

● **Other estimated costs**

 None.

REFERENCES

1 Royal College of Radiologists. *Staffing and Standards in Departments of Clinical Oncology and Clinical Radiology*. London: RCR, 1994.

SUBMITTED BY

Miss D Bratcher (Senior Radiographer) and Dr J Tawn, Royal Bournemouth Hospital.

51 | IVU Radiograph Series

THE AUDIT

Number of radiographs obtained during intravenous urography (IVU).

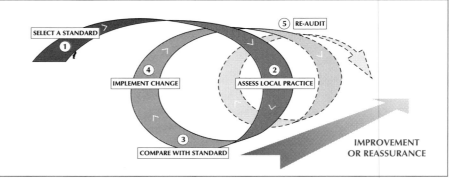

BACKGROUND

● **Why this audit is worth doing**

IVUs comprise 1% of medical radiographic examinations, but contribute 11% of the collective medical radiation dose. When an IVU is indicated, there is no universally accepted film sequence in the UK. However, limiting the number of radiographs obtained in a routine IVU can significantly reduce the collective radiation dose.

THE CYCLE

1 THE STANDARD

● **A locally agreed standard**

All uncomplicated IVU radiographic sequences should contain a maximum of 6 radiographs.

2 ASSESS LOCAL PRACTICE

● **The indicator**

% of routine IVUs where more than 6 radiographs were obtained.

● **Data items to be collected**

For each IVU performed, the number of radiographs taken. Whether this number is greater than 6.

● **Suggested number**

50 consecutive (routine) IVUs.

THE CYCLE (continued)

3   COMPARE FINDINGS WITH THE STANDARD

4   CHANGE

● **Some suggestions**

Presentation of the results of the audit to the entire department. Emphasise that the agreed policy is that routine IVUs consist of no more than six radiographs. Address any difficulties or misconceptions that may arise. Develop an agreed IVU routine radiographic sequence to limit the number of radiographs.

5   RE-AUDIT Every 12–24 months.

RESOURCES   FIRST CYCLE   £

● **Data collection**

Retrospective film review.

● **Assistance required**

Audit staff to pull x ray packets and count the number of films in each IVU series.

● **Estimated radiologists' and radiographers' time to complete stages 1–3 of the first cycle**

Radiologist: 2 hours.

● **Other estimated costs**

None.

REFERENCES

1   National Radiological Protection Board. *Patient Dose Reduction in Diagnostic Radiology*. Didcot: NRPB, 1990.

2   Dunnick NR *et al. Textbook of Uroradiology*. Baltimore, Williams & Wilkins, 1991:41–5.

SUBMITTED BY

Dr AM Cook, Dundee Royal Infirmary.

THE AUDIT

Use of radiology journals within a training department.

(See Appendix, pages 257–258)

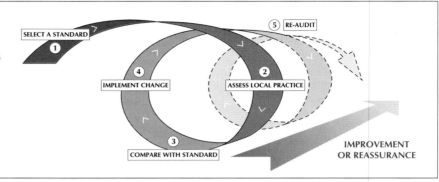

BACKGROUND

● **Why this audit is worth doing**

To keep abreast of current radiological literature is a basic requirement for both postgraduate (PGME) and continuing medical education (CME). Introducing changes into everyday medical practice depends in large part on an awareness of the results of current research. Good practice (i.e. the regular reading of journals) is best introduced during the early years of training.

THE CYCLE

1   THE STANDARD

● **A locally agreed standard**

All the specialist registrars should regularly scrutinise a minimum of four radiology journals each month.

2   ASSESS LOCAL PRACTICE

● **The indicator**

Number of specialist registrars who have scrutinised at least four journals.

● **Data items to be collected**

The front sheet from each journal recording signatures of trainees (see Appendix, page 258).

The consultant's notes from the Journal Club (see Appendix, page 257).

Record for each specialist registrar:

• which journals he or she has signed to say that he or she has read;

• which journals the consultant has concluded that the specialist registrar has read adequately.

If a specialist registrar has signed to say that he or she has read a journal, and if the consultant judges that he or she has read that journal adequately, then the registrar can be said to have scrutinised that journal.

● **Suggested number**

The current issue of each of eight radiology journals.

All specialist registrars.

THE CYCLE (continued)

3 COMPARE FINDINGS WITH THE STANDARD

4 CHANGE

● **Some suggestions**

Increase the accessibility of journals within the department.

Improve the organisation and attendance of the Journal Club.

Presentation of the audit results every 6 months.

The Head of Training should monitor the use of the two half days per week which are assigned for personal study and research (Ref. 1).

5 RE-AUDIT Every month.

RESOURCES

FIRST CYCLE £

● **Data collection**

Ongoing data collection.

● **Assistance required**

Secretarial.

● **Estimated radiologists' and radiographers' time to complete stages 1–3 of the first cycle**

Radiologists: 2 hours for the consultant who carries out the assessment.

● **Other estimated costs**

None.

REFERENCES

1 Temple J *et al*. Study leave for postgraduate trainees. A paper prepared for the Committee of Medical Postgraduate Deans. *Brit J Hosp Med* 1994;**51**:308–9.

2 Royal College of Radiologists. *Guidelines to Assist with RCR Visits to Training Schemes*. London: RCR, 1995.

SUBMITTED BY

Dr E Elson and Dr D Remedios, Northwick Park & St. Mark's Hospitals, Harrow.

53 Leg Venograms and Patient Management

THE AUDIT

Effect of the results of leg venograms on patient management.

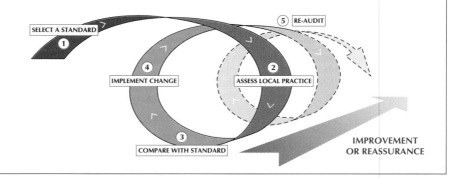

BACKGROUND

● **Why this audit is worth doing**

The number of leg venograms is increasing, particularly outside normal working hours. The perception within the Department of Clinical Radiology is that the results do not influence management unless they confirm the existing clinical diagnosis. The result of an investigation should alter or confirm the appropriateness of patient management (Ref. 1).

THE CYCLE

1 THE STANDARD

● **A locally agreed standard**

In all cases, the result of a radiological investigation should either alter or confirm the appropriateness of patient management.

2 ASSESS LOCAL PRACTICE

● **The indicator**

% of cases where it is judged that the result of the venogram has either altered the management of the patient, or confirmed that management is correct.

● **Data items to be collected**

For each venogram:

- clinical presentation (leg swelling, leg pain or chest pain);
- result of venogram (positive or negative);
- initial clinical diagnosis (positive, negative or equivocal);
- final clinical diagnosis (positive, negative or equivocal);
- management of patient;
- whether result has altered management;
- whether result has confirmed that management is appropriate.

● **Suggested number**

100 consecutive lower limb venograms.

THE CYCLE (continued)

3 COMPARE FINDINGS WITH THE STANDARD

4 CHANGE

- **Some suggestions**

Discussion with Medical Directorate of their policy on management of localised below-knee DVT – if anticoagulation is not considered necessary then ultrasound (US) doppler scanning may be adequate as the first line investigation.

Discussion of findings with clinicians to encourage venography only when the result is likely to influence management.

Education of junior medical staff in the clinical signs and management of leg DVT.

Introduction of cross-charging of Medical Directorate for examinations.

5 RE-AUDIT Every 6–12 months.

RESOURCES   FIRST CYCLE   £

- **Data collection**

Notes search for clinical information.

Review of request cards for venography.

- **Assistance required**

Audit Assistant for notes search.

Clerical staff for request cards.

- **Estimated radiologists' and radiographers' time to complete stages 1–3 of the first cycle**

Radiologist: 6 hours.

- **Other estimated costs**

None.

REFERENCES

1 Royal College of Radiologists. *Making the Best Use of a Department of Clinical Radiology*. Guidelines for Doctors. Third edition. London: RCR; 1995.

2 Verstraete M. The diagnosis and treatment of deep vein thrombosis. Editorial. *N Engl J Med* 1994;**329**:1418–20.

SUBMITTED BY

Dr D Rose and Dr A Manhire, Nottingham City Hospital.

54 | Low Osmolar Contrast Media

THE AUDIT

The use of low osmolar
contrast agents.

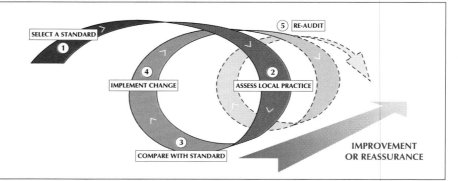

BACKGROUND

● **Why this audit is worth doing**

Low osmolar contrast agents offer a reduction in the incidence of adverse reactions in comparison with high osmolar agents, but they are not usually given for all contrast injections because of cost. Specific groups of patients who have a higher risk of contrast injection have been identified (Ref. 1). In these groups, a duty of care exists to ensure that only low osmolar contrast media (LOCM) is used.

THE CYCLE

1 | THE STANDARD

● **A locally agreed standard**

All patients identified by the Royal College of Radiologists' Guidelines (Ref. 1) as requiring a low osmolar contrast agent injection will receive LOCM.

2 | ASSESS LOCAL PRACTICE

● **The indicator**

% of the patients identified by the RCR Guidelines (Ref. 1) as requiring low osmolar contrast agents, who actually received LOCM.

● **Data items to be collected**

For each patient investigated, whether high or low osmolar contrast medium was used.

● **Suggested number of cases/patients**

100 consecutive patients requiring LOCM as indicated by Ref. 1.

THE CYCLE (continued)

3 COMPARE FINDINGS WITH THE STANDARD

4 CHANGE

● **Suggested change**

The results of the audit should be presented to all radiology staff.

The Royal College of Radiologists' guidelines on the use of low osmolar contrast agents (Ref. 1) should be circulated to all radiologists.

The Clinical Director should devise a local strategy which will ensure that all the staff adhere to the agreed departmental policy for the use of LOCM.

5 RE-AUDIT Every 6 months if standard is not being met, otherwise every 12–24 months.

RESOURCES   FIRST CYCLE £

● **Data collection**

Review of request cards for the relevant patient information.

Notes search for patient details where necessary.

Review of examination reports to establish whether high or low osmolar contrast medium was used.

● **Assistance required**

Audit Assistant to obtain request cards and radiology reports, also to obtain patient notes where necessary.

● **Estimated radiologists' and radiographers' time to complete stages 1–3 of the first cycle**

Radiologist: 20 hours.

● **Other estimated costs**

None.

REFERENCES

1 Royal College of Radiologists. *Guidelines for Use of Low Osmolar Intravascular Contrast Agents.* London: RCR,1991.

2 Grainger RG and Dawson P. Low osmolar contrast media: an appraisal. *Clin Radiol* 1990;**42**:1–5.

3 Dawson P and Grainger RG. High or low osmolar contrast media? Letter. *Clin Radiol* 1991;**43**:435–6.

SUBMITTED BY

Dr AM Cook, Dundee Royal Infirmary.

THE AUDIT

Lumbar spine radiography.

(See Appendix, page 259)

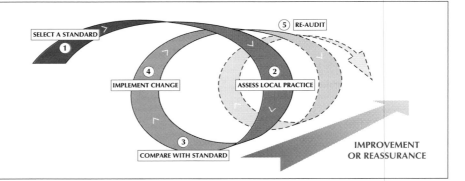

BACKGROUND

- **Why this audit is worth doing**

Lumbar spine radiography contributes 15% of the total radiation dose received by patients attending Diagnostic Imaging Departments (Ref. 1). Compliance with NRPB and RCR guidelines (Refs 1 and 2) would minimise the collective radiation dose to the population. If there is poor compliance with the guidelines then remedial action can be targeted to where it is most needed (Ref. 3).

THE CYCLE

1 THE STANDARD

- **The local standard has two components**

All requests should comply with the guidelines provided by the Royal College of Radiologists (Ref. 2).

All patients aged 20–55 years should have a single radiographic view only (Ref. 1).

See the Appendix, page 259 for a summary of the guidelines.

2 ASSESS LOCAL PRACTICE

- **The indicators**

% of requests in which the clinical information on the request form justifies radiography, complying with the Royal College of Radiologists' guidelines.

% of cases in which the number and type of radiographs obtained is appropriate to the patient's age and symptoms (see the Appendix, page 259).

- **Data items to be collected:**

For each lumbar spine examination, an assessment of:

- whether the clinical information on the request form justifies radiography;
- the precise radiographs obtained.

- **Suggested number**

200 consecutive patients referred for lumbar spine radiography.

THE CYCLE (continued)

3   COMPARE FINDINGS WITH THE STANDARD

4   CHANGE

● **Suggested change**

Present the audit results at the monthly departmental meeting, and reinforce the guidelines. Post the NRPB guidelines (Ref. 1) in the examination rooms. Make sure all requesting doctors are aware of the Royal College of Radiologists' guidelines (Ref. 2). Target remedial action (Ref. 3) where it is needed.

5   RE-AUDIT   Every 6–12 months.

RESOURCES   FIRST CYCLE   £

● **Data collection**

Review request forms.

Review radiographs.

● **Assistance required**

Clerk (film pulling and obtaining the request forms).

● **Estimated radiologists' and radiographers' time to complete stages 1–3 of the first cycle**

Radiologist: 16 hours.

Radiographer: 8 hours.

● **Other estimated costs**

None.

REFERENCES

1   National Radiological Protection Board. *Patient Dose Reduction in Diagnostic Radiology*. Didcot: NRPB, 1990.

2   Royal College of Radiologists. *Making the Best Use of a Department of Clinical Radiology*. Third edition. London: RCR, 1995.

3   Halpin SFS *et al*. Radiographic Examination of the Lumbar Spine in a Community Hospital: An Audit of Current Practice. *BMJ* 1991;**303**:813–15.

4   Waddell G. An approach to backache. *Br J Hosp Med* 1982;**28**:187–219.

5   Eisenberg RL *et al*. Single, well centred view of Lumbosacral Spine: is coned view necessary? *AJR* 1979;**133**:711–13.

SUBMITTED BY

Dr C Charlesworth, Wycombe General Hospital, High Wycombe.

<table>
<tr><td>

56

</td><td>

Lumbar Spine Radiation Dose

</td><td>

☐ Structure
■ Process
☐ Outcome

</td></tr>
</table>

Radiation dose received by a patient during a lumbar spine examination.

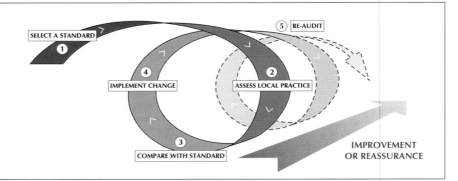

BACKGROUND

● **Why this audit is worth doing**

Lumbar spine radiography contributes 15% of the UK collective effective dose resulting from medical radiography (Ref.1). Regular patient dose monitoring is essential in order to keep the radiation dose as low as reasonably achievable.

THE CYCLE

1 THE STANDARD

● **A locally agreed standard**

In all patients, the dose area product will be below 15 Gy cm^2 (i.e. the rounded third quartile value in Table 5 of Ref. 1).

2 ASSESS LOCAL PRACTICE

● **The indicator**

% of patients in whom the dose area product is below 15 Gy cm^2.

● **Data items to be collected**

In each room where lumbar spine radiography is carried out, the dose area product should be assessed for all films in the series of each patient. For each patient record:

- age;
- weight (each patient should weigh between 60 and 80 kg, see page 8 of Ref. 1);
- each radiographic projection obtained;
- repeat exposures;
- the patient's dose area product reading.

● **Suggested number**

A minimum of 10 consecutive adult patients attending for radiography of the lumbar spine – for each room audited.

THE CYCLE (continued)

3 COMPARE FINDINGS WITH THE STANDARD

4 CHANGE

● **Some suggestions**

Circulate local and Royal College of Radiologists (Ref. 3) guidelines to Hospital Clinicians and GPs on when to perform radiography.

Reinforce the local radiographic protocol to be followed by the radiographers and the radiologists (e.g. a single long lateral view in only certain categories of patients, Ref. 2).

Perform regular quality assurance checks on all aspects of the radiographic equipment.

Regularly review radiographers' practice (e.g. audit of the quality of lumbar spine radiographs and reject analysis).

Assess the sensititivity of the film-screen combinations and assess the need for change to another combination.

Doses well below the standard may be reasonably achievable and efforts to reduce patient doses further should not be relaxed simply because this reference level has been achieved (Ref. 1).

5 RE-AUDIT Every 12 months.

RESOURCES   FIRST CYCLE £

● **Data collection**

Ongoing data recording.

● **Assistance required**

Physicist, to calibrate the diamentor.

● **Estimated radiologist's and radiographer's time to complete the first cycle (stages 1-3)**

Radiologist: 2 hours.
Radiographer: 4 hours.

● **Other estimated costs**

None.

REFERENCES

1 Dosimetry Working Party of the Institute of Physical Sciences in Medicine. *National Protocol for Patients Dose Measurements in Diagnostic Radiology.* Didcot: NRPB, 1992.

2 Eisenberg RL *et al.* Single, well centred view of lumbosacral spine : is coned view necessary? *AJR* 1979;**133**:711–13.

3 The Royal College of Radiologists. *Making the Best Use of a Department of Clinical Radiology. Guidelines for Doctors.* Third Edition. London: RCR, 1995.

4 Plaut S. *Radiation Protection in the X-ray Department.* Oxford: Butterworth-Heinemann, 1993.

5 Cosman M. Managing radiation safety in imaging departments. *Rad* 1995;**21**:32.

SUBMITTED BY

Dr G Kaplan, Mr L Taylor (Radiographer), and Dr C Green (Medical Physicist) of Northwick Park and St. Mark's Hospitals, Harrow.

RECIPES

Whether the language used in lung scan reports is understood by the referring clinicians.

(See Appendix, pages 260–261)

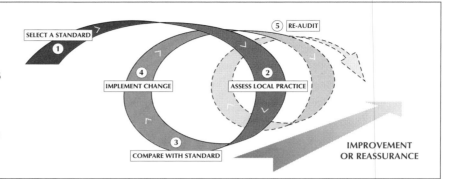

SELECT A STANDARD — 1

5 RE-AUDIT

4 IMPLEMENT CHANGE

2 ASSESS LOCAL PRACTICE

3 COMPARE WITH STANDARD

IMPROVEMENT OR REASSURANCE

BACKGROUND

● **Why this audit is worth doing**

It is important that all radiology reports are understood by the referring clinician (Ref. 1), and it is necessary that the clinicians also understand the language used based on the Prospective Investigation of Pulmonary Embolism Diagnosis (PIOPED) classification (Ref. 2). Lack of understanding may not be appreciated and the necessary changes will not take place unless something such as this audit instigates it.

THE CYCLE

1 THE STANDARD

● **A locally agreed standard with four parts**

All clinicians should:

- be aware of PIOPED;

- understand the recommendations of PIOPED;

- have understood the most recent report they have received;

- feel that they do not need further clarification of the Department of Clinical Radiology's use of language.

2 ASSESS LOCAL PRACTICE

● **The indicators**

% of clinicians who are aware of PIOPED.

% of clinicians who express an understanding of the PIOPED recommendations.

% of clinicians who did understand the most recent lung scan report received by them.

% of clinicians who feel that they do not need clarification of the Department of Clinical Radiology's use of language.

● **Data items to be collected**

Send out the questionnaire (Appendix, page 260) to each referring clinician. Make sure that each clinician receives the questionnaire once only.

● **Suggested number**

All clinicians who regularly request lung scans.

THE CYCLE (continued)

3 COMPARE FINDINGS WITH THE STANDARD

4 CHANGE

● **Suggested change**

Improved communication between radiologists and the referring clinicians can be achieved by:

- explanation of the PIOPED recommendations (in terms of reporting the probability of a pulmonary embolus, Ref. 2).
- agreement between all the Radiologists to use standard language for all lung scan reports.

5 RE-AUDIT Every 6 months.

RESOURCES   FIRST CYCLE £

● **Data collection**

Questionnaire.

● **Assistance required**

Secretarial.

● **Estimated radiologists' and radiographers' time to complete stages 1–3 of the first cycle**

Radiologist: 10 hours.

Radiographer: 20 hours.

● **Other estimated costs**

None.

REFERENCES

1 Orrison WW *et al*. The language of certainty: proper terminology for the ending of the radiologic report. *AJR* 1985;**145**:1093–5.

2 PIOPED Investigators. Value of the Ventilation/Perfusion Scan in Acute Pulmonary Embolism. *JAMA* 1990;**263**:2753–9.

3 Gray HW *et al*. Lung Scan reports: Interpretation by Clinicians. *Nuclear Medicine Communications* 1993;**14**:989–94.

SUBMITTED BY

Ms J Ryder (Superintendent Radiographer) and Dr L Wilkinson, Northwick Park & St. Mark's Hospitals, Harrow.

THE AUDIT

Speed of performing and reporting lung scintigraphy.

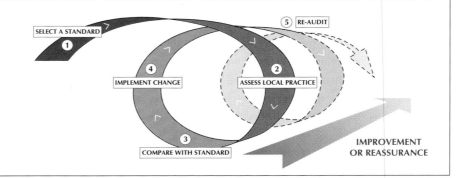

BACKGROUND

● **Why this audit is worth doing**

The rapid and accurate diagnosis of pulmonary embolism is clinically important for effective management (Ref. 1). Prompt exclusion of pulmonary embolus reduces the likelihood of inappropriate treatment (Ref. 2) and an unnecessary in-patient stay.

THE CYCLE

1 THE STANDARD

● **A locally agreed standard**

90% of in-patient requests for lung scans should be performed and reported within one working day of receipt and acceptance of the request form.

2 ASSESS LOCAL PRACTICE

● **Data items to collect**

For each request, record:

- the date and time of receipt of the request form;
- the date and time of the scan;
- the date and time of issue of the report.

● **Suggested number**

All requests accepted over a 3-month period.

3 COMPARE FINDINGS WITH THE STANDARD

THE CYCLE (continued)

4 CHANGE

● **Some suggestions**

Increase the availability of lung scintigraphy, e.g. if it is performed only on certain days of the week.

Formulate clinical guidelines to assist with the initiation of requests, in order to reduce unnecessary examinations and avoid the need for discussion. Scrutinise requests more carefully.

Scrutinise the organisational aspects of the nuclear medicine service.

Write all reports in the patient's notes on completion of the examination, as well as producing a typed report.

5 RE-AUDIT Every 6–12 months.

RESOURCES

FIRST CYCLE £

● **Data collection**

Ongoing data recording.

● **Assistance required**

None.

● **Estimated radiologists' and radiographers' time to complete stages 1–3 of the first cycle**

Radiologist: 8 hours.

Radiographer: 24 hours.

● **Other costs**

None.

REFERENCES

1 PIOPED Investigators. Value of the Ventilation/Perfusion Scan in Acute Pulmonary Embolism. *JAMA* 1990;**263**:2753–9.

2 Davies HTO, Crombie IK. Assessing the quality of care: measuring well supported processes may be more enlightening than monitoring outcomes. *BMJ* 1995;**311**:766.

3 Royal College of Radiologists. *Clinical Radiology Quality Specification for Purchasers*. London: RCR, 1995.

SUBMITTED BY

Dr D Remedios and Ms J Ryder (Superintendent Radiographer), Northwick Park and St. Mark's Hospitals, Harrow.

THE AUDIT

Department of Clinical Radiology call-in list for use in case of a major accident (majax).

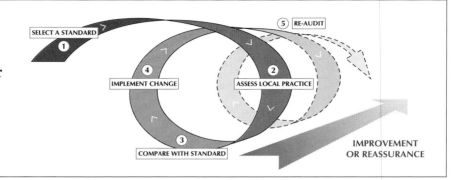

BACKGROUND

● **Why this audit is worth doing**

All major and medium sized hospitals may expect to be involved in a major accident at some time. An up-to-date and accurate list of all staff members should be readily available within the department and should contain the correct information in order to effect the prompt call-in of staff in the event of a major accident.

THE CYCLE

1 THE STANDARD

● **A locally agreed standard**

An up-to-date and accurate list of all staff members should be readily available within the department. It should include:

* correct home telephone numbers;

* addresses (which may be needed in case of telephone failure).

All staff should know where the list is posted.

2 ASSESS LOCAL PRACTICE

● **The indicators**

% of staff who know the correct whereabouts of the staff call-in list.

% of correct telephone numbers on the call-in list.

% of correct addresses on the call-in list.

● **Data items to be collected**

A blitz audit (unannounced, during any part of the day) of staff members. Using a check list of selected staff, identify for each member of staff:

* whether they know the whereabouts of the list;

* whether their correct telephone number is on the list;

* whether their correct address is on the list.

● **Suggested number**

20 members of staff, randomly selected.

THE CYCLE (continued)

3 COMPARE FINDINGS WITH THE STANDARD

4 CHANGE

● **Some suggestions**

To make the call-in list's whereabouts easily known to staff, create a *majax cupboard* in the staff room. It should be bright red, with a key available in the department key cupboard. It should contain:

- the correct list of staff telephone numbers and addresses;
- any other majax information or policy documents belonging to the hospital.

Identify one named individual to be responsible for maintaining an up-to-date call-in list.

5 RE-AUDIT every 12 months.

RESOURCES   FIRST CYCLE   £

● **Data collection**

Ongoing data recording.

● **Assistance required**

Audit officers to examine lists and carry out the blitz audit.

● **Estimated radiologists' and radiographers' time to complete stages 1–3 of the first cycle**

Radiologist: 1 hour to discuss the results of the audit and any changes required.

● **Other estimated costs**

None.

REFERENCES

1 Wallace WA *et al. Management of Disasters and their Aftermath.* London: BMJ Publications, 1994.

2 Walsh M. *Disasters – Current Planning and Recent Experience.* London: Edward Arnold, 1989.

SUBMITTED BY

Dr RJ Godwin, West Suffolk Hospital, Bury St Edmunds.

60	Mammography	☐ Structure
		■ Process
		☐ Outcome

Optical density used for symptomatic mammograms.

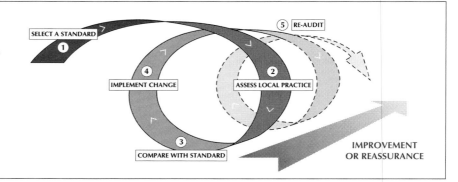

BACKGROUND

● **Why this audit is worth doing**

The ability to detect small cancers by mammography is influenced by the quality of the mammograms (Ref. 1). One factor influencing mammographic quality is the optical density. In screening mammography, the detection of small cancers increases significantly if the optical density is over 1.2 D. Breast screening units aim for an optical density between 1.4 D to 1.8 D. Ensuring that a high optical density is being used in symptomatic patients may lead to a higher detection rate for small cancers.

THE CYCLE

1 THE STANDARD

● **A locally agreed standard**

The optical density of a test mammogram should be between 1.4 D and 1.8 D in departments carrying out symptomatic mammography.

2 ASSESS LOCAL PRACTICE

● **The indicator**

The optical density of a test mammogram.

● **Data items to be collected**

Measure the optical density of the test mammograms using standard phantom techniques. Use current mammography unit settings and processing for symptomatic mammograms.

● **Suggested number of cases/patients**

One test mammogram.

THE CYCLE (continued)

3 COMPARE FINDINGS WITH THE STANDARD

4 CHANGE

● **Some suggestions**

Change the setting and calibration of the density control of the automatic exposure control of the mammogram unit.

Change the processing temperature.

Change the processing time.

Use a different film / screen combination.

5 RE-AUDIT Continuous. At the beginning of each day on which symptomatic mammography is conducted.

RESOURCES

● **Data collection**
Ongoing data recording.

● **Assistance required**
None.

● **Estimated radiologists' and radiographers' time to complete stages 1–3 of the first cycle**
Radiographer: 5 minutes.

● **Other estimated costs**
A step wedge, a densitometer and a phantom (e.g. Leeds) will need to be purchased or borrowed.

REFERENCES

1 Young KC *et al*. Mammographic film density and detection of small breast cancers. *Clin Radiol*; 1994;**49**; 461–5.

2 Davies HTO, Crombie IK. Assessing the quality of care: measuring well supported processes may be more enlightening than monitoring outcomes. *BMJ* 1995;**311**:766.

SUBMITTED BY

Dr AM Cook, Dundee Royal Infirmary.

<table>
<tr><td>

61 | Missing Films

</td><td>

☐ Structure
■ Process
■ Outcome

</td></tr>
</table>

THE AUDIT

Missing films causing unnecessary repeat radiography.

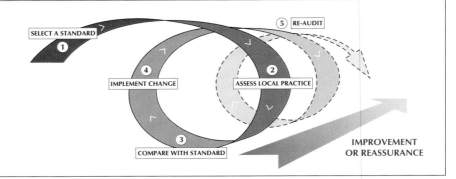

BACKGROUND

● **Why this audit is worth doing**

There has been concern that repeat x ray examinations are performed solely because original films are missing (Refs 1 and 2).

High levels of unnecessary repeat radiography may occur when x ray facilities are situated remote from the main Hospital (Refs 3 and 4). However, this problem may also exist even when x ray facilities are not remote.

THE CYCLE

1 THE STANDARD

● **A locally agreed standard**

Repeat x ray examinations because of missing films should occur in less than 1% of all patients referred for radiography from the out-patient clinic (Ref. 4).

2 ASSESS LOCAL PRACTICE

● **The indicator**

Using the orthopaedic clinics as an example, % of x ray requests arising because previous films are missing at the time of attendance at the orthopaedic clinics.

● **Data items to be collected**

X ray reception clerks and radiographers complete a short proforma for each orthopaedic request recording whether:

• previous radiography had occurred;

• those radiographs are presently available to the clinic;

• the previous films are missing/unavailable and the repeat radiography duplicates the missing radiographs.

● **Suggested number**

Survey all orthopaedic clinic referrals over a 3-week period.

THE CYCLE (continued)

3 COMPARE FINDINGS WITH THE STANDARD

4 CHANGE

● **Some suggestions**

Discussions between the relevant clinical directors should explain why the standard has not been met. Improvements which may be indicated include alterations to:

- the system of film storage;
- film filing;
- organisation of the film pulling lists for orthopaedic clinics;
- the system for film envelope retrieval from other hospital departments.

5 RE-AUDIT every 6 months if standard has not been met, otherwise every 12 months.

RESOURCES   FIRST CYCLE   £

● **Data collection**

Ongoing data recording.

● **Assistance required**

Reception staff to help complete the proforma.

● **Estimated radiologists' and radiographers' time to complete stages 1–3 of the first cycle**

Radiographer: 8 hours.

● **Other estimated costs**

None.

REFERENCES

1 Gifford D. Reducing radiation exposure to patients. *Br Med J* 1990;**301**:451–2.

2 National Radiological Protection Board and Royal College of Radiologists. *Patient dose reduction in diagnostic radiology. Documents of the National Radiological Protection Board No.3.* Didcot: NRPB, 1990.

3 Bransley-Zachary MAP, Sutherland GR. Unnecessary X-ray examinations. *Br Med J* 1989;**298**:1294.

4 de Lacey G, McQueen A. Unnecessary radiology. *Br Med J* 1992;**304**:572–3.

SUBMITTED BY

Dr G de Lacey and Ms A McQueen (Superintendent Radiographer), Northwick Park and St Mark's Hospitals, Harrow.

<table>
<tr><td>

62

</td><td>

MRI Patients and Metal

</td><td>

☐ Structure
■ Process
☐ Outcome

</td></tr>
</table>

THE AUDIT

Patient inquiry regarding the presence of ferro-magnetic materials prior to magnetic resonance imaging (MRI).

(See Appendix, page 262)

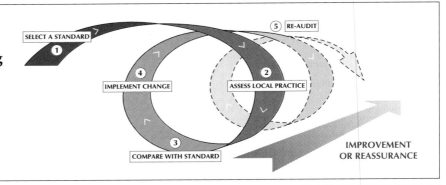

BACKGROUND

● **Why this audit is worth doing**

Ferro-magnetic materials, either iatrogenic or incidental, may move within the magnetic field of the scanner. This can cause injury to the patient, produce artefacts on the images or damage the scanner. Examples include aneurysm clips, components of pacemakers, house or car keys and metal fragments within the orbit.

THE CYCLE

1 THE STANDARD

● **A locally agreed standard**

All patients should be asked about the possibility of metallic foreign bodies anywhere in the body or in clothing prior to entering the scanner room, and the answers should be recorded on a form (Appendix, page 262) filed in the MRI Office.

2 ASSESS LOCAL PRACTICE

● **The indicator**

% of patients who are asked, and whose answers are recorded.

● **Data items to be collected**

For each patient, record whether there is a completed questionnaire, held with the MRI Office's records.

● **Suggested number**

All patients examined during a 2-week period.

THE CYCLE (continued)

3 COMPARE FINDINGS WITH THE STANDARD

4 CHANGE

● **Some suggestions**

Present the results of the audit to the MRI staff.

Re-emphasise the importance of the information to the radiographers and other staff members.

Put up a notice in the patients' waiting room both to inform and to warn patients.

Design a special MRI request form with an integral questionnaire.

5 RE-AUDIT Every 3 months if the standard is not met, otherwise every 12 months.

RESOURCES

FIRST CYCLE £

● **Data collection**
Computer records. File review.

● **Assistance required**
MRI Office clerks.

● **Estimated radiologists' and radiographers' time to complete stages 1–3 of the first cycle**
Radiologist: 2 hours.

● **Other estimated costs**
None.

REFERENCES

Shellock F. *Pocket Guide to MR Procedures*. New York: Raven Press, 1994.

SUBMITTED BY

Mr A Cooper (Superintendent Radiographer) and Dr A Manhire, Lister Bestcare and Nottingham City Hospital MRI Unit.

RECIPES

THE AUDIT

Detection of neural tube defect (NTD) by ultrasound (US).

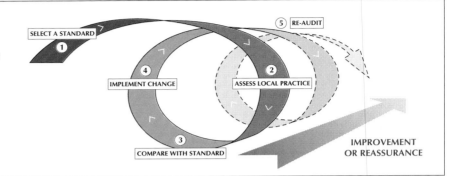

BACKGROUND

● **Why this audit is worth doing**

With recent technical advances and improved examination protocols it has become possible to detect NTDs with an accuracy approaching 100% without needing to resort to more invasive techniques such as amniocentesis.

THE CYCLE

1 THE STANDARD

● **A locally agreed standard**

All patients booking at the antenatal clinic should be offered an anomaly scan if and when the pregnancy reaches 18–20 weeks.

There should be no false positive diagnoses.

All scans of fetuses with NTD should identify that a defect is present.

2 ASSESS LOCAL PRACTICE

● **The indicators**

% of patients offered second trimester anomaly scan.

% of false positive diagnoses of NTD.

% of false negative diagnoses of NTD.

● **Data items to be collected**

The number of pregnancies reaching 18–20 weeks gestation. Of these:

- the number offered anomaly scanning.

- the number of fetuses in which a diagnosis of NTD is made at the anomaly scan. The number of these subsequently shown at delivery or at post mortem to have NTD.

- the number of fetuses in whom a diagnosis of NTD was not made at the second trimester anomaly scan but in whom at delivery or post mortem NTD was diagnosed.

● **Suggested number**

Because the incidence of NTD is low (approximately 2 in 1,000), in order for this audit to be of value it will either need to extend over a 1 year period for an average (3,000–4,000 deliveries per year) department, or be part of a multi-hospital audit.

THE CYCLE (continued)

3 COMPARE FINDINGS WITH THE STANDARD

4 CHANGE

● **Suggested change**

Discuss the audit results with all staff involved in obstetric management. Re-organise the booking protocol to ensure an anomaly scan is actually offered to all women at 18–20 weeks. Identify sonographers who miss NTD, and re-train. Consider upgrading equipment. Consider videotaping scans for review purposes.

5 RE-AUDIT Alternate years if standard is met, otherwise continuous.

RESOURCES   FIRST CYCLE £

● **Data collection**

Computer records (Antenatal Clinic, US Unit, Labour Ward and Neonatal Paediatrics).

Review of US reports and patient notes.

Pathology post mortem results.

● **Assistance required**

Audit office to obtain information from the computer records and to review patient notes.

● **Estimated radiologists' and radiographers' time to complete stages 1–3 of the first cycle**
Radiologist: 2 hours.

● **Other estimated costs**
None.

REFERENCES

1 Chitty L *et al*. Effectiveness of routine ultrasonography in detecting fetal structural abnormalities in a low risk population. *Br Med J* 1991;**303**:1165–9.

2 Shirley I *et al*. Routine radiographer screening for fetal abnormalities by ultrasound in an unselected low risk population. *Br J Radiol* 1992;**65**:654–9.

SUBMITTED BY

Dr M Gowland, Bolton General Hospital.

THE AUDIT

Appropriateness of out-of-hours examinations.

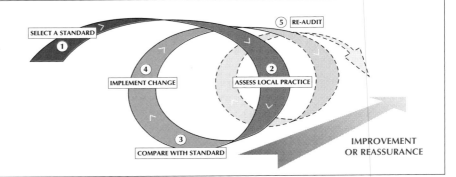

BACKGROUND

● **Why this audit is worth doing**

The number of requests for out-of-hours examinations has been rising steadily leading to an increase in radiographer on-call costs, difficulties in obtaining patient escorts and increased portering costs. It often causes distress to the patient without a change in management (Ref. 1).

THE CYCLE

1   THE STANDARD

● **A locally agreed standard**

All out-of-hours examinations should make a difference to patient management – and the change in management will have occurred – before the next available in-hours routine examination.

2   ASSESS LOCAL PRACTICE

● **The indicator**

% of out-of-hours examinations which make a difference to patient management before the next available routine examination.

● **Data items to be collected**

For each out-of-hours radiographic examination, determine:

- whether a change in management resulted or whether there was a recorded confirmation of the provisional diagnosis;
- whether any change in management occurred before the next available in-hours routine examination;
- the type of radiographic examination;
- the referring consultant.

● **Suggested number**

100 consecutive out-of-hours examinations.

THE CYCLE (continued)

3 COMPARE FINDINGS WITH THE STANDARD

4 CHANGE

● **Some suggestions**

Discussion with clinical consultants regarding the use of out-of-hours investigations and their effect on subsequent management. Encourage the delay of investigations until an in-hours routine list. Seek agreement as to when out-of-hours investigations are appropriate.

Arrange a trial period during which only specialist registrars can request these examinations.

5 RE-AUDIT Every 6–12 months.

RESOURCES   FIRST CYCLE £

● **Data collection**

Review of request cards.

Review of patient notes.

● **Assistance required**

Audit Officer to obtain notes (4 hours).

Clerical staff to retrieve request cards.

● **Estimated radiologists' and radiographers' time to complete stages 1–3 of the first cycle**

Radiologist: 12 hours.

Audit assistant: 4 hours.

● **Other estimated costs**

None.

REFERENCES

1   Charny MC *et al*. Out of hours radiology, a suitable case for audit? *Br J Radiol* 1987;**60**:553–6.

SUBMITTED BY

Dr A Ceccherini and Dr A Manhire, Nottingham City Hospital.

<table>
<tr><td>

65

</td><td>

Painful Hip

</td><td>

☐ Structure
■ Process
☐ Outcome

</td></tr>
</table>

Adherence to a protocol
for the investigation of
children presenting with
a painful hip.

(See Appendix, page 263)

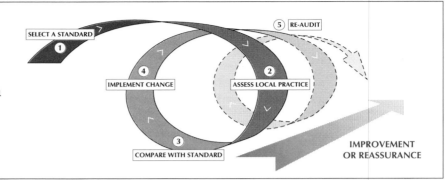

BACKGROUND

● **Why this audit is worth doing**

Hospital admission for the investigation of children with painful hips can be avoided in most cases. A local protocol should be utilised so that this condition is safely managed on an out-patient basis (Refs 1 and 2).

THE CYCLE

1 THE STANDARD

● **A locally agreed standard**

In all cases of children presenting with a painful hip in the absence of trauma, the protocol in the Appendix (page 263) should be followed.

2 ASSESS LOCAL PRACTICE

● **The indicator**

% of cases of children presenting with a painful hip in the absence of trauma in which the protocol is followed.

● **Data items to be collected**

For each child attending the hospital with a painful hip in the absence of trauma, record whether:
- an AP radiograph of the pelvis is obtained;
- this plain radiograph is abnormal;
- the child undergoes an ultrasound (US) examination;
- an effusion is detected;
- an aspiration is performed;
- the gram stain is negative;
- the child is sent home or admitted;
- the child attends the follow up clinic one week later.

● **Suggested number**

20 consecutive children attending hospital with a painful hip and no history of trauma.

THE CYCLE (continued)

3 COMPARE FINDINGS WITH THE STANDARD

4 CHANGE

● **Some suggestions**

Reinforce the protocol agreed between the paediatricians, orthopaedic surgeons, Accident and Emergency (A&E) consultant, and radiologists. Present the results of the audit to each of these clinical teams (preferably at a meeting with all the teams present) and take appropriate action.

Publicise the protocol in each department, post it up in A&E (Ref. 4) and include it in the GP handbook.

Identify and publish the average bed stay as an in-patient for those cases *not* thought to adhere to the protocol.

5 RE-AUDIT Every 12–24 months.

RESOURCES   FIRST CYCLE £

● **Data collection**

Computer records to identify the children.

Review case notes.

Review radiologists' reports.

● **Assistance required**

Clerk (film pulling and case note pulling).

● **Estimated radiologists' and radiographers' time to complete stages 1–3 of the first cycle**

Radiologist: 9 hours.

● **Other estimated costs**

None.

REFERENCES

1 Fink, AM *et al*. The irritable hip: immediate ultrasound guided aspiration and prevention of hospital admission. *Arc Dis Child* 1995;**72**:110–14.

2 Raby N, Berman L, de Lacey G. Accident and Emergency Radiology: A Survival Guide. London: WB Saunders, 1995:240–41.

3 Berman L *et al*. Technical note: identifying and aspirating hip effusions. *Brit J Rad* 1995;**68**:306–10.

4 National Radiological Protection Board. *Patient Dose Reduction in Diagnostic Radiology*. Didcot: NRPB, 1990.

SUBMITTED BY

Dr L Berman and Dr A Fink, Addenbrookes Hospital, Cambridge; Dr T Johnson-Smith, Northwick Park and St. Mark's Hospitals, Harrow.

66 Patient Arrival Times

Patient arrival times for appointments.

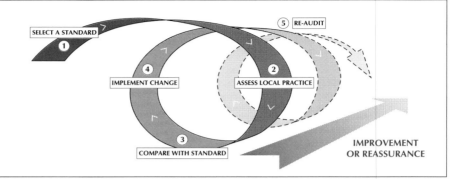

BACKGROUND

● **Why this audit is worth doing**

Early or late arrival of patients in the department for their appointments can disrupt the operation of the appointment system and the use of radiography rooms, and can cause congestion in waiting areas. This audit can help to minimise this problem, by identifying the reasons for very early or very late arrival.

THE CYCLE

1 THE STANDARD

● **A locally agreed standard**

100% of patients should be registered at reception within 5 minutes of their scheduled appointment time.

2 ASSESS LOCAL PRACTICE

● **The indicator**

% of patients who are registered at reception within 5 minutes of their appointment time.

● **Data items to be collected**

The total number of appointments, the number of patients arriving more than five minutes early, and the number of patients arriving more than five minutes late. In each individual case, the reason for late arrival (e.g. parking, signposting, appointment letter), or for early arrival.

● **Suggested number**

All booked appointments over a one-month period.

3 COMPARE FINDINGS WITH THE STANDARD

THE CYCLE (continued)

4 CHANGE

● **Some suggestions**

If patients are not arriving within 5 minutes of their appointment time, the problem is often within the hospital. The following should be reviewed, and improved if possible:

- the efficiency of the booking system and allocation of appointment times;
- the clarity of the appointment letter and other information supplied to patients;
- the ease of parking;
- the ease of registering an arrival:
- the Hospital or Departmental signposting;
- the portering arrangements;
- the adequacy of local transport services.

5 RE-AUDIT   Every 12 months.

RESOURCES   FIRST CYCLE £(££)

● **Data collection**

Ongoing data recording, on a simple proforma.

● **Assistance required**

Reception Clerk to collect information.

Audit staff to collate the results (up to 20 hours).

● **Estimated radiologists' and radiographers' time to complete stages 1–3 of the first cycle**

None.

● **Other estimated costs**

None necessary; though a Dymo time/date stamp at £160.00 might be helpful in some hospitals.

REFERENCES

1   The Audit Commission. *Improving your Image. How to Manage Radiology Services More Effectively.* London: Audit Commission, 1995.

2   Department of Health. *The Patient's Charter.* London: DoH, 1991.

SUBMITTED BY

Dr D Wheatley and Mrs C Soar (Audit Officer), Nottingham City Hospital.

<table>
<tr><td>

67

</td><td>

Patient Privacy

</td><td>

☐ Structure
☐ Process
■ Outcome

</td></tr>
</table>

THE AUDIT

Patients' satisfaction with privacy whilst in the Department of Clinical Radiology.

(See Appendix, pages 264–265)

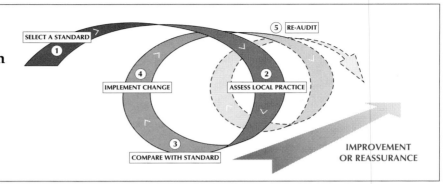

BACKGROUND

● **Why this audit is worth doing**

The preservation of privacy and dignity are basic requirements for all patients whilst in hospital (Ref. 1). Privacy is essential in the clinical areas. It is also essential in the public areas, especially during reception or when discussing referral details and appointment arrangements (Ref. 2). The right to privacy and dignity should be respected during procedures – even if the patient is unconscious.

The questionnaire on pages 264–265 can help to identify problems of privacy and dignity and will enable the department to make changes. It can also help to draw the attention of staff to specific problems.

THE CYCLE

1 THE STANDARD

● **A locally agreed standard**

All patients should feel that they have their need for privacy met and their confidentiality protected during their visit to the radiology department (Ref. 1).

2 ASSESS LOCAL PRACTICE

● **The indicator**

% of patients who feel that they have their need for privacy met and their confidentiality protected during their visit to the radiology department.

● **Data items to be collected**

A questionnaire (Appendix, pages 264–265) should be completed by each patient attending the department. For each patient, regard a score of 5 or 6 on the question at the bottom of page 264 as indicating that they feel that they had their need for privacy met and their confidentiality protected.

● **Suggested number**

All patients attending the department during 1 week.

THE CYCLE (continued)

3 COMPARE FINDINGS WITH THE STANDARD

4 CHANGE

● **Some suggestions**

Appropriate change will depend on the problem areas identified through the questionnaire. Improvements may be required in:

- reception area skills (e.g. reception staff training);
- the environment at reception (e.g. sound proofing);
- privacy for bed patients (e.g. creation of new bed areas with screens);
- privacy in changing areas (e.g. purchase of new gowns).

5 RE-AUDIT Every 12–24 months.

RESOURCES   FIRST CYCLE   £

● **Data collection**

Questionnaire (Appendix, pages 264–265).

● **Assistance required**

Audit assistant for analysis of results of questionnaire.

● **Estimated radiologists' and radiographers' time to complete stages 1–3 of the first cycle**

Radiologist: 3 hours for discussion of problems.

● **Other estimated costs**

None.

REFERENCES

1 Royal College of Nursing . *Standards of Care – Radiology Nursing. The Royal College of Nursing Radiology & Cardiology Forum.* London: RCN, 1993.

2 UKCC. *Confidentiality. A UKCC Advisory paper.* London: UKCC, 1987.

SUBMITTED BY

Sister C Whelan (Sister, Department of Radiology) and Dr RJ Godwin, West Suffolk Hospital, Bury St Edmunds.

RECIPES

68	Patient Satisfaction I	☐ Structure
		☐ Process
		■ Outcome

The level of satisfaction felt by patients with the way they were treated (by the doctors) in the Department of Clinical Radiology.

(See Appendix, pages 266–267)

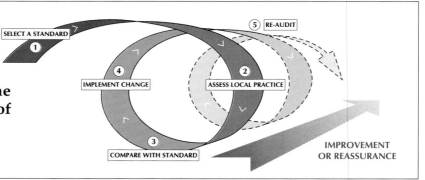

BACKGROUND

● **Why this audit is worth doing**

We need to know what our patients think of the way in which we have treated them.

This survey can be useful in encouraging medical staff to take seriously issues that intuitively they suspect may be a problem (Ref. 1).

A standardised questionnaire can be a useful off-the-shelf tool (Refs 1, 2 and 3) for surveys both across different hospitals, and across different departments within one hospital.

THE CYCLE

1 THE STANDARD

● **A locally agreed standard**

90% of patients who answer questions 2, 3b, 3d, 3e, 3f and 3g of the questionnaire should mark their answers as 4–6 (*good* to *very good*). See Appendix, pages 266–267.

2 ASSESS LOCAL PRACTICE

● **The indicator**

% of patients who mark their answers to all of 2, 3b, 3d, 3e, 3f and 3g as 4–6 (i.e. *good* to *very good*).

● **Data items to be collected**

Collect responses to the questionnaire.

Telephone follow up, as Ref. 1.

● **Suggested number**

Post the questionnaire to 500 consecutive attenders within two weeks of their visit. Post as an enquiry from the Clinical Audit Department with a SAE – i.e. the enquiry is seen as being at arm's length from the Department of Clinical Radiology.

THE CYCLE (continued)

3 COMPARE FINDINGS WITH THE STANDARD

4 CHANGE

● **Suggested change**

Present the results of the audit to all consultants. Some re-training may be necessary in order to improve the communication skills of the Radiologists.

5 RE-AUDIT Every 12–24 months

RESOURCES
FIRST CYCLE ££

● **Data collection**

Questionnaire. Telephone follow up as Ref. 1.

● **Assistance required**

Data analysis and presentation of results by the Clinical Audit Office.

● **Estimated radiologists' and radiographers' time to complete stages 1–3 of the first cycle**

Superintendent Radiographer: 2–4 hours (to provide patient names to the Clinical Audit Office).

● **Other estimated costs**

Postage. Stationery. Telephone follow up.

REFERENCES

1 Bamford C, Jacoby A. Development of patient satisfaction questionnaires: I. Methodological issues. *Quality in Health Care* 1992;**1**:153–7.

2 Jones L, Leneman L, Maclean U. *Consumer Feedback for the NHS*. London: Kings Fund, 1987.

3 Fitzpatrick R. Surveys of patient satisfaction. I. Important general considerations. *BMJ* 1991;**302**:887–9.

4 Rowland M, Shanks J. Broader definitions of clinical effectiveness are needed. *BMJ* 1995;**311**:808.

5 Davies HTO, Crombie IK. Assessing the quality of care. *BMJ* 1995;**311**:766.

SUBMITTED BY

Dr G de Lacey, Mrs J Chapman (Quality Development Manager) and Ms A McQueen (Superintendent Radiographer), Northwick Park and St. Mark's Hospitals, Harrow.

<table>
<tr><td>

69

</td><td>

Patient Satisfaction II

</td><td>

☐ Structure

☐ Process

■ Outcome

</td></tr>
</table>

THE AUDIT

Determining the satisfaction of patients (referred by GPs) with the hospital's organisation of their visit to the Department of Clinical Radiology.

(See Appendix, pages 268–269)

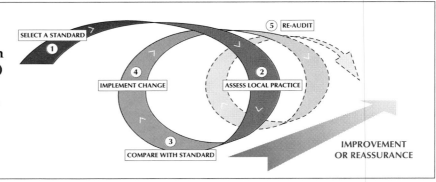

BACKGROUND

● **Why this audit is worth doing**

We need to know what our patients think of the way we have treated them.

This survey can be useful in encouraging staff to take seriously issues that intuitively they suspect may be a problem (Ref. 1).

A standardised questionnaire can be useful as an off-the-shelf tool (Refs 1–3) for surveys both across different hospitals, and across different departments within one hospital.

THE CYCLE

1 THE STANDARD

● **A local standard:**

At least 90% of patients should rate each of six specific questions in the questionnaire (Appendix, pages 268–269) as follows:

- question 3a between 4 and 6 (*polite* and *very polite*);
- question 3b between *ontime* and *15 minutes delay*;
- question 4a between 5 and 6 (*enough seats*);
- question 4b between 4 and 6 (*adequate decoration*);
- question 4c between 5 and 6 (*clean* and *very clean*);
- question 5 between 5 and 6 (*good* and *very good*).

2 ASSESS LOCAL PRACTICE

● **The indicator**

% of patients who indicate on the questionnaire that all of the questions have met the target specified in the standard.

● **Data items to be collected**

Responses to questionnaire.

Telephone follow up as per Ref 1.

THE CYCLE (continued)

● **Suggested number**

Post the questionnaire to 500 consecutive attenders within 2 weeks of their visit. Post as an enquiry from the Clinical Audit Department with an SAE, i.e. the enquiry is seen as being at arm's length from the Department of Clinical Radiology.

3 COMPARE FINDINGS WITH THE STANDARD

4 CHANGE

● **Suggested change**

Present the results of the audit to the entire staff. The Clinical Director and Business Manager should address problems of patient flow and/or communication as revealed by the audit. Use training videos to improve staff–patient communication skills.

5 RE-AUDIT Every 12–24 months.

RESOURCES

FIRST CYCLE ££

● **Data collection**

Questionnaire. Telephone follow up as Ref. 1.

● **Assistance required**

Data analysis and presentation of results by the Clinical Audit Office.

● **Estimated radiologists' and radiographers' time to complete stages 1–3 of the first cycle**

Superintendent Radiographer: 2–4 hours (to provide patient names to the Clinical Audit Office).

● **Other estimated costs**

Postage. Stationery. Telephone follow up.

REFERENCES

1 Bamford C, Jacoby A. Development of patient satisfaction questionnaires: I. Methodological issues. *Quality in Health Care* 1992;**1**:153-7.

2 Jones L *et al. Consumer Feedback for the NHS*. London: Kings Fund, 1987.

3 Fitzpatrick R. Surveys of patient satisfaction. I. Important general considerations. *BMJ* 1991; **302**:887-9.

4 Rowland M, Shanks J. Broader definitions of clinical effectiveness are needed. *BMJ* 1995;**311**:808.

5 Davies HTO, Crombie IK. Assessing the quality of care. *BMJ* 1995;**311**:766.

6 Handy C. Understanding Organisations. Fourth edition. Harmondsworth: Penguin, 1992:43–4.

SUBMITTED BY

Dr G de Lacey, Mrs J Chapman (Quality Development Manager), and Ms A McQueen (Superintendent Radiographer), Northwick Park and St. Mark's Hospitals, Harrow.

THE AUDIT

Patient satisfaction in patients aged over 60 years.

(See Appendix, pages 270–271)

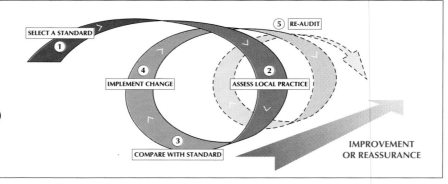

BACKGROUND

● **Why this audit is worth doing**

Some elderly patients require special care and attention when faced with unfamiliar surroundings and events (Ref. 1). This audit can help to evaluate whether they are given the extra attention they may require and to suggest areas which may need improvement.

THE CYCLE

1 THE STANDARD

● **A locally agreed standard**

At least 85% of patients aged over 60 years should give a score of 4 or 5 for all of questions 1–17 of the questionnaire (Appendix, pages 270–271).

2 ASSESS LOCAL PRACTICE

● **The indicator**

% of patients who give a score of 4 or 5 for all of questions 1–17 of the questionnaire (Appendix, pages 270–271).

● **Data items to be collected**

For each patient collect responses to the questionnaire, using the semi-interview technique (Ref. 2).

● **Suggested number**

20 consecutive patients over 60 years of age in each of five groups – i.e. those undergoing:

* chest radiography;
* lumbar spine radiography;
* urography;
* barium meal;
* barium enema.

THE CYCLE (continued)

3 COMPARE FINDINGS WITH THE STANDARD

4 CHANGE

● **Suggested change**

Discuss the results with all departmental staff.

Consider arranging a communication skills course for staff members.

Improve explanation of procedures, including how patients will receive their results.

Introduce a comments box for patients. Invite them to indicate when they have been well treated. Have an award for staff member of the month.

Review cubicle privacy, and adequacy of access for wheelchairs and the disabled.

Obtain arm protectors for patients with fragile skin, and use mattresses on hard examination tables.

5 RE-AUDIT every 12–24 months.

RESOURCES

FIRST CYCLE £

● **Data collection**

Data collection

Questionnaire (Appendix, page 270).

● **Assistance required**

X ray helper to assist patients with completion of the questionnaire (Ref. 2).

Audit assistant for data analysis.

● **Estimated radiologists' and radiographers' time to complete stages 1–3 of the first cycle**

Radiologist: 4 hours.
Radiographer or x ray helper: 25 hours.

● **Other estimated costs**

None.

REFERENCES

1 The Audit Commission. *Improving your Image. How to Manage Radiology Services More Effectively.* London: HMSO, 1995.

2 Fitzpatrick R, Hopkins A. *Measurement of Patient Satisfaction with their care.* London: Royal College of Physicians, 1993.

3 Department of Health. The Patient's Charter. London: DoH, 1991.

SUBMITTED BY

Miss A Forbes (Senior Radiographer) and Dr J Tawn, Poole Hospital.

RECIPES

71 Patient's Charter

THE AUDIT

Adherence to (locally modified) Patient's Charter standards.

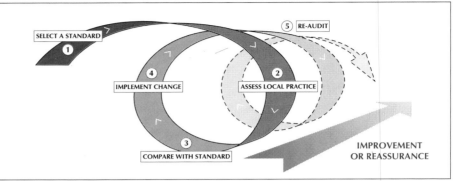

BACKGROUND

● **Why this audit is worth doing**

The Patient's Charter (Ref. 1) sets out the rights to care in the National Health Service and also includes the National and local Charter Standards which individual Hospitals are expected to achieve.

Purchasers of radiological services are seeking evidence that Patient's Charter standards are being met (Ref. 2).

Payment on contracts with purchasers may be linked to evidence that the agreed quality standards (i.e. waiting times and turn-round times for imaging investigations) are being met.

THE CYCLE

1 THE STANDARD

● **A locally agreed standard**

For all out-patients, all of the following should occur:
• they should be informed of their appointment times within 10 working days of the request being received;
• their appointment should be within 6 weeks of the request being received;
• their radiological/radiographic examination should commence within 30 minutes of their appointment time;
• their report should be dispatched within 7 days of the examination.
These four elements represent locally modified – i.e. improved – Patient's Charter (Ref. 1) standards.

2 ASSESS LOCAL PRACTICE

● **The indicator**

% of patients for whom all of the criteria in the standard are met.

● **Data items to be collected**

For each patient:
• the date the request was received;
• the date the appointment was sent out;
• the date the appointment was received by the patient;
• the date of the appointment;
• the scheduled time of the appointment;
• the time the patient arrived;
• the time the examination actually commenced;
• the date the report was dispatched.

● **Suggested number**

50 consecutive out-patient bookings from each of the sections in the Department of Clinical Radiology (e.g. 50 general radiography, 50 CT, 50 ultrasound, 50 nuclear medicine, 50 MRI).

THE CYCLE (continued)

3 COMPARE FINDINGS WITH THE STANDARD

4 CHANGE

● **Suggested change**

Present the results to all staff. Action with regard to failure to meet the standard will need to be taken by the Clinical Director, sometimes after discussion with the Chief Executive Officer. Ways to improve the booking and reporting systems may include:

- book fewer patients with more realistic time intervals;
- open the department for longer hours;
- employ more staff;
- development of innovative practices – e.g. involving changes in skill mix (Ref. 3);
- obtain extra imaging equipment.

5 RE-AUDIT Every 12 months.

RESOURCES   FIRST CYCLE £

● **Data collection**

Computer records.

Ongoing data recording.

Questionnaires.

● **Assistance required**

Clerical staff and radiographers to complete parts of the questionnaire.

● **Estimated radiologists' and radiographers' time to complete stages 1–3 of the first cycle**

Radiographer: 12 hours for each Section Head.

● **Other costs**

None.

REFERENCES

1 *Patient's Charter* (1995). London: National Charter Standards, Department of Health, Richmond House, 79 Whitehall, SW1A 2NS.

2 Harker P. Is money wasted on audit? Report of meeting of Forum on Quality in Health Care. *J of Roy Soc Med* 1994;**87**:55.

3 Irving H. No change is no option. *Radiology Now* 1995; **12**:17–18.

4 The Audit Commission. *Improving your Image. How to Manage Radiology Services More Effectively.* London: Audit Commission, 1995.

5 Robinson R. Accrediting hospitals. *BMJ* 1995; **310**:755–6.

SUBMITTED BY

Ms A McQueen (Superintendent Radiographer) and Ms A Paris (Radiology Services Manager), Northwick Park and St. Mark's Hospitals, Harrow.

<table>
<tr><td>

72

</td><td>

Pelvimetry

</td><td>

☐ Structure
■ Process
☐ Outcome

</td></tr>
</table>

Pelvimetry in cases of breech presentation.

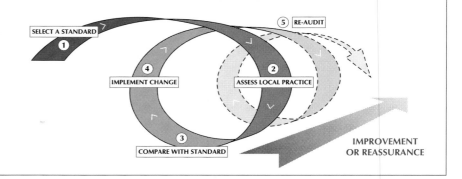

BACKGROUND

● **Why this audit is worth doing**

The most common indication for pelvimetry is to assist with the assessment of a pregnancy in which there is a breech presentation (Refs 1 and 2). In some instances magnetic resonance imaging (MRI) is used (Ref. 3), but in many hospitals pelvimetry involves the x ray irradiation of the fetus and maternal gonads. Breech presentation may be misdiagnosed clinically, causing unnecessary radiation exposure or wasted MRI scanner time. This audit can help to prevent such occurrences.

THE CYCLE

1 THE STANDARD

● **A locally agreed standard**

All cases, where the clinical indication for pelvimetry is a breech presentation, should indeed be breech at the time of pelvimetry.

2 ASSESS LOCAL PRACTICE

● **The indicator**

% of cases where breech presentation is confirmed on the pelvimetry study.

● **Data items to be collected**

For each case, presentation on pelvimetry.

● **Suggested number**

20 consecutive cases of singleton pregnancy breech presentation.

THE CYCLE (continued)

3   COMPARE FINDINGS WITH THE STANDARD

4   CHANGE

● **Suggested change**

If the standard is not met: introduce a routine prior ultrasound examination (US) at the time of attendance for pelvimetry so as to avoid unnecessary radiation and / or wasted examination time. Pre-booking should not be required as the US examination time is extremely short.

5   RE-AUDIT Every 12–24 months.

RESOURCES   FIRST CYCLE   £

● **Data collection**

Ongoing data collection.

● **Assistance required**

None.

● **Estimated radiologists' and radiographers' time to complete stages 1–3 of the first cycle**

Radiographer: 2 hours.

● **Other estimated costs**

None.

REFERENCES

1   Christian SS *et al*. Vaginal breech delivery: a five year prospective evaluation of a protocol using computed tomographic pelvimetry. *Am J Obstet Gynecol* 1990; **163(3)**:848–55.

2   Gimovsky ML *et al*. Assessment of computed tomographic pelvimetry within a selective breech presentation management protocol. *J Reprod Med* 1994;**39(7)**:489–91.

3   van Loon AJ *et al*. Pelvimetry by magnetic resonance imaging in breech presentation. *Am J Obstet Gynecol* 1990;**163(4)**:1256–60.

SUBMITTED BY

Dr C Charlesworth, Wycombe General Hospital, High Wycombe; Dr RL Shaw, Inverclyde Royal Hospital, Greenock.

<table>
<tr><td>

73

</td><td>

Percutaneous Biopsy Procedures

</td><td>

☐ Structure
■ Process
☐ Outcome

</td></tr>
</table>

THE AUDIT

The success of imaging guided biopsy procedures.

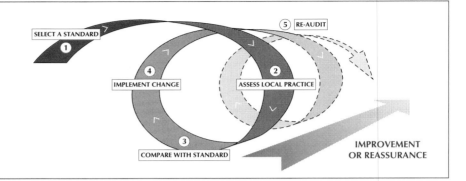

BACKGROUND

● **Why this audit is worth doing**

The majority of percutaneous biopsy procedures are now performed under imaging guidance in the Department of Clinical Radiology. It is essential to check that specimens so obtained are adequate for diagnosis and are representative of the lesion.

THE CYCLE

1   THE STANDARD

● **A locally agreed standard**

An adequate specimen from the biopsy site should be provided for histological/cytological assessment in at least 95% of cases.

2   ASSESS LOCAL PRACTICE

● **The indicator**

% of specimens which are adequate and representative for histological/cytological diagnosis.

● **Data items to be collected**

The number of patients with adequate tissue samples, as defined by the pathologist.

The number of patients with positive pathological results.

The number of patients with a negative pathological result, benign result, or normal tissue, but an adequate specimen.

Record for each patient:
• the site or organ biopsied;
• the size of the lesion or organ;
• the type of lesion (focal, diffuse);
• the imaging technique (CT, US, Fluoroscopy);
• the biopsy technique (cutting needle, automated biopsy device, fine needle aspiration);
• the type and size of needle used;
• the pathology result (definite diagnosis, normal tissue, inadequate specimen);
• any complications;
• coded identifier for the radiologist.

● **Suggested number**

30 consecutive cases.

THE CYCLE (continued)

3 COMPARE FINDINGS WITH THE STANDARD

4 CHANGE

● **Some suggestions**

Present the results at an audit meeting, and discuss the possible reasons for failure to meet the standard. Consider changing the size of needle used, or the number of biopsies taken at each procedure. Consider using a mechanical biopsy technique as routine. Record the position of the needle with hard copy to check the accuracy. Arrange a training visit to a department with better results. Also see suggestions included in Recipe 18, on page 36.

5 RE-AUDIT Every 3 months if standard is not met, otherwise every 12 months.

RESOURCES   FIRST CYCLE £

● **Data collection**

Ongoing data recording.

● **Assistance required**

Secretarial.

● **Estimated radiologists' and radiographers' time to complete stages 1–3 of the first cycle**

Radiologist: 6–12 hours.

● **Other estimated costs**

None.

REFERENCES

1 Bernadino ME. Percutaneous biopsy. *AJR* 1984;**142**:41–5.

2 Burbank F et al. Image guided automated core biopsies of the breast, chest, abdomen and pelvis. *Radiology* 1994;**191**:165–71.

3 Moulton JS, Moore PT. Coaxial percutaneous biopsy technique with automated biopsy devices: value in improving accuracy and negative predictive value. *Radiology* 1993;**186**:515.

4 Labadie M, Liaras A. Percutaneous biopsy: cytology. In: Dondelinger *et al.*, eds. *Interventional Radiology*. New York: Thieme Medical Publishers, 1990:2–8.

SUBMITTED BY

Dr J Tawn, Royal Bournemouth Hospital.

THE AUDIT

Incidence of pneumothoraces occurring after lung biopsy and the requirement for chest drain insertion.

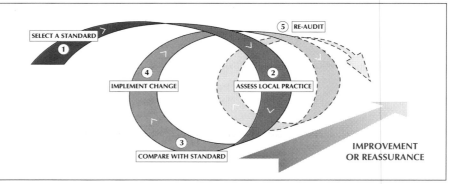

BACKGROUND

● **Why this audit is worth doing**

This audit will help to determine whether lung biopsies are resulting in more pneumothoraces than the figures quoted in the medical literature (Refs 1–3). It will also help to ascertain whether there is a greater incidence of large pneumothoraces requiring chest drains than is acceptable. The study may suggest whether alterations in technique are required.

THE CYCLE

1 THE STANDARD

● **A locally agreed standard**

Less than 20% of lung biopsies should produce pneumothoraces. Chest drains should be required in no more than 8% of lung biopsies.

2 ASSESS LOCAL PRACTICE

● **The indicators**

% of lung biopsies resulting in pneumothorax.

% of lung biopsies after which a chest drain is required.

● **Data items to be collected**

For each lung biopsy, record:

• a patient identifier;

• an operator identifier;

• the needle size;

• whether a pneumothorax was produced;

• whether a chest drain was required.

● **Suggested number**

All lung biopsies over a 1-year period.

THE CYCLE (continued)

3 COMPARE FINDINGS WITH THE STANDARD

4 CHANGE

● **Suggested change**

To reduce the number of pneumothoraces, there is a need for smaller needles and fewer passes. The latter may be achieved by examination of the material by the cytologist at the time of biopsy. Discussion with the cytologist may enable smaller needles to be used. Performing CT scans prior to biopsy provides better localisation. Staff re-training in biopsy technique may also be required.

5 RE-AUDIT Every 12–24 months.

RESOURCES   FIRST CYCLE £

● **Data collection**

Notes search.

Review of radiology reports.

● **Assistance required**

Audit staff to obtain and search the notes and review post-biopsy chest radiograph reports (30 hours).

● **Estimated radiologists' and radiographers' time to complete stages 1–3 of the first cycle**

Radiologist: 3 hours.

● **Other estimated costs**

None.

REFERENCES

1 Labadie M, Liaras A. Percutaneous biopsy: cytology. In: Dondelinger RF et al., eds. *Interventional Radiology* New York: Thieme Medical Publishers 1990:2–8.

2 Flower CD, Verney GI. Percutaneous needle biopsy of thoracic lesions – an evaluation of 300 biopsies. *Clin Radiol* 1979;**30**:215–18.

3 Stanley JH *et al*. Lung lesions – cytologic diagnosis by fine needle biopsy. *Radiology* 1987;**162**:389–91.

4 Harrison BDW *et al*. Percutaneous thoracic lung biopsy in the diagnosis of localized pulmonary lesions. *Thorax* 1984;**39**:493–9.

SUBMITTED BY

Dr A Nair and Dr A Manhire, Nottingham City Hospital.

<table>
<tr><td>

75

</td><td colspan="2">

Portering

</td><td>

☐ Structure
■ Process
☐ Outcome

</td></tr>
</table>

THE AUDIT

The portering needs of in-patients.

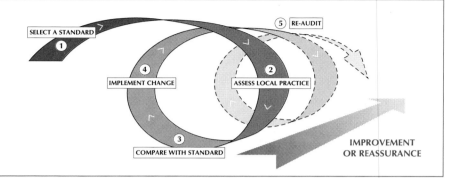

BACKGROUND

● **Why this audit is worth doing**

Knowledge of the availability, dependence, and special needs of any patient prior to bringing them to the Department of Clinical Radiology is essential to:

- enable efficient planning of lists;
- make the most efficient use of portering staff;
- ensure that the correct number of porters are available for each transfer;
- avoid wasted porter visits to wards;
- decrease patient waiting time in the department (especially for very ill patients);
- improve relationships with the ward staff;
- speed up the overall processing of in-patients;
- empower the hard working portering staff.

THE CYCLE

1 THE STANDARD

● **A locally agreed standard**

On all occasions when in-patients require transfer to the Department of Clinical Radiology, the patient should have their portering needs correctly identified and should be transferred on time and effectively.

2 ASSESS LOCAL PRACTICE

● **The indicator**

% of occasions when in-patients require transfer to the Department of Clinical Radiology, in which the patient has their portering needs correctly identified and is transferred on time and effectively.

● **Data items to be collected**

For each occasion when an in-patient is required to be transferred to the department, record:

- the ward and specialty group;
- the time of planned transfer;
- actual time of transfer;
- whether a correct assessment is judged to have been made;
- whether the patient was transferred on time and effectively.

THE CYCLE (continued)

If a correct assessment was not made, or the patient was not transferred on time and effectively, classify the problem encountered from the following list:

- the patient was unavailable (e.g. in physiotherapy);
- the patient was unfit for transfer;
- the patient status was incorrect (e.g. bed not chair required);
- a nurse was required to accompany patient (e.g. on oxygen), and was unavailable;
- other.

● **Suggested number**

Over a one week period, during normal working hours, all patients requiring transfer to the department by the portering staff.

3 COMPARE FINDINGS WITH THE STANDARD

4 CHANGE

● **Some suggestions**

Institute regular telephone assessment of portering needs of in-patients prior to transfer.

Request more portering information on request forms for in-patients.

Publish the audit results by ward and specialty group and discuss the results with nursing and Department of Clinical Radiology staff.

5 RE-AUDIT Every 6–12 months.

RESOURCES — FIRST CYCLE £

● **Data collection**
Ongoing data recording.

● **Assistance required**
Porters: 1 hour each day for 1 week, for recording data.

● **Estimated radiologists' and radiographers' time to complete stages 1–3 of the first cycle**
Radiologist: 1 hour.

● **Other estimated costs**
None.

REFERENCES

1 The Audit Commission. *Improving your Image. How to Manage Radiology Services More Effectively.* London: Audit Commission, 1995.

SUBMITTED BY

W King, B Hall and PW Smith (radiology portering staff), West Suffolk Hospital, Bury St Edmunds.

76 Pregnancy Questioning

☐ Structure
■ Process
☐ Outcome

THE AUDIT

The exclusion of pregnancy in patients who are undergoing radiography (application of the 28 day rule).

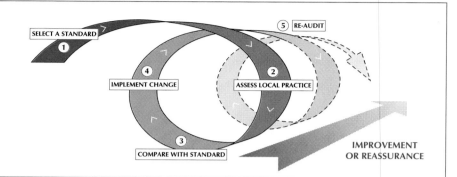

BACKGROUND

● **Why this audit is worth doing**

As part of risk management (Ref. 1) within a department, a regular audit of the effectiveness of the local processes for avoiding irradiation of the pregnant woman is essential. There is still some confusion over the current advice given to the professions following the change from the 10 day rule to the 28 day rule (Refs 2–4), and over the precise responsibilities of individual staff members. This audit can:

- identify local misconceptions;
- identify which examinations are overlooked when making pregnancy enquiries (e.g. operating theatre cases undergoing fluoroscopic screening);
- improve local practice by acting as an educational tool.

THE CYCLE

1 THE STANDARD

● **An agreed standard with two parts**

All females (age 12 to 50 inclusive) who are to undergo radiography to areas between the knees and the diaphragm should be asked about the possibility of their being pregnant.

In all cases in which it is known that the patient is, or might be pregnant, and radiography does take place, the request form should be countersigned by a doctor to that effect.

2 ASSESS LOCAL PRACTICE

● **The indicators**

% of females within the age groups and examination group asked about the possibility of their being pregnant.

Of cases where possibility of pregnancy exists and radiography takes place, % where the request form has been countersigned by a doctor.

● **Data items to be collected**

For each request, using the information on the request form, identify the presence or absence of:
- the patient's signature indicating that she is not pregnant;
- the signature of the radiographer carrying out the examination;
- a signature of a doctor indicating that the radiographic examination should be undertaken despite the possibility of pregnancy.

● **Suggested number**

100 consecutive examination request forms in which:
- the age of a female patient lies between 12 years and 50 years;
- the field of examination lies between the knees and diaphragm.

THE CYCLE (continued)

3 COMPARE FINDINGS WITH THE STANDARD

4 CHANGE

● **Suggested change**

A joint audit meeting should be held with all radiographic staff to discuss the results of the audit. By means of a confidential code enable individual staff members to identify their own errors from the audit results. Identify those examinations in which errors have occurred, and take appropriate steps to see that they do not occur again. Include a written policy for pregnancy questioning within the departmental radiographic techniques and processes file. Increase the number and distribution of pregnancy posters within the department; site the posters in the examination, changing and waiting rooms.

5 RE-AUDIT every 6–12 months.

RESOURCES   FIRST CYCLE £

● **Data collection**

Computer records, to identify the patients.

Review of request forms.

● **Assistance required**

Note pulling by audit staff.

Computer records search.

● **Estimated radiologists' and radiographers' time to complete stages 1–3 of the first cycle**

Radiologist or radiographer: 5 hours for checking the radiography request forms.

● **Other estimated costs**

None.

REFERENCES

1 Royal College of Radiologists. *Risk Management in Clinical Radiology*. London: RCR, 1995.

2 College of Radiographers and Royal College of Radiologists. *Guidelines for implementation of ASP8*. Didcot: NRPB, 1986.

3 Bury B et al. Radiation and Women of child bearing potential. *BMJ* 1995;**310**:1022–3.

4 National Radiological Protection Board. *Board Statement on Diagnostic Medical Exposures to Ionising Radiation during Pregnancy and Estimates of Late Radiation Risks to the UK Population*. Didcot: NRPB, 1993.

SUBMITTED BY

Dr RJ Godwin, West Suffolk Hospital, Bury St Edmunds.

<table>
<tr><td>

77

</td><td>

Pre-Op Chest X Rays for Elective Surgery

</td><td>

☐ Structure
■ Process
☐ Outcome

</td></tr>
</table>

THE AUDIT

Pre-operative chest radiographs prior to elective surgery.

(See Appendix, page 272)

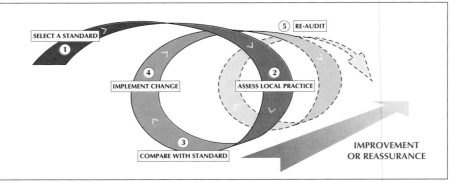

BACKGROUND

● **Why this audit is worth doing**

Many pre-operative chest radiographs contribute little to patient management in elective surgery. The Royal College of Radiologists has formulated guidelines (Refs 1 and 2), but these may be ignored. This audit can help to reduce unneccessary radiography by encouraging the stricter application of these guidelines (Ref. 3).

THE CYCLE

1 THE STANDARD

● **A locally agreed standard with two elements**

The pre-operative chest radiography rate should be below 12% for all patients scheduled for elective surgery (Ref. 1).

All requested radiographs should be viewed pre-operatively by the surgical or anaesthetic team.

2 ASSESS LOCAL PRACTICE

● **The indicators**

% of elective surgery patients having pre-operative chest radiography.

% of films viewed pre-operatively by the surgical or anaesthetic team.

● **Data items to be collected**

During the review period, record for each specialty:

- the total number of patients having elective surgery;

- the number of these patients for whom a chest radiograph is requested;

- the number of radiographs which are not viewed pre-operatively.

For the method of obtaining these data items, see Appendix, page 272.

● **Suggested number**

A review period of 2 weeks is adequate. Occasionally, for smaller units, 4 weeks may be necessary.

THE CYCLE (continued)

3 COMPARE FINDINGS WITH THE STANDARD

4 CHANGE

● **Some suggestions**

Meetings with surgical teams.

Guidelines should be circulated, for example those from the Royal College of Radiologists (Ref. 2). Local variations may be incorporated (Ref. 4). Following this, those requests which do not adhere to the locally agreed guidelines should be returned, with an explanation, and radiography not carried out.

5 RE-AUDIT 6 months after the guidelines have been issued.

RESOURCES   FIRST CYCLE £

● **Data collection**

Retrospective (See Appendix, page 272).

● **Assistance required**

Theatre office staff, to provide operation lists for review period.

Film Library Clerks, to identify those patients who have undergone radiography, and to collect film envelopes from wards for reporting.

● **Estimated radiologists' and radiographers' time to complete stages 1–3 of the first cycle**

Radiologist: 15 hours.

● **Other estimated costs**

None.

REFERENCES

1   Royal College of Radiologists. Pre-operative Chest Radiography: a National Study by the Royal College of Radiologists. *Lancet* 1979;**ii**:83–6.

2   Royal College of Radiologists. *Making the Best Use of a Department of Clinical Radiology.* Third edition. London: RCR, 1995.

3   Royal College of Radiologists Working Party. Influence of the Royal College of Radiologists' Guidelines on Hospital Practice: a Multicentre Study. *BMJ* 1992;**304**:740–43.

4   Walker D *et al.* Audit of Requests for Pre-Operative Chest Radiography. *BMJ* 1994;**309**:772–3

SUBMITTED BY

Dr J Tawn, Royal Bournemouth Hospital.

THE AUDIT

Speed of turnaround of unbooked radiography referrals for out-patients in a private healthcare hospital.

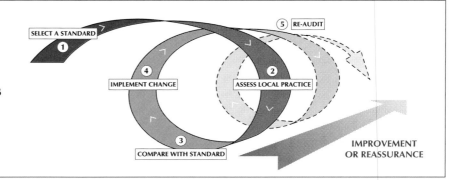

BACKGROUND

● **Why this audit is worth doing**

Fast access to radiography is valued as it often:

- meets the wishes of the referring consultants;
- is expected by the patients;
- increases the efficiency of other sectors involved in patient care (e.g. use of consulting rooms).

THE CYCLE

1 THE STANDARD

● **A locally agreed standard**

90% of all patients who attend the consulting rooms and who are then sent to the Department of Clinical Radiology (unbooked) for an immediate plain film examination (mammography excluded) will be greeted, undergo radiography, and leave the department within 20 minutes of arrival.

2 ASSESS LOCAL PRACTICE

● **The indicator**

% of unbooked out-patients sent for immediate plain film radiography who leave the department within 20 minutes of arrival.

● **Data items to be collected**

For each patient:

- the time of arrival within the Radiology Department;
- the time of departure from the Radiology Department.

● **Suggested number**

All patients attending during 7 consecutive days.

THE CYCLE (continued)

3 COMPARE FINDINGS WITH THE STANDARD

4 CHANGE

● **Some suggestions**

Re-organise the bookings in the x ray rooms, so as to provide more time when the number of unbooked patients is likely to be high.

Improve the efficiency of:

• patient documentation;

• the process of patient registration;

• radiographer work practice.

Increase staffing levels, particularly at times of peak demand.

5 RE-AUDIT
Every 2 months. Whatever the result of the audit, this standard will be monitored on a regular basis.

RESOURCES
FIRST CYCLE £

● **Data collection**
Ongoing data recording.

● **Assistance required**
None.

● **Estimated radiologists' and radiographers' time to complete stages 1–3 of the first cycle**
Radiographer's time: 1 hour.

● **Other estimated costs**
None.

REFERENCES

1 Editor's choice: Patient power. *BMJ* volume 310; 13th May 1995.

2 The Audit Commission. *Improving your Image. How to Manage Radiology Services More Effectively.* London: HMSO, 1995.

3 Handy C. *Understanding Organizations.* Fourth edition. Harmondsworth: Penguin, 1993.

SUBMITTED BY

Mr K Tyrrell (Superintendent Radiographer and Radiology Department Manager), Clementine Churchill Hospital, Harrow-on-the-Hill.

THE AUDIT

In-patient satisfaction with radiology services in a private healthcare hospital.

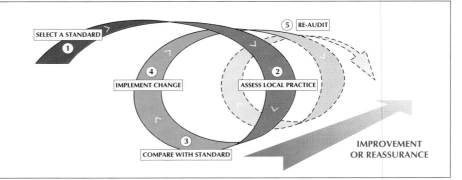

BACKGROUND

● **Why this audit is worth doing**

It is important to be aware of patients' perceptions of the radiology service in order to:

• identify areas that require improvement;

• inform each hospital within the Healthcare Group how well it is doing relative to the other hospitals;

• identify trends and thereby enable early corrective action.

• identify good practices as an encouragement to staff.

THE CYCLE

1 THE STANDARD

● **A locally agreed standard**

In-patients in all the hospitals within the Healthcare Group are surveyed and the results are presented to each individual hospital 4 times per year. The precise standard varies because it depends on the percentage of all in-patients in all the hospitals who rate two specific aspects of radiology services (from a pool of items) as excellent. The actual standard which is required to be met (four times per year) represents the mean of the last four quarterly surveys and this mean is expressed as a percentage of those who have rated the services as excellent during the period. This % is then taken as the benchmark to be met within each hospital. Thus in (for example) October 1994 the two elements of the standard could have been defined as follows:

1 30% of in-patients should rate the communication (i.e. the explanation given to them about their radiological examination) as *excellent*.

2 40% of in-patients should rate the x ray service overall as *excellent*.

2 ASSESS LOCAL PRACTICE

● **The indicators**

This will vary with the standard. For the example given above:

% of patients who rate the communication/explanation about their radiological examinations as excellent.

% of patients who rate the x ray service overall as excellent.

THE CYCLE (continued)

● **Data items to be collected**

Scores between excellent and poor are collected by telephone interviews carried out with a random selection of in-patients who have been recently discharged from the hospital. Comments are recorded as to why scores are good or poor.

● **Suggested number**

A random selection of in-patients. The precise number will be determined by the external company carrying out the survey.

3 COMPARE FINDINGS WITH THE STANDARD

4 CHANGE

● **Some suggestions**

Improve communication (i.e. explanation of examinations and procedures) to the patients, by leaflets and by encouraging staff to discuss examination technique.

Improve overall delivery of the service. The Radiology Manager should address and review waiting times, radiography standards, and the attitude and demeanour of staff.

5 RE-AUDIT The audit is continuous. Results are presented four times per year.

RESOURCES   FIRST CYCLE ££

● **Assistance required**

External company carries out the audit (BMRB, Customer Satisfaction Measurements, Hadley House, 79–81 Uxbridge Road, W5 5SU).

● **Estimated radiologists' and radiographers' time to complete stages 1–3 of the first cycle**

None.

● **Other estimated costs**

Fee to the external company for carrying out the interviews and preparing the data for presentation to each hospital in the Healthcare Group. The total fee includes the full report on other (non-radiological) services in the hospital.

REFERENCES

1 The Audit Commission. *Improving your Image. How to Manage Radiology Services More Effectively.* London: HMSO, 1995.

2 Peters T, Waterman RH. *In Search of Excellence.* London: Harper-Collins, 1995:chapter 6.

SUBMITTED BY

Mr K Tyrrell (Superintendent Radiographer and Radiology Manager), Clementine Churchill Hospital, Harrow-on-the-Hill.

THE AUDIT

Radiation dose to the eyes and thyroid of radiologists during contrast media injections for dynamic CT scanning.

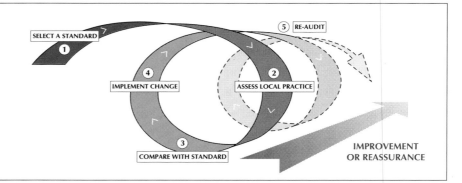

BACKGROUND

● **Why this audit is worth doing**

During dynamic contrast enhanced CT scans, if no pump injector is available, a radiologist may stand close to the patient during scanning. Thyroid and eye radiation protection measurements may be necessary.

THE CYCLE

1 THE STANDARD

The maximum annual average dose equivalent for the lens of the eye for employees aged 18 years or over (150 mSv) and for other individual organs (500 mSv) should not be exceeded for any radiologist (Refs 1 and 2).

2 ASSESS LOCAL PRACTICE

● **The indicator**

% of radiologists who receive more than the annual dose equivalents stated in the standard.

● **Data items to be collected**

For each radiologist, use a thermoluminescent dosemeter (TLD) taped to the forehead to measure radiation dose to the eyes and thyroid acquired during all dynamic scanning over a 3-month period. Pro rata extension of this dose will give the dose for a 12-month period.

● **Suggested number**

All contrast media injections for dynamic CT scans over a 3-month period.

THE CYCLE (continued)

3 COMPARE FINDINGS WITH THE STANDARD

4 CHANGE

● **Suggested changes**

The radiation dose to the eyes and thyroid of radiologists may be reduced through:

- presentation of the audit results to all Radiologists and Radiographers;
- refresher course/tutorials on radiation protection to all Radiologists and Radiographers;
- use of improved lead protection devices;
- purchase of an injection pump.

5 RE-AUDIT Every 12 months.

RESOURCES   FIRST CYCLE £

● **Data collection**

TLD.

● **Assistance required**

None.

● **Estimated radiologists' and radiographers' time to complete stages 1–3 of the first cycle**

Radiologist: 2 hours.

● **Other costs**

None.

REFERENCES

1 *The Ionising Radiations Regulations.* (SI 1333). London: HMSO, 1985.

2 *1990 Recommendations of the International Commission on Radiological Protections* (IRCP 60). London: Pergamon Press, 1991.

SUBMITTED BY

Dr C Charlesworth, Wycombe General Hospital, High Wycombe.

THE AUDIT

Requests for lumbar spine radiography in patients with acute low back pain.

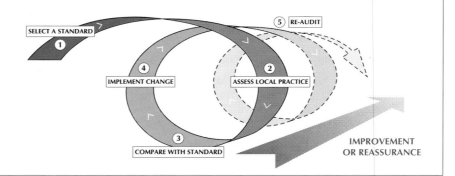

SELECT A STANDARD ①
⑤ RE-AUDIT
④ IMPLEMENT CHANGE
② ASSESS LOCAL PRACTICE
③ COMPARE WITH STANDARD
IMPROVEMENT OR REASSURANCE

BACKGROUND

● **Why this audit is worth doing**

In the UK, plain lumbar spine radiographs contribute 15% of the collective radiation dose from medical imaging. Lumbar spine radiography represents 3% of all radiographs taken. Most patients with acute low back pain and a clinical picture suggesting a mechanical cause improve within 6 weeks of conservative management, and imaging is required only for continuing symptoms. Plain lumbar spine radiography should not be performed during the period of conservative management as it serves no useful purpose and represents an unnecessary radiation dose.

THE CYCLE

1 THE STANDARD

● **A locally agreed standard**

Lumbar spine radiography should not be performed in patients within 6 weeks of the onset of acute low back pain when the clinical picture suggests a mechanical cause only (Ref. 1).

2 ASSESS LOCAL PRACTICE

● **The indicators**

% of plain film examinations of the lumbar spine performed on patients within 6 weeks of the onset of acute low back pain. The % of *these* examinations for which the clinical picture suggests a mechanical cause only.

● **Data items to be collected**

For each plain film examination of the lumbar spine, perform a request card review so as to assess the clinical history; if necessary review the GP/clinic notes for the full clinical history. Record:

• the date of onset of pain;

• the date of examination;

• whether or not the clinical picture suggests a mechanical cause.

● **Suggested number**

100 consecutive plain film examinations of the lumbar spine.

THE CYCLE (continued)

3 COMPARE FINDINGS WITH THE STANDARD

4 CHANGE

- **Some suggestions**

If inappropriate lumbar spine radiography is being performed:

- circulate the Royal College of Radiologists' guidelines (Ref. 1) to GPs and clinicians, and discuss them at meetings;

- check all request cards for lumbar spine radiography before the patient is radiographed, to ensure that each request meets the standard. Refer inappropriate requests back to the GPs and clinicians.

5 RE-AUDIT Every 12 months.

RESOURCES
FIRST CYCLE £

- **Data collection**

Review of request cards.

- **Assistance required**

Audit staff, to obtain 100 consecutive request cards.

- **Estimated radiologists' and radiographers' time to complete stages 1–3 of the first cycle**

Radiologist: 10 hours.

- **Other estimated costs**

None.

REFERENCES

1 Royal College of Radiologists. *Making the Best Use of a Department of Clinical Radiology*. Third edition. London: RCR, 1995.

2 National Radiological Protection Board. *Patient Dose Reduction in Diagnostic Radiology*. Didcot: NRPB, 1990.

3 Butt WP. Radiology for back pain. *Clin Radiol* 1989;**40**:6–10.

SUBMITTED BY

Dr A M Cook, Dundee Royal Infirmary.

RECIPES

<table>
<tr><td>

82

</td><td>

Radiography Referral Rate from A&E

</td><td>

☐ Structure
■ Process
☐ Outcome

</td></tr>
</table>

Referral rate for radiography of first time attenders to the Accident and Emergency (A&E) Department.

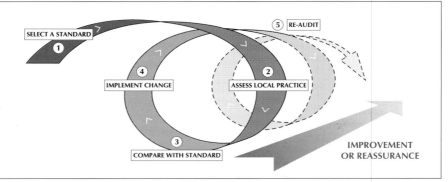

IMPROVEMENT OR REASSURANCE

BACKGROUND

● **Why this audit is worth doing**

Radiography should be strongly discouraged unless clinically indicated (Refs 1 and 2). There is evidence that the referral rates for radiography from A&E can vary by a factor of two (Ref. 3). It appears that a referral rate of approximately 40–50% of all first time attenders for radiography represents an average rate (Ref. 3). This audit will indicate the level of referral. If the average rate is exceeded then steps can be taken to lower the referral rate (Refs 4 and 5).

THE CYCLE

1 THE STANDARD

● **A locally agreed standard**

No more than 45% of patients attending A&E should be referred for radiography (Ref. 3).

2 ASSESS LOCAL PRACTICE

● **The indicator**

% of first-time attenders to A&E referred for radiography.

● **Data items to be collected**

The number of patients attending A&E for the first time (i.e. repeat or follow-up attendances to be excluded).

The number of patients referred for radiography.

● **Suggested number**

All patients attending over a period of 4 consecutive weeks.

RECIPES

THE CYCLE (continued)

3 COMPARE FINDINGS WITH THE STANDARD

4 CHANGE

● **Suggested change**

Presentation of the audit results to the staff in A&E, the introduction of guidelines (Ref. 4), and the development of strategies which reinforce the guidelines (Ref. 5).

5 RE-AUDIT Every 6 months if the results are well outside the standard. Otherwise use a longer time interval.

RESOURCES   FIRST CYCLE £

● **Data collection**

Computer records.

● **Assistance required**

Full cooperation of A&E staff.

Audit Officer to retrieve the computer information.

● **Estimated radiologists' and radiographers' time to complete stages 1–3 of the first cycle**

Radiologists: 6 hours.

● **Other estimated costs**

None.

REFERENCES

1 National Radiological Protection Board and Royal College of Radiologists. *Patient Dose Reduction in Diagnostic Radiology*. Didcot: NRPB, 1990

2 de Lacey GJ. Too much radiology? *Current Imaging* 1989;**1**:141–5.

3 de Lacey GJ. Number of casualty attenders referred for x ray examination. *Brit J Radiol* 1979;**52**:332.

4 Royal College of Radiologists. *Making the Best Use of a Department of Clinical Radiology. Guidelines for Doctors*. Third edition. London: RCR, 1995.

5 McNally E et al. Posters for accident departments: simple method of sustaining reduction in x ray examinations. *BMJ* 1995;**310**:640–2.

SUBMITTED BY

Dr J Tawn, Royal Bournemouth Hospital.

83 | Radiological Errors

THE AUDIT

Errors of interpretation in radiology imaging reports.

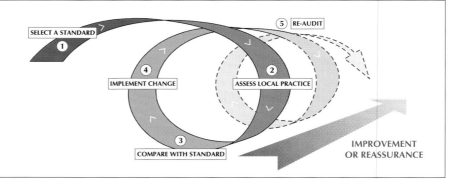

BACKGROUND

● **Why this audit is worth doing**

Errors in diagnostic radiology are inevitable. The absolute number of radiological errors that are made is difficult to quantify. Nevertheless an attempt can be made at *assessing the type of error* (Ref. 1) and this can then lead to changes in approach which might assist in their reduction.

THE CYCLE

1 THE STANDARD

● **A locally agreed standard**

Errors of *interpretation* should constitute less than 25% of all recorded errors (Ref. 1).

2 ASSESS LOCAL PRACTICE

● **The indicator**

% of errors which are errors of interpretation.

● **Data items to be collected**

Keep a confidential record (Refs 2–4) of all errors. In order to ensure anonymity, records of errors should contain no names but should allow classification as follows.

For each examination, record:

- the type of error (perception – false negative or false positive; interpretive; misuse of language; technical);

- the type of examination (chest, trauma, skeletal, barium, ultrasound, CT, MRI, other).

● **Suggested number**

All errors during a 3-month period.

THE CYCLE (continued)

3 COMPARE FINDINGS WITH THE STANDARD

4 CHANGE

● **Some suggestions**

Target those examinations with a high percentage of interpretation error as part of the local programme (Ref. 5) of Continuing Medical Education (CME). In training departments, direct tutorials and teaching towards these areas. Arrange for double reporting of those procedural examinations shown to be associated with a persistently high percentage of interpretation errors.

5 RE-AUDIT Audit three consecutive months each year.

RESOURCES   FIRST CYCLE £

● **Data collection**

Review of the Errors Book (Refs 2 and 3).

● **Assistance required**

Complete confidentiality regarding the record keeping (Refs 2 and 3), and when analysing and presenting the results of the audit. This requires the goodwill, co-operation and understanding of colleagues, both senior and junior.

● **Estimated radiologists' and radiographers' time to complete stages 1–3 of the first cycle**

Radiologist: 6 hours.

● **Other estimated costs**

None.

REFERENCES

1 Renfrew AL *et al*. Error in Radiology: Classification and Lessons in 182 cases presented at a Problem Case Conference. *Radiology* 1992;**183**:145–50.

2 Brighton Health Authority. *Guidelines on Medical Audit and Confidentiality*. Brighton: Brighton Health Authority, 1991:appendix C.

3 de Lacey G *et al*. Setting up hospital audit – One model. *Hosp Update* 1992;**18**:670–76.

4 Dingle AF, Flood LM. The implementation of audit in an ENT unit. *J Laryngology and Otology* 1991;**105**:611–13.

5 Mitchell MW, Fowkes FGR. Audit reviewed. Does feedback on performance change clinical behaviour? *J R Coll Physicians London* 1985;**19**:251–4.

SUBMITTED BY

Dr D Remedios, Northwick Park and St. Mark's Hospitals, Harrow.

THE AUDIT

Time taken for radiologists to attend the Nuclear Medicine (NM) Department to give injections.

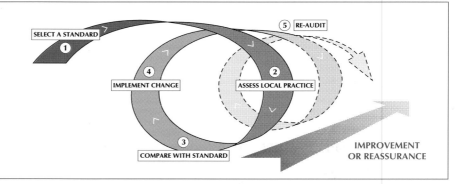

BACKGROUND

● **Why this audit is worth doing**

Long delays in attending to give injections interfere with patient appointment times, disrupt the organisation of the NM Department, and are unfair to patients. This audit can help to identify where and why delays are taking place, and so minimise these problems.

THE CYCLE

1 THE STANDARD

● **A locally agreed standard**

All calls for a radiologist should result in a 5-minute (or less) response time.

2 ASSESS LOCAL PRACTICE

● **The indicator**

% of calls with a response time of 5 minutes or less.

● **Data items to be collected:**

For each examination:

- the day of the week;
- the time the radiologist was called (24 hour clock);
- the time the radiologist attended;
- the type of examination;
- a coded identifier for the radiologist.

● **Suggested number**

100 consecutive examinations.

THE CYCLE (continued)

3 COMPARE FINDINGS WITH THE STANDARD

4 CHANGE

● **Suggested change**

Present the results of the audit to all staff. The importance of a prompt response time should be stressed, and the reasons for delays in response times should be identified. Consider also:

- alterations to the rostering of the radiologists on the weekly timetable;

- using appointments for procedures requiring injections;

- extension of the role of the radiographers (Ref. 1) to include the administration of injections – specifically Lasix and lung scan injections. This will not change response times but may remove the need for radiologists to attend.

5 RE-AUDIT Every 3 months if the standard is not met, otherwise every 6 months.

RESOURCES   FIRST CYCLE   £

● **Data collection**

Ongoing data collection.

● **Assistance required**

None.

● **Estimated radiologists' and radiographers' time to complete stages 1–3 of the first cycle**

Radiologist: 1 hour.

Radiographer: 16 hours.

● **Other estimated costs**

None.

REFERENCES

1 Paterson A. Developing and expanding practice in radiography. *Radiography Today* 1994;**60**:9–11.

2 Winter M. Extended role: hope, scope and a jump. *Nursing Stand* 1994;**8**:53.

3 Holmes S. Extended role: weathering the storm. *Nursing Stand* 1992;**6**:22–3.

4 Irving H. No change is no option. *Radiology Now* 1995;**12**:17–18.

5 de Lacey G. Clinical audit: don't look a gift horse in the mouth. *Clin Radiol* 1995;**50**:815–17.

SUBMITTED BY

Ms J Ryder (Superintendent Radiographer) and Dr L Wilkinson, Northwick Park & St. Mark's Hospitals, Harrow.

85 Radiologists' Availability

☐ Structure
■ Process
☐ Outcome

THE AUDIT

Availability of a radiologist to give an opinion during the working day.

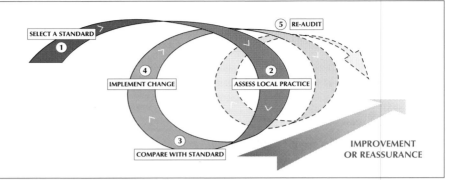

BACKGROUND

● **Why this audit is worth doing**

Having a radiologist readily available to give an opinion during the working day will:

- facilitate the implementation of departmental guidelines for referral for radiological investigation (Refs 1 and 2);
- avoid wasting colleagues' valuable time;
- facilitate the correct planning of patient management in difficult or urgent cases.

It may also (dramatically) improve the department's image within the local medical community (Ref. 3). Identifying a radiologist with specific responsibility for answering incoming queries can:

- avoid interrupting other colleagues in difficult situations (e.g. whilst scrubbed up for an angiographic or interventional procedure);
- enable him or her to deal with problems, have rapid access to current waiting time information and to patient records.

THE CYCLE

1 THE STANDARD

● **A locally agreed standard**

A radiologist will be available for the discussion of referrals or results at all times during the working day. This does not include on-call arrangements.

2 ASSESS LOCAL PRACTICE

● **The indicator**

% of occasions on which attempts to see or speak to a radiologist are successful.

● **Data items to be collected**

During the working day the reception and secretarial staff should record the number of requests to speak to a radiologist, and the number of these which are successful. For each request, record:

- the time of the call;
- the name of the caller;
- if a radiologist is unavailable, the reason why this is so (e.g. answering another telephone, out of the department with notification, out of the department with no prior notification).

● **Suggested number**

Continuous monitoring during 1 week.

THE CYCLE (continued)

3 COMPARE FINDINGS WITH THE STANDARD

4 CHANGE

● **Some suggestions**

Discuss the results of the audit amongst the consultant radiologists.

Identify a named radiologist on the weekly roster, who has the specific task of answering incoming queries during the working session.

Change the rota to create a *duty radiologist* to be available to answer calls. Make him or her more accessible, with reporting as his or her sole activity during these periods. The duty radiologist should work in an office near to the reception/secretarial area.

Increase the number of telephone lines, and identify a specific telephone number for medical enquiries.

Improve internal communications. Install an internal intercom system.

5 RE-AUDIT Every 12–24 months.

RESOURCES   FIRST CYCLE   £

● **Data collection**

Ongoing data recording.

● **Assistance required**

Secretarial and reception staff.

Data analysis by audit staff (2 hours).

● **Estimated radiologists' and radiographers' time to complete stages 1–3 of the first cycle**

None.

● **Other costs**

None.

REFERENCES

1 *Principles for the Purchase and Provision of Imaging Services.* Yorkshire Regional Health Authority, November 1993.

2 Royal College of Radiologists. *Making the Best Use of a Department of Clinical Radiology – Guidelines for Doctors.* Third edition. London: RCR, 1993.

3 The Audit Commission. *Improving your Image. How to Manage Radiology Services More Effectively.* London: Audit Commission, 1995.

SUBMITTED BY

Dr RJ Godwin, West Suffolk Hospital, Bury St Edmunds.

86

Radiology Reporting by Other Doctors

THE AUDIT

Effectiveness of arrangements to transfer the responsibility for the reporting of specified plain radiographs to referring clinicians.

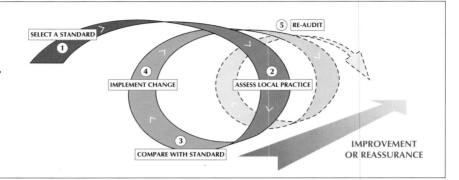

BACKGROUND

● **Why this audit is worth doing**

Every examination which utilises ionising radiation must be reported by a doctor trained for the purpose (Ref. 1). All radiological examinations should be reported either by a trained radiologist or a specialist registrar in an accredited programme, or by a process of proper delegation to a non-medical member of the Department of Clinical Radiology staff. However, some departments have insufficient resources (Ref. 2) to support this level of service, and responsibility for reporting some plain radiographs may be transferred by written agreement with the clinician(s) concerned and the approval of management, to the referring doctor (Ref. 3). This audit is designed to determine whether such arrangements for delegation are being properly implemented (Ref. 3).

THE CYCLE

1 THE STANDARD

● **A locally agreed standard**

All examinations where the radiograph is issued to the referring doctor as the result of a written agreement that a radiologist's report is not necessary (Ref. 1) should be formally reported by a doctor in the patient's case notes.

2 ASSESS LOCAL PRACTICE

● **The indicator**

Of examinations in which plain radiographs are issued without a radiologist's report by written agreement, % which are formally reported by a doctor in the patient's case notes.

● **Data items to be collected**

For each examination, record whether or not a report has been written in the case notes of the patient.

● **Suggested number**

100 consecutive plain radiographic examinations (in-patients or out-patients) issued without a radiologist's report under a written agreement.

THE CYCLE (continued)

3 COMPARE FINDINGS WITH THE STANDARD

4 CHANGE

● **Suggested change**

Discuss the results of the audit with the referring clinicians and review the delegating agreement. If radiographs are not being formally reported as agreed, then changes need to be made so as to achieve improved compliance with the agreement. Improve the organization of clinical service and the training of requesting doctors. Consider increases in resources for radiology (Ref. 4).

5 RE-AUDIT
Every 12 months if standard is met. Otherwise re-audit 6 months after implementation of changes.

RESOURCES   FIRST CYCLE £

● **Data collection**

Computer records.

Review of case notes.

● **Assistance required**

Data analysis by audit staff.

● **Estimated radiologists' and radiographers' time to complete stages 1–3 of the first cycle**

Radiologist: 2 hours.

● **Other estimated costs**

None.

REFERENCES

1 *The Ionising Radiation (Protection of Persons Undergoing Medical Examination or Treatment) Regulations.* London: HMSO, 1988.

2 Royal College of Radiologists. *Medical Staffing and Workload in Clinical Radiology in the United Kingdom NHS.* London: RCR, 1993.

3 Royal College of Radiologists. *Statement on Reporting in Departments of Clinical Radiology.* London: RCR, 1995.

4 Royal College of Radiologists. *Risk Management in Clinical Radiology.* London: RCR, 1995.

SUBMITTED BY

Dr MJ Brindle, The Queen Elizabeth Hospital, King's Lynn.

<table>
<tr><td>

87

</td><td>

Radiology Workload

</td><td>

☐ Structure
■ Process
☐ Outcome

</td></tr>
</table>

THE AUDIT

The number of
examinations performed
by a consultant
radiologist.

(See Appendix, pages 273–278)

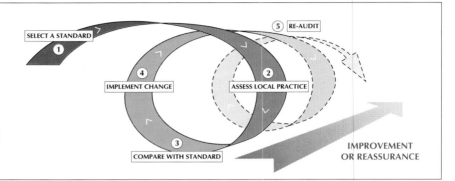

BACKGROUND

● **Why this audit is worth doing**

Managers, and those who pay for health care have a justifiable interest in the work carried out by
hospital consultants (Refs 1–4). Radiological practice has undergone considerable change in recent
years and now involves a high proportion of complex hands-on procedures and time-consuming
examinations, which require close and personal supervision. These responsibilities necessarily limit the
annual number of examinations (Refs 5 and 6) which can be expected of some individual consultants.
This audit is useful because (a) it can provide reassurance to employers that consultants are meeting an
important part of the duties expected of them (b) it will allow a regular re-assessment of the changing
balance between local workload and the available manpower (c) it will act as a focus for the regular
and informed (Ref. 7) reappraisal of existing work practices with a view to determining whether
innovative and imaginative changes should be introduced (Ref. 6) and (d) it can assist in identifying
and protecting those doctors who (for whatever reason) feel compelled to work far too hard for their
own good (Refs 8–14).

THE CYCLE

1   THE STANDARD

Preliminary note: This audit is carried out by measuring against a locally proposed standard and not
against a Royal College of Radiologists, nor any other, standard. This standard adopts an approach in
which the number of radiological examinations to be expected per annum of the hospital's consultant
radiologists will be determined by a prospective and separate assessment of each consultant's actual
clinical practice; the number thus arrived at will represent a manageable workload for that individual
(see examples in the Appendix, page 274).

Thus, the local standard has two elements:

1   The number of examinations carried out per annum should not fall below that individual's expected
norm.

2   The number of examinations carried out per annum should not unsafely exceed an individual's
expected norm (i.e. it should not represent worrying personal overstretch which may be detrimental
to either the individual consultant, to patients, or to the working of the department). If an individual
exceeds his or her agreed norm by more than 10% then this will be regarded as raising the
possibility of personal overstretch.

2   ASSESS LOCAL PRACTICE

● **The indicator**

The number of consultants whose completed patient examinations either falls below or unsafely
exceeds that individual's expected norm.

THE CYCLE (continued)

● **Data items to be collected**

For each consultant record:

- the total number of reports generated;

- how many of each examination group (CT, MRI, nuclear medicine, plain film, barium, mammography, ultrasound, procedural/minor, middle range, major) are generated.

- actual absences for annual holiday leave, illness, study leave or other NHS business;

- the contracted sessional commitment, and agreed job plan.

● **Suggested number**

Assess 12 months' work.

3 COMPARE FINDINGS WITH THE STANDARD

4 CHANGE

● **Some suggestions**

The results should be presented to all the consultant radiologists in a closed session; full and frank discussion should follow. If the standard has not been met:

- too few examinations: the Clinical Director should examine the other legitimate NHS work or roles that the individual performs within or without the hospital and consider whether adequate time has been allocated for these within that individual's job plan. Advise on alterations to the job plan. Increase the number of examinations booked for the individual consultant. Organisational aspects may need to be addressed: e.g. improved portering arrangements, adequate number of clerks to carry out film retrieval and preparation of film bags, adequate secretarial staff to carry out the administrative work, provision of multi-viewers, improved reporting facilities, precluding of interruptions during reporting sessions.

- too many (excessively high) examinations : the appropriate solution will vary – increase the number of Consultants or decrease the number of patient examinations so that manpower more closely matches workload (Ref. 7). Delegation of specific duties and developing innovative approaches including supervised skill mix solutions in certain areas of practice (Refs 6, 15–22). Increase ease of access to, and funding for, study leave. Obtain management's assistance in seeing that the full annual holiday entitlement is taken up (Refs 10 and 14). Provide counselling and introduce other initiatives which recognise and address the dangers which can result from personal overstretch (Refs 8–14).

5 RE-AUDIT
If the standard is not met then repeat the audit in 6 months, otherwise repeat the audit every 12 months.

Resources and References for this recipe appear in the Appendix, pages 273–278.

SUBMITTED BY

Dr G de Lacey, Northwick Park and St. Mark's Hospitals, Harrow; Dr AEA Joseph, St George's Hospital, London.

<table>
<tr><td>

88
</td><td>

RCR Guideline Distribution
</td><td>

☐ Structure
■ Process
☐ Outcome
</td></tr>
</table>

THE AUDIT

Distribution of Royal College of Radiologists' Guidelines to hospital staff.

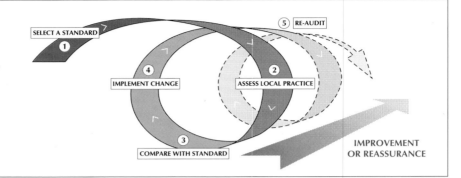

BACKGROUND

● **Why this audit is worth doing**

The Royal College of Radiologists' guidelines, *Making the Best Use of a Department of Clinical Radiology* (Ref. 1) are based on a multidisciplinary approach. However, they can only be effective if they are distributed and brought to the attention of referring clinical staff. This audit will determine whether distribution has occurred.

THE CYCLE

1 THE STANDARD

● **A locally agreed standard**

All medical staff in the hospital who request imaging investigations should receive a copy of *Making the Best Use of a Department of Clinical Radiology*.

2 ASSESS LOCAL PRACTICE

● **The indicator**

% of the medical staff in the hospital who request radiological imaging who have received a copy of *Making the Best Use of a Department of Clinical Radiology*.

● **Data items to be collected**

For each member of staff, whether they have received a copy of *Making the Best Use of a Department of Clinical Radiology*.

● **Suggested number**

A random sample (10%) of all staff who request radiological imaging investigations.

3 COMPARE FINDINGS WITH THE STANDARD

4 CHANGE

● **Some suggestions**

If any member of staff has not received a copy of the guidelines, this should be rectified. A system should be established to ensure that in future the guidelines are distributed efficiently (e.g. in the induction pack for new doctors). Discussion with clinicians and managers should reveal the best way to ensure complete distribution. Purchase of additional copies of the guidelines may be necessary.

5 RE-AUDIT Every 12–24 months.

RESOURCES   FIRST CYCLE £

● **Data collection**

Identification of staff who request imaging investigations.

A simple questionnaire to each staff member, enquiring whether he or she has received a copy.

● **Assistance required**

Audit staff, to identify clinicians who request imaging investigations, to circulate the questionnaire, and to analyse the results (5 hours).

● **Estimated radiologists' and radiographers' time to complete stages 1–3 of the first cycle**
None.

● **Other estimated costs**
None.

REFERENCES

1 Royal College of Radiologists. *Making the Best Use of a Department of Clinical Radiology.* Third edition. London: RCR, 1995.

2 Roberts CJ *et al.* A multicentre audit of hospital referral for radiological investigation in England and Wales. *BMJ* 1991;**303**:809–12

3 The Audit Commission. *Improving your Image. How to Manage Radiology Services More Effectively.* London: Audit Commission, 1995.

SUBMITTED BY

Dr AM Cook, Dundee Royal Infirmary.

89

Reject Analysis of Radiographs

THE AUDIT

Reject analysis of non-fluoroscopy films.

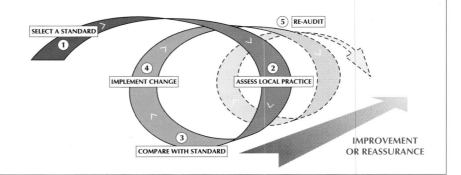

SELECT A STANDARD ① ⑤ RE-AUDIT

④ IMPLEMENT CHANGE ② ASSESS LOCAL PRACTICE

③ COMPARE WITH STANDARD

IMPROVEMENT OR REASSURANCE

BACKGROUND

● **Why this audit is worth doing**

This audit can help to assess the department's performance against recommended standards and to reduce rejection rates where appropriate. This could reduce film cost and patient radiation exposure by limiting repeat examinations (Refs 1–3).

THE CYCLE

1 THE STANDARD

● **A locally agreed standard**

Less than 10% of non-fluoroscopy films should be rejected (Ref. 1).

2 ASSESS LOCAL PRACTICE

● **The indicators**

Less than 10% of non-fluoroscopy films should be rejected (Ref. 1).

● **Data items to be collected**

For each of the 20 most frequently performed types of examination, record the total number of films taken, and the number of rejected films. For each rejected film, record:

- the reason for rejection (underexposure, overexposure, malposition, motion artefact, or other specified cause);
- where the film was processed.

Add the results together to give total figures for the department.

● **Suggested number**

All examinations undertaken during 1 week.

THE CYCLE (continued)

3 COMPARE FINDINGS WITH THE STANDARD

4 CHANGE

● **Suggested change**

Identify which types of examination have reject rates higher than the standard. Review the positioning technique and the processing of these films, check the equipment for consistent performance, and retrain radiographers if necessary. Consider the need for a change of film screen combination, the introduction of digital imaging, acquisition of automatic exposure devices, and/or a revised local radiographic positioning policy.

5 RE-AUDIT Every 6 months.

RESOURCES

● **Data collection**

Ongoing data recording of total number of films.

Collection and review of all reject films.

● **Assistance required**

None.

● **Estimated radiologists' and radiographers' time to complete stages 1–3 of the first cycle**

Radiographer: 3 hours for film assessment.

● **Other estimated costs**

None.

REFERENCES

1 Rogers K D *et al*; Variation in repeat rates beween 18 radiology departments. *Br J Radiol* 1987;**60**:463–8.

2 National Radiological Protection Board. *Patient Dose Reduction in Diagnostic Radiology*. Didcot: NRPB, 1990.

3 Watkinson S *et al*. Reject analysis: its role in quality assurance. *Radiography* 1984;**50**:189–94.

SUBMITTED BY

Mr G Ramsey (Superintendent Radiographer) and Mr P Davis (Radiology Audit Officer), Nottingham City Hospital.

<table>
<tr><td>

90

</td><td>

Reporting Skills

</td><td>

☐ Structure
■ Process
☐ Outcome

</td></tr>
</table>

THE AUDIT

Specialist registrars' reporting skills.

(See Appendix, page 279)

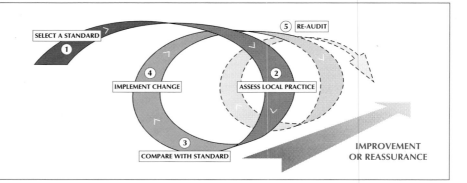

IMPROVEMENT OR REASSURANCE

BACKGROUND

● **Why this audit is worth doing**

The radiology report is the major path of communication between the radiologist and the referring clinician. There is a close relationship between the structure of the report and its accuracy (Ref. 1), so radiologists should strive to present information clearly and concisely in all circumstances (Ref. 2). There is often no change in an individual's reporting style as a result of training beyond the first year (Ref. 1). Good practices are best introduced during the early years of training.

THE CYCLE

1   THE STANDARD

● **A locally agreed standard**

All reports on intravenous urograms, barium examinations, non-obstetric ultrasound or CT examinations by specialist registrars in their first three years of training should:

* indicate the precise imaging examination;

* state the drugs used (including intravenous contrast medium);

* briefly describe the relevant findings;

* provide a differential diagnosis of the likely pathology;

* advise on further appropriate imaging;

* end with a conclusion, impression or summary which includes only the significant diagnostic probabilities, excludes any repetition, and addresses any question posed on the request form.

2   ASSESS LOCAL PRACTICE

● **The indicator**

% of reports which achieved 10 points on the audit assessment sheet. See Appendix (page 279).

● **Data items to be collected**

For each examination, complete an assessment sheet (Appendix, page 279), and record a coded identifier for the reporting specialist registrar. Keep the results anonymised.

● **Suggested number**

10 randomly selected examinations carried out by each trainee in years 1–3 of training.

THE CYCLE (continued)

3 COMPARE FINDINGS WITH THE STANDARD

4 CHANGE

● **Some suggestions**

Refresher course in reporting skills (Refs 1–4).

Formal teaching of reporting skills during the local FRCR I course and further reinforcement during the FRCR II course.

Encourage all *trainers* to develop (for themselves) a local reporting format which matches the standard.

The Head of Training should address the particular needs of those specialist registrars who continue to fall below the standard.

5 RE-AUDIT Every six months if the standard is not met, otherwise every 12 months.

RESOURCES   FIRST CYCLE £

● **Data collection**

Review of reports.

● **Assistance required**

Clerk (Film pulling).

● **Estimated radiologists' and radiographers' time to complete stages 1–3 of the first cycle**

Radiologist: 1 hour per specialist registrar.

● **Other estimated costs**

None.

REFERENCES

1 Hessel S J *et al.* The composition of the radiologic report. *Invest Rad 1975;***10**:385–90.

2 Sierra A E *et al.* Readability of the radiologic reports. *Invest Rad 1992;***27**:236–9.

3 Lafortune M *et al.* The radiological report. *J. Can Assoc Rad 1982;***33**:255–66.

4 Orrison W W *et al.* The language of certainty: proper terminology for the ending of the radiologic report. *AJR 1985;***145**:1093–5.

SUBMITTED BY

Professor G Roberts, University of Wales College of Medicine, Dr G de Lacey and Dr D Remedios, Northwick Park & St. Mark's Hospitals, Harrow.

THE AUDIT

Availability and
acceptability of
resuscitation equipment.

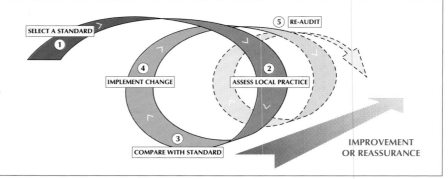

BACKGROUND

● **Why this audit is worth doing**

Patients attending the Department of Clinical Radiology may require resuscitation or life support at any time, either because of a deterioration of their clinical condition or from a complication following an investigation. All clinical areas within the department should be adequately equipped to deal with these events. Regular audit of resuscitation equipment represents sensible risk management.

THE CYCLE

1 THE STANDARD

● **A locally agreed standard based on Royal College of Radiologists guidelines**

The Department of Clinical Radiology should at all times have:

- appropriate and functional emergency equipment available, including a defibrillator and paediatric and adult airways.
- a supply of emergency drugs, in date, and approved by both the Clinical Head of Service and a designated anaesthetist.
- an established routine for checking the equipment and drugs and a method for recording the results of these regular inspections.

This standard is based on Ref. 1, Sections 4.3 and 4.4.

2 ASSESS LOCAL PRACTICE

● **The indicator**

Compliance with the standard on the day of the audit.

● **Data items to be collected**

On the day of the audit, record whether:

- all emergency equipment is present and functional;
- emergency equipment is well maintained and in a safe condition;
- all emergency drugs are present and in date;
- drugs correspond to the list approved by the designated anaesthetist (Ref. 1);
- written records with regard to routine checking are available for inspection and kept in good order.

● **Suggested number**

Carry out the whole audit on one day. The day should be chosen at random (a blitz audit).

THE CYCLE (continued)

3 COMPARE FINDINGS WITH THE STANDARD

4 CHANGE

● **Some suggestions**

Designate a named consultant anaesthetist to have a responsibility within the Department of Clinical Radiology, who should list in detail the appropriate resuscitation drugs to have available. Update the defibrillation equipment if the anaesthetist deems it necessary (e.g. external pacing capability).

Introduce a formal nursing rota for checking of resuscitation equipment and drugs. Keep written records.

Ask the Hospital Pharmacy to perform a regular check on resuscitation drugs, checking both their date and their condition.

Provide identical equipment at suitable positions if the department is multi-storey (Ref. 1, section 4.3).

Re-site resuscitation equipment if accessibility is considered inadequate. Seek advice from the Hospital Resuscitation Training Officer (RTO) on siting the equipment within the department.

Ascertain that clear lines of responsibility and accountability are fully understood in regard to regular checking and the action to be taken on any deficiencies.

5 RE-AUDIT Every 3 months.

RESOURCES   FIRST CYCLE   £

● **Data collection**

Scrutiny and completion of an inspection proforma. The inspection to be carried out by the RTO.

● **Assistance required**

Nursing staff.

Consultant anaesthetist.

RTO (3–4 hours).

● **Estimated radiologists' and radiographers' time to complete stages 1–3 of the first cycle**

None.

● **Other costs**

None.

REFERENCES

1 Royal College of Radiologists. *Guidelines for the Management of Reactions to Intravenous Contrast Media.* London: RCR, 1993.

2 Royal College of Anaesthetists and Royal College of Radiologists. *Sedation and Anaesthesia in Radiology. Report of a Joint Working Party.* London: RCR, 1992.

3 Royal College of Nursing. *Standards of Care: Radiology Nursing (Topic 4: Safety).* London: RCN, 1993.

4 Royal College of Radiologists. *Risk Management in Clinical Radiology.* London: RCR, 1995.

SUBMITTED BY

Dr M O'Driscoll, Dr D Remedios and Dr E Elson, Northwick Park & St. Mark's Hospitals, Harrow.

92 Resuscitation Skills

THE AUDIT

Resuscitation skills within the Department of Clinical Radiology. A risk management audit.

(See Appendix, page 280)

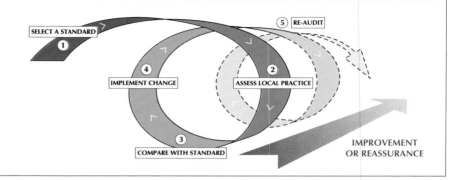

BACKGROUND

● **Why this audit is worth doing**

A large number of the patients who attend the Department of Clinical Radiology are very ill. Many are given intravenous (IV) contrast medium, and a number undergo invasive procedures. Adverse clinical events requiring resuscitation are to be expected. Early institution of appropriate treatment improves clinical outcome.

Resuscitation skills rapidly disappear and need to be relearned (Ref. 1). This audit will ensure that resuscitation skills are being maintained at a satisfactory level.

THE CYCLE

1 THE STANDARD

● **A locally agreed standard**

All staff should possess the following level of resuscitation skills as detailed in the Appendix (page 280):

- level 1: all staff;
- level 2: nurses and radiographers;
- level 3: doctors.

2 ASSESS LOCAL PRACTICE

● **The indicator**

% of staff members who have reached the expected level of competence as defined in the standard.

● **Data items to be collected**

See Appendix, page 280.

● **Suggested number**

All staff.

THE CYCLE (continued)

3 COMPARE FINDINGS WITH THE STANDARD

4 CHANGE

● **Suggested change**

Train all new members of staff during their first week of work in the department. Institute a rolling programme for re-training of resuscitation skills – every 6 months. Booking for imaging procedures should be reduced to allow for this training to take place.

5 RE-AUDIT Every 6–12 months.

RESOURCES | FIRST CYCLE | £

● **Data collection**

The Hospital Resuscitation Training Officer (RTO) should arrange the precise method of assessment. In most cases it will be oral and practical.

● **Assistance required**

Testing by RTO (in Hospitals with no RTO, seek assistance from a consultant anaesthetist).

● **Estimated radiologists' and radiographers' time to complete stages 1–3 of the first cycle**

Radiologists and radiographers: 30 minutes each for assessment by RTO.

● **Other costs**

None.

REFERENCES

1 Berden H *et al*. How frequently should basic cardiopulmonary resuscitation training be repeated to maintain adequate skills? *BMJ* 1993;**306**:1576–7.

2 Royal College of Radiologists. *Guidelines for the Management of Reactions to Intravenous Contrast Media*. London: RCR, 1993.

3 A Report of the Royal College of Physicians. Resuscitation from Cardiopulmonary Arrest; Training and Organisation. *J R Coll Physicians* 1987;**21**:175–82.

4 Royal College of Anaesthetists and Royal College of Radiologists. *Sedation and Anaesthesia in Radiology. Report of a Joint Working Party*. London: RCR, 1992.

5 Colquhoun MC *et al*. (eds) *ABC of Resuscitation*. Third edition. London: BMJ Publishing Group, 1995.

6 Davies HTO, Crombie IK. Assessing the quality of care: measuring well supported processes may be more enlightening than monitoring outcomes. *BMJ* 1995;**311**:755.

SUBMITTED BY

Dr M O'Driscoll, Dr D Remedios and Dr E Elson, Northwick Park & St. Mark's Hospitals, Harrow.

93 | Return of ICU Radiographs

☐ Structure
■ Process
☐ Outcome

THE AUDIT

Time taken to return reported radiographs to the ICU.

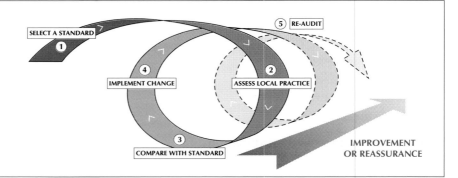

BACKGROUND

● **Why this audit is worth doing**

Patients in ICU have a rapidly changing clinical course, and radiography will frequently have an important effect on management decisions. The prompt return of radiographs with a radiological report to ICU is essential in order to assist with these decisions.

THE CYCLE

1 THE STANDARD

● **A locally agreed standard**

During working hours, all radiographs taken for ICU should be delivered to ICU with a radiological report within 1 hour of receiving the request.

2 ASSESS LOCAL PRACTICE

● **The indicator**

% of reported radiographs delivered to ICU during working hours within 1 hour of receiving the request.

● **Data items to be collected**

For each ICU radiography request:

- the time of receipt of the request;
- the time the film arrives for reporting;
- the time that processed film and report are ready for transport to ICU;
- the time the reported film arrives in ICU;
- the total time elapsed between receipt of the request and arrival of the report;
- whether the time elapsed is less than 1 hour.

● **Suggested number**

100 consecutive radiology requests from ICU during working hours.

THE CYCLE (continued)

3 COMPARE FINDINGS WITH THE STANDARD

4 CHANGE

● **Some suggestions**

If the radiographs are taking longer than the time specified in the standard, then change will be required at one or more points in the chain of events. For example:

- the time taken to perform radiography after the request is received;
- the time to process the radiographs;
- the time to delivery of films to the radiologist;
- the time to type and verify the report;
- the time to return the reported radiographs.

Discussion with all professional groups before and after carrying out the audit will reveal where improvements need to be made. Recommendations can then be circulated.

5 RE-AUDIT Every 12 months.

RESOURCES   FIRST CYCLE £

● **Data collection**

Ongoing data recording.

● **Assistance required**

Audit staff for collection of information and data analysis.

● **Estimated radiologists' and radiographers' time to complete stages 1–3 of the first cycle**

Radiologist and radiographer: 3 hours each for discussion with professional groups.

● **Other estimated costs**

None.

REFERENCES

1 Royal College of Radiologists. *Clinical Radiology Quality Specification for Purchasers*. London: RCR, 1995.

SUBMITTED BY

Dr AM Cook, Dundee Royal Infirmary.

94

Second Trimester Screening

☐ Structure
■ Process
☐ Outcome

Management of patients in whom anomalies are suspected at the second trimester screening examination.

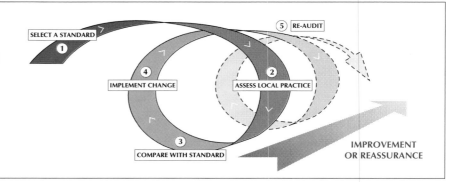

SELECT A STANDARD ①
④ IMPLEMENT CHANGE
② ASSESS LOCAL PRACTICE
⑤ RE-AUDIT
③ COMPARE WITH STANDARD
IMPROVEMENT OR REASSURANCE

BACKGROUND

● **Why this audit is worth doing**

A second trimester anomaly scan is now offered to the majority of pregnant women attending an antenatal clinic. It may be difficult for the radiographer performing the scan to give a full explanation of the abnormality detected – particularly in regard to details relating to the prognosis. To avoid maternal distress it is important that as much accurate information as possible is given to the patient as soon as possible.

THE CYCLE

1 THE STANDARD

● **A locally agreed standard**

All patients in whom an abnormality is suspected should be informed of this by the sonographer at the end of the examination.

All such patients should have a follow-up scan by an appropriately qualified doctor within 2 working days of the screening examination.

Details of the findings and prognosis should be given at the end of the follow-up scan.

2 ASSESS LOCAL PRACTICE

● **The indicators**

Of the patients in whom an abnormality is suspected:

• % who are informed at the end of the examination that an abnormality is suspected.

• % who have a follow-up scan by an appropriately qualified doctor within 2 working days.

• % who are given an explanation of the findings and prognosis at the end of the follow-up scan.

● **Data items to be collected**

For each patient in whom the sonographer suspects an anomaly at the end of the second trimester anomaly scan:

• the information given to the patient by the sonographer at the initial anomaly scan;

• the time interval between the sonographer's scan and the follow-up scan by a doctor;

• the information given to the patient by the examining doctor at the follow-up scan;

• the fetal abnormality found.

THE CYCLE (continued)

● **Suggested number**

In a centre where there are 3,000 deliveries per year there will be approximately 150 fetal anomalies of varying degrees of severity. Ongoing data recording should be performed for a 3–4 month period in order to audit approximately 40 affected patients.

3 COMPARE FINDINGS WITH THE STANDARD

4 CHANGE

● **Suggested change**

More frequent medical scanning sessions may be required, to enable medical scanning within 2 days. Training for ultrasonographers and doctors in breaking bad news may also be required. Use of a proforma to record details of the first scan, and this will also provide a prompt to action a follow-up scan. Also keep a written record of all the information given to the patient.

5 RE-AUDIT Every 12–24 months.

RESOURCES | FIRST CYCLE | £

● **Data collection**

Ongoing data recording to identify the patients and the time interval between sonographer and doctor examinations.

Review of case notes to ascertain what information was given at the time of the two examinations.

● **Assistance required**

Sonographers to identify the patients.

Audit staff to assist with data analysis.

● **Estimated radiologists' and radiographers' time to complete stages 1–3 of the first cycle**

Radiologist: 8 hours for analysis of results.

● **Other estimated costs**

None.

REFERENCES

1 Marteau TM *et al*. The psychological effects of false-positive results in prenatal screening for fetal abnormality: a prospective study. *Prenat Diagn* 1992; **12**:205–14.

2 Evans MI. The choices women make about prenatal diagnosis. *Fetal Diagn Ther* 1993; **8 Suppl.1**:70–80.

SUBMITTED BY

Dr M Gowland, Bolton General Hospital.

<table>
<tr><td>

95

</td><td>

Security – Staff ID

</td><td>

☐ Structure
■ Process
☐ Outcome

</td></tr>
</table>

**Departmental security –
staff identification (ID).**

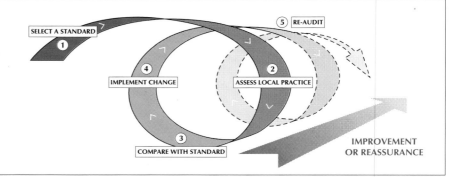

BACKGROUND

● **Why this audit is worth doing**

If all staff wear identification badges:

* patients and staff will know with whom they are dealing;

* visitors (and others who are not staff members) will be more easily identified and, if needs be, challenged;

* improved monitoring of departmental security both in and out-of-hours will be possible.

THE CYCLE

1 THE STANDARD

● **A locally agreed standard**

All members of staff of the Department of Clinical Radiology (employed or voluntary) and all official visitors should be wearing hospital-approved identification badges which are in date, in view, and legible.

2 ASSESS LOCAL PRACTICE

● **The indicator**

% of staff and official visitors who are wearing hospital-approved identification badges which are in date, in view and legible.

● **Data items to be collected**

This is a blitz audit. All staff should be surveyed at a random time and date. All staff levels (clerks, secretaries, porters, radiographers, doctors, nurses) should be surveyed, and also official visitors. No warning should be given, and the audit can occur in- or out-of-hours.

● **Suggested number**

All staff (employed or voluntary) and all official visitors in the department at the time of the blitz audit.

THE CYCLE (continued)

3 COMPARE FINDINGS WITH THE STANDARD

4 CHANGE

● **Some suggestions**

Make sure that the ID policy requirements are widely known.

Make sure that locum staff and visitors are given IDs. All visitors should be encouraged to report to departmental reception for allocation of visitor ID badges (booked in and out).

The ID policy should be part of the induction process for all staff.

Senior staff should take on the responsibiity of ensuring that their staff are wearing their IDs at all times.

All staff should be encouraged to challenge courteously non-ID-wearing personnel – particularly out-of-hours.

Warn visitors and locums in their appointment letters that they will be expected to wear an ID badge.

5 RE-AUDIT Every 3–6 months.

RESOURCES   FIRST CYCLE £

● **Data collection**

Blitz audit, using a simple proforma.

● **Assistance required**

Audit officers to carry out the blitz audit.

● **Estimated radiologists' and radiographers' time to complete stages 1–3 of the first cycle**

Radiologist: 2 hours to analyse the results and prepare the results for presentation.

● **Other estimated costs**

None.

REFERENCES

1 National Association of Health Authorities & Trusts. *National Association of Health Authorities & Trusts. Security Manual.* London: NAHAT, 1992:134–43.

SUBMITTED BY

Dr RJ Godwin, Miss J Wright (Radiology Services Manager) West Suffolk Hospital, Bury St Edmunds.

THE AUDIT

Speaker's technique at radiology conferences.

(See Appendix, pages 281–283)

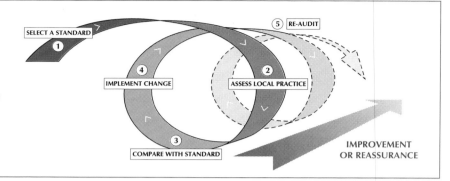

SELECT A STANDARD ①
④ IMPLEMENT CHANGE
② ASSESS LOCAL PRACTICE
③ COMPARE WITH STANDARD
⑤ RE-AUDIT
IMPROVEMENT OR REASSURANCE

BACKGROUND

● **Why this audit is worth doing**

All speakers need to pay careful attention to slide presentation. Conference and meeting organisers have a responsibility (to the attenders) in seeing that the invited lecturers adhere to some basic standards. Some speakers appear unaware of the fundamentals of slide presentation (Refs 1–5).

THE CYCLE

1 THE STANDARD

● **A conference or meeting standard**

The audio-visual presentation of 90% of speakers should score 15 points (or more) overall on the evaluation sheet (see Appendix, pages 281–283).

2 ASSESS LOCAL PRACTICE

● **The indicator**

% of speakers whose presentations score 15 points or more overall on the evaluation sheet.

● **Data items to be collected**

Completion of an assessors' questionnaire (see Appendix, page 283).

● **Suggested number**

In a large congress – random selection and assessment of (say 20%) of speakers.

3 COMPARE FINDINGS WITH THE STANDARD

THE CYCLE (continued)

4 CHANGE

● **Some suggestions**

Deliver guidelines to all speakers 4 months prior to the conference.

Inform all speakers that an audit (by an independent assessor) will occur during the conference.

Delivery of anonymised results to all the speakers taking part in the conference; each speaker will know his or her own conference number.

Give a prize for the speaker who scores highest on the assessors' questionnaire.

Make alterations as appropriate to the lighting or lectern arrangements within the hall.

5 RE-AUDIT Every conference.

RESOURCES   FIRST CYCLE £

● **Data collection**

Assessment sheet (see Appendix, page 283).

● **Assistance required**

None.

● **Estimated radiologists' and radiographers' time to complete stages 1–3 of the first cycle**

Radiologist: 3 hours for each batch of 20 completed evaluation sheets.

● **Other estimated costs**

None.

REFERENCES

1 Heyderman E et al. Down with double projection. *The Lancet* 1991;**338**:1463.

2 Harden RM. Twelve tips on using double slide projection. *Med Teach* 1991;**13**:267–71.

3 Cull P. Making and using medical slides. *BJ Hosp Med* 1992;**47**:132–5.

4 Kodak Ltd. *Let's Stamp out Awful Lecture Slides. Kodak Publication No. S-22 (H)*. Hemel Hempstead: Kodak, 1982.

5 Spinler SA. How to prepare and deliver pharmacy presentations. *Amer J Hosp Pharm* 1991; **48** : 1730-1738.

6 Lee N. Illustrating and Presenting your Data. *BMJ* 1995;**311**:319–22.

7 Simmonds D, Reynolds L. *Data Presentationa and Visual Literacy in Medicine and Science*. London: Butterworth-Heinemann, 1995.

8 Evans M. The use of slides in teaching – a practical guide. Medical Education Booklet No. 134. *Medical Education* 1981;**15**:186–91.

SUBMITTED BY

Dr G de Lacey, Dr L Wilkinson and Dr N Ridley, Northwick Park & St. Mark's Hospitals, Harrow.

97 | Staff Dosimetry

☐ Structure
■ Process
☐ Outcome

THE AUDIT

Wearing of film badges during fluoroscopic procedures.

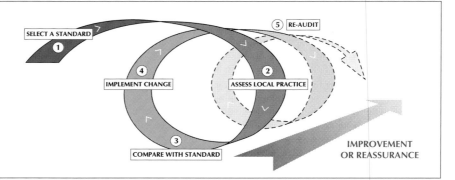

BACKGROUND

● **Why this audit is worth doing**

Although the wearing of a personal dosemeter is not obligatory for diagnostic radiology personnel (Ref. 1), the Ionising Radiation Regulations (Ref. 2) require every Department of Clinical Radiology to prepare local rules which define when staff should wear their dosemeters.

In interventional radiology there is the potential to receive radiation doses approaching or exceeding the classification dose levels (Ref. 3). If personnel do not wear their dosemeters during all other (i.e. non-interventional) procedures then it can lead to an under-estimate of the dose received.

In interventional radiology there is a need for routine monitoring which is additional to the standard single dosemeter worn under the apron (Ref. 4). If radiology personnel do not wear even a single dosemeter they are even less likely to wear two.

Radiology personnel should not be complacent about the dose they receive.

THE CYCLE

1 THE STANDARD

● **A locally agreed standard**

All radiology personnel present during fluoroscopy should be wearing a personal dosemeter at all times.

2 ASSESS LOCAL PRACTICE

● **The indicator**

% of personnel who are wearing a personal dosemeter during fluoroscopy.

● **Data items to be collected**

This is a blitz audit. At a specified time known only to the Radiation Protection Officer (RPO), record the total number of staff present in the fluoroscopy rooms. Of these, record the number of members of staff who are wearing their dosemeters.

● **Suggested number**

All staff in the fluoroscopy rooms.

THE CYCLE (continued)

3 **COMPARE FINDINGS WITH THE STANDARD**

4 **CHANGE**

● **Suggested change**

Present the results of this on-going audit at the department's monthly audit meetings. Hold a refresher meeting on staff exposure and the effects of radiation.

5 **RE-AUDIT** An assessment should be made on 2 random half days every 6 months, to be selected by the RPO.

RESOURCES

● **Data collection**

Ongoing data collection.

● **Assistance required**

RPO to carry out blitz audit.

● **Estimated radiologists' and radiographers' time to complete stages 1–3 of the first cycle**

None.

● **Other estimated costs**

None.

REFERENCES

1 Plaut S. *Radiation Protection in the X-Ray Department.* London: Butterworth-Heinemann Ltd, 1993:113–14.

2 The Ionising Radiations Regulations (S.I. 1985 No. 1333). London. HMSO, 1985.

3 Faulkner K. *Radiation Protection in Interventional Radiology – a Summary of the Discussion. Radiation Protection in Interventional Radiology.* London: British Institute of Radiology, 1995.

4 Goldstone KE. *Occupational Exposures in Interventional Radiology. Radiation Protection in Interventional Radiology.* London: British Institute of Radiology, 1995.

SUBMITTED BY

Dr G Kaplan and Dr T Johnson-Smith, Northwick Park and St. Mark's Hospitals, Harrow.

98	# Staff Radiation Dose in Angiography	☐ Structure
		■ Process
		☐ Outcome

Eye and thyroid radiation dose to staff during angiography.

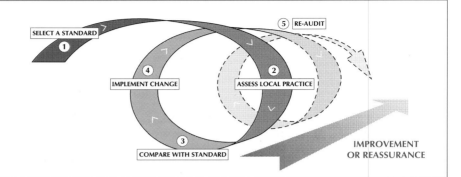

SELECT A STANDARD 1 · 5 RE-AUDIT · 4 IMPLEMENT CHANGE · 2 ASSESS LOCAL PRACTICE · 3 COMPARE WITH STANDARD · IMPROVEMENT OR REASSURANCE

BACKGROUND

● **Why this audit is worth doing**

The angiography room is staffed by a multidisciplinary team, some of whom (e.g. nurses) have no formal training with regard to the hazards of ionising radiation or radiation protection practice. Radiologists/interventionalists are performing an increasing number and range of complex procedures, and this can result in longer periods of exposure to radiation. All staff are routinely monitored by means of film badges worn at hip level under a protective lead rubber apron, but this does not monitor the radiation dose received by the eyes and thyroid, dose limits for which are prescribed in the Ionising Radiations Regulations (Ref. 1). This audit can help to ensure compliance with these limits and help to educate staff in the avoidance of unnecessary exposure.

THE CYCLE

1 THE STANDARD

● **A locally agreed standard**

No member of staff working in the angiographic room should receive a measurable radiation dose to the eyes and thyroid during any period of four consecutive weeks that is greater than 0.2 mSv (Ref. 1).

2 ASSESS LOCAL PRACTICE

● **The indicator**

% of members of staff who exceed a total radiation dose of more than 0.2 mSv to the eyes and thyroid during a monitored 4-week period.

● **Data items to be collected**

The radiation dose for each worker will be measured by a thermoluminescent dosemeter (TLD) which is taped to the forehead whenever the person is in the angiography room.

● **Suggested number**

All individuals working in the angiography room over a 4-week period.

3 COMPARE FINDINGS WITH THE STANDARD

4 CHANGE

● **Some suggestions**

Discuss the audit results so as to increase the awareness of staff to the important aspects of radiation exposure. Make sure all staff are clear that the best way to reduce dose is to distance themselves from the x ray source. Doubling the distance reduces the dose by $^3/_4$.

Lead protective devices (e.g. lead glass shield, thyroid shield, lead protective eye wear) should be available. All staff, including non-radiologists and non-radiographers, should be trained in their use.

Change working practices so that no one staff member is working constantly in the area.

Purchase new imaging equipment (e.g. pulsed fluoroscopy, frame grabbing).

Draw a line on the floor 1 metre from the table. All staff must stand behind this line unless they must be closer by virtue of their duty or task.

5 RE-AUDIT Every 3 months if standard is not met, otherwise every 12 months.

RESOURCES   **FIRST CYCLE** **££**

● **Data collection**

Ongoing data collection.

● **Assistance required**

Regional Radiation Physics and Protection Service.

● **Estimated radiologists' and radiographers' time to complete stages 1–3 of the first cycle**

Radiographer: 6 hours.

● **Other estimated costs**

Dosimetry Service and costs of dosemeters.

REFERENCES

1 The Ionising Radiations Regulations (SI No 1333). London: HMSO, 1985.

2 Faulkner K, Trunen D. *Radiation Protection in Interventional Radiology*. London: British Institute of Radiology, 1995.

3 Cosman M. Managing radiation safely in imaging departments. *RAD Magazine* 1995;**21**:32.

4 *RAD Review of protection and safety. RAD Magazine* 1995;**21**:34.

5 *Ionising Radiations (Protection of Persons Undergoing Medical Examination Treatment) Regulations.* (SI 1980 No. 778). London: HMSO, 1988.

SUBMITTED BY

Ms J Brown (Superintendent Radiographer), Mr M West (Radiation Protection Adviser), Northwick Park & St. Mark's Hospitals, Harrow.

99 | Study Leave for Consultants

■ Structure
□ Process
□ Outcome

THE AUDIT

The amount of study leave taken up by the consultants.

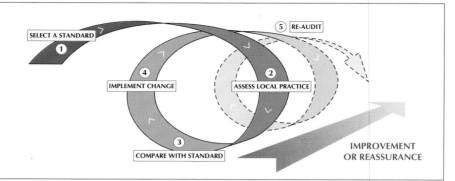

SELECT A STANDARD ①

⑤ RE-AUDIT

④ IMPLEMENT CHANGE

② ASSESS LOCAL PRACTICE

③ COMPARE WITH STANDARD

IMPROVEMENT OR REASSURANCE

BACKGROUND

● Why this audit is worth doing

Continuing medical education (CME) is now a formal requirement of all consultants in Departments of Clinical Radiology. It is evolving, but at the present time much CME will be carried out away from the base hospital. It is important that there are no restrictions on legitimate study leave arrangements for Consultants. Study leave is fundamental to seeing that time is available for CME (Ref. 1). If obstructions are put in the way of study leave applications, then CME is unlikely to occur. This audit will indicate whether legitimate study leave applications are being refused.

THE CYCLE

1 THE STANDARD

● This standard is taken from the Red Book (Ref. 2)

Study leave is granted for postgraduate purposes approved by the employing authority, and includes study (usually, but not exclusively or necessarily, on a course), research, teaching, examining and taking examinations, visiting clinics and attending professional conferences. Study leave will normally be granted to the maximum extent consistent with maintaining essential services ... leave with pay and expenses, within a maximum of thirty days (including off duty days falling within the period of leave) in any period of three years for professional purposes within the United Kingdom.

Thus, the standard is that all consultants should have been able to take up to thirty days for study leave over a period of three years, and all study leave expenses (within the UK) that have been applied for should have been met by the employer.

2 ASSESS LOCAL PRACTICE

● The indicators

% of consultants who have not had legitimate study leave requests refused.

% of legitimate study leave expense claims that have been met by the employers.

● Data items to be collected

A simple questionnaire should be completed by each consultant. The questionnaire should be based on the standard above.

● Suggested number

All consultants in the Department of Clinical Radiology.

THE CYCLE (continued)

3 COMPARE FINDINGS WITH THE STANDARD

4 CHANGE

● **Some suggestions**

Clinical work re-arranged/locum cover provided during study leave periods.

Local Consultant leaders install local arrangements for monitoring applications for study leave.

CEO and (hospital) employers make representations to the NHS Executive so that a mechanism is put in place which is effective in ensuring that the necessary funds are made available to meet the Red Book (Ref. 2) standard.

5 RE-AUDIT Every 12 months.

RESOURCES   FIRST CYCLE   £

● **Data collection**

Questionnaire.

● **Assistance required**

Secretarial.

● **Estimated radiologists' and radiographers' time to complete stages 1–3 of the first cycle**

Radiologists: less than 1 hour each to complete the questionnaire.

● **Other costs**

None.

REFERENCES

1. Peaston MJT. Consultant Perceptions of CME and teaching time. *Hospital Update* 1994;**20**: 414–17.

2. Department of Health. *NHS Hospital Medical and Dental Staff (England & Wales) Terms and Conditions of Service*. London: DoH, 1986.

3 Ward S. Education for Life. *BMA News Review* 1994:18–19.

4 Department of Health. Hospital Medical and Dental Staff: Study Leave. *HC* (**79**) 10 April 1979.

5 NHS Management Executive. *Working for Patients. Postgraduate and Continuing Medical and Dental Education*. Health Publications Unit 1991:7.

6 Kerr DNS *et al*. Continuing medical education: experience and opinions of consultants. *BMJ* 1993;**306**:1398–402.

7 Toghill PJ. Are consultants up to date? *Hospital Update* 1994;**20**:66–7.

SUBMITTED BY

Dr G de Lacey, Northwick Park and St. Mark's Hospitals, Harrow.

<table>
<tr><td>

100

</td><td>

Study Time for Trainees

</td><td>

■ Structure
□ Process
□ Outcome

</td></tr>
</table>

Protected study time for
specialist registrars.

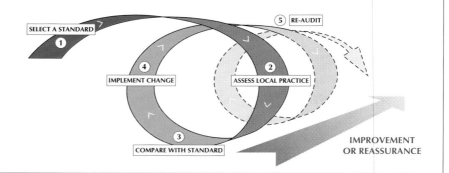

BACKGROUND

● **Why this audit is worth doing**

Specialist registrars need protected time for individual study and research. Department of Health guidelines have been provided (Refs 1 and 2) though these are not always followed (Ref. 3). Ensuring that this requirement is met is an obligation for those responsible for training (Ref. 4).

THE CYCLE

1 THE STANDARD

● **A locally agreed standard**

All specialist registrars should have one day per week for individual study and specific research projects (Ref. 2). For the purpose of this audit this standard will be applied to all those in their third, fourth and fifth years of training.

2 ASSESS LOCAL PRACTICE

● **The indicator**

% of specialist registrars who had taken an average of 1 day per week off service work and devoted this protected time to individual study or research.

● **Data items to be collected**

For each specialist registrar record the number of days that were used for study over a 6-month period.

● **Suggested number**

All specialist registrars in years 3, 4 and 5 of training, over the same six-month period.

THE CYCLE (continued)

3 COMPARE FINDINGS WITH THE STANDARD

4 CHANGE

● **Some suggestions**

Re-organisation of individual work schedules:

- alter workload so as to match the available manpower;
- reappraise consultants' work patterns and patient bookings on specialist registrar study days.

Re-organisation of weekly timetables:

- on the same day each week take all specialist registrars in years 3, 4 and 5 off service work and reduce routine bookings accordingly.

5 RE-AUDIT Every 12–24 months.

RESOURCES

FIRST CYCLE £

● **Data collection**

Weekly duty rotas.

Also post a simple proforma in the department. Each specialist registrar should add an entry each week to record that their protected study periods had been truly protected.

● **Assistance required**

None.

● **Estimated radiologists' and radiographers' time to complete stages 1–3 of the first cycle**

RCR Tutor: 2–3 hours.

● **Other costs**

None or minimal.

REFERENCES

1 Temple J *et al*. Study leave for postgraduate trainees. A paper prepared for the Committee of Medical Postgraduate Deans. *Brit J Hosp Med* 1994;**51**:308–9.

2 Department of Health. NHS Hospital Medical and Dental Staff (England and Wales). Terms and conditions of service. *HC* 1986. Reprinted 31-12-92.

3 Standing Committee on Postgraduate Medical Education. *Uptake and Costs of Study Leave. Results of a retrospective study of 15 health districts in England*. London: SCOPME, 1991.

4 Royal College of Radiologists. *Higher Training in Clinical Radiology*. London: RCR, 1991.

SUBMITTED BY

Dr L King, Dr L Jelly, and Dr S Sohaib, St Bartholomew's Hospital, London; Dr P Scott-Mackie, Guy's and St Thomas' Hospitals, London; Dr B Shah, Northwick Park and St Mark's Hospitals, Harrow.

101 | Swimmer's Views

☐ Structure
■ Process
☐ Outcome

THE AUDIT

Demonstration of the C7/T1 junction and the radiographic quality of swimmer's views in the Accident and Emergency (A&E) Department.

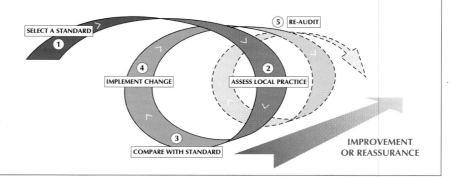

BACKGROUND

● **Why this audit is worth doing**

A significant proportion of cervical spine injuries occur at C7/T1 and it is essential that the top of the T1 vertebra is well shown in all patients (Refs 1 and 2). Sometimes this requires a Swimmer's view. A technically good Swimmer's view can be hard to obtain and subluxation occurring as a result of positioning has been reported (Ref. 3). Too many repeat exposures increase the radiation dose.

THE CYCLE

1 THE STANDARD

● **A locally agreed standard**

The top of the T1 vertebra should be adequately seen in all patients in the finally accepted radiograph. When a Swimmer's view is obtained, no more than two attempts will have occurred in 90% of these patients.

2 ASSESS LOCAL PRACTICE

● **The indicators**

% of patients in whom the finally accepted radiograph shows the top of the T1 vertebra.

Of patients who had a Swimmer's view, % in whom more than two attempts were needed to obtain a satisfactory Swimmer's view.

● **Data items to be collected**

For each patient record:

• whether the top of the T1 vertebra was adequately seen;

• whether a Swimmer's view was required;

• the number of attempts at a Swimmer's view.

● **Suggested number of cases/patients**

50 consecutive patients.

THE CYCLE (continued)

3   COMPARE FINDINGS WITH THE STANDARD

4   CHANGE

● **Some suggestions**

Present the results of the audit to the radiographers.

Educate radiographers in the mechanisms of, and findings in, cervical spine injury.

Re-train radiographers who are having difficulty obtaining adequate views.

Review radiographic techniques.

Consider changing from Swimmer's view to lateral oblique views in certain patients (Refs 4 and 5).

5   RE-AUDIT   Every 6–12 months.

RESOURCES   FIRST CYCLE   £

● **Data collection**

Ongoing data recording.

● **Assistance required**

Radiographers to record number of attempts at obtaining a satisfactory Swimmer's view.

● **Estimated radiologists' and radiographers' time to complete stages 1–3 of the first cycle**

Radiologists: 5 hours.

● **Other costs**

None.

REFERENCES

1   Nichols CG *et al*. Evaluation of Cervicothoracic Junction Injury. *Annals of Emergency Medicine* 1987;**16**:640–42.

2   McCall IW *et al*. The Radiological Demonstration of Acute Lower Cervical Injury. *Clin Radiol* 1973;**24**:235–40.

3   Davis JW. Cervical Injuries – Perils of the Swimmer's View: Case Report. *The Journal of Trauma* 1989;**29**:891–3.

4   Raby N, Berman L, de Lacey G. *Accident and Emergency Radiology – A Survival Guide*. London: WB Saunders, 1995:112.

5   Turetsky DB *et al*. Technique and use of supine oblique views in acute cervical spine trauma. *Am Emerg Med* 1993;22:685–9.

SUBMITTED BY

Dr C Charlesworth, Wycombe General Hospital, High Wycombe.

102 | Teaching Course Assessment

■ Structure
□ Process
□ Outcome

THE AUDIT

Effectiveness of a radiology teaching course.

(See Appendix, pages 284–285)

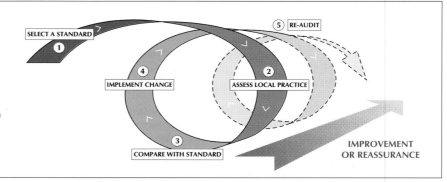

BACKGROUND

● **Why this audit is worth doing**

All courses need evaluation so as to determine whether:

• the training is cost-effective;

• the needs and expectations of the attenders are being met.

THE CYCLE

1 THE STANDARD

● **A locally agreed standard**

In the questionnaire (Appendix, page 284) the course should be rated between *good* and *very good* (4, 5 or 6) by at least 90% of the participants, in each of the following areas:

• usefulness of the course;

• pre-course information;

• lectures;

• small group work;

• hand-outs and notes;

• venue;

• catering.

2 ASSESS LOCAL PRACTICE

● **The indicator**

For each aspect of the course identified in the standard, % of participants who graded that particular aspect between 4 and 6 (i.e. from *good* to *very good*).

● **Data items to be collected**

Responses to the questionnaire (Appendix, page 284).

● **Suggested number**

All participants attending the course.

THE CYCLE (continued)

3 COMPARE FINDINGS WITH THE STANDARD

4 CHANGE

● **Suggested change**

The course organiser should act on the audit findings by addressing those aspects where less than 90% of participants rated the course good or better. Required improvements may include:

- improvements to the pre-course information;
- alterations to the content;
- change in the amount of small group work;
- elimination or reduction in length of particular lectures;
- replacement of teachers;
- improvements in lecture notes;
- change of venue;
- change of caterer.

Some of these may need to be underpinned by an increase in the course registration fee.

5 RE-AUDIT Every time the course is held.

RESOURCES   FIRST CYCLE   £

● **Data collection**

Questionnaire (Appendix, page 284).

● **Assistance required**

None.

● **Estimated radiologists' and radiographers' time to complete stages 1–3 of the first cycle**

Radiologist: 3 hours for a course with 50 registrants.

● **Other estimated costs**

None.

REFERENCES

1 Seednom BB *et al. Devise a Course for Overseas Visitors who don't Speak English Well. How to do it (2).* London: BMA Publishing, 1987.

2 Youngman MB. *Designing and Analysing Questionnaires. (Rediguide 12).* Nottingham: University of Nottingham, 1978.

3 Anderson AH. *Successful Training Practice.* London: Blackwell, 1993:chapter 8.

4 Harrison R. *Training and Development.* London: Institute of Personnel Management, 1989:chapter 15.

SUBMITTED BY

Dr G de Lacey, Northwick Park and St. Mark's Hospitals, Harrow; Mr R Knowles, Educational Consultant, 6 Carmalt Gardens, SW15.

103 | Trainee Assessment

THE AUDIT

The organisation of the annual assessment of trainees.

(See Appendix, pages 286–287)

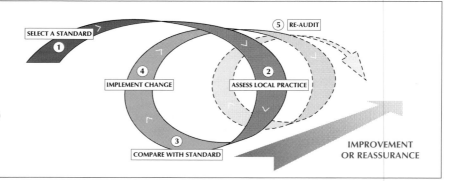

BACKGROUND

● **Why this audit is worth doing**

The majority of doctors want well structured postgraduate training programmes with pre-determined rotations and structured educational content (Ref. 1). There have been criticisms by junior doctors of the extent to which the educational component of a training post is regarded as secondary to the service commitment (Ref. 1). There is evidence that careers advice, information, and counselling in the postgraduate years has often been haphazard or non-existent (Ref. 1). A regular programme of Assessment is necessary so that the effectiveness of the training programme and the progress of the individual trainee can be monitored and any need for changes can be identified (Refs 2 and 3). Assessment is a requirement laid down by the Royal College of Radiologists (see Appendix, page 286) and the responsibility for overseeing the assessment process rests with the Head of Training (Ref. 4). For these reasons it is necessary to regularly scrutinise (i.e. audit) the local arrangements for trainee assessment.

THE CYCLE

1 | THE STANDARD

● **A locally agreed standard**

All trainees should answer *yes* to all of questions 1–7 of the questionnaire (Appendix, page 287).

This standard is based in part on the recommendations of the Royal College of Radiologists (Refs 2 and 4).

2 | ASSESS LOCAL PRACTICE

● **The indicator**

% of trainees for whom the training and assessment given satisfies the requirements in the Appendix.

● **Data items to be collected**

The local College Tutor should arrange for the Clinical Audit Department to distribute, collect and analyse the Questionnaire (Appendix, page 287).

● **Suggested number**

All trainees.

206

THE CYCLE (continued)

3 COMPARE FINDINGS WITH THE STANDARD

4 CHANGE

Some of the following may be necessary

Overhaul the existing assessment procedure by seeking advice and help from the Regional Post-Graduate Dean (Ref. 2) and/or the Royal College of Radiologists Regional Adviser (Refs 2 and 4). Training in the methods of assessment should be available to all trainers. The Clinical Director should allocate protected time for assessors to carry out the assessment. Include an external assessor in the annual assessment (Ref. 2).

5 RE-AUDIT 12–24 months depending on the result of the audit.

RESOURCES

FIRST CYCLE £

- **Data collection**

Questionnaire.

- **Assistance required**

Audit Officer ($^1/_4$ hour per trainee).

- **Estimated radiologists' and radiographers' time to complete stages 1–3 of the first cycle**

None.

- **Other estimated costs**

None.

REFERENCES

1 Allen I. *Doctors and their Careers: a New Generation.* Poole: BEBC Distribution Ltd, 1994.

2 Royal College of Radiologists. *Structured Training in Clinical Radiology.* London: The Royal College of Radiologists, 1996.

3 NHS Executive. *Report of the Working Party on the Unified Training Grade.* London: Department of Health, 1994.

4 Royal College of Radiologists. *Curriculum Framework for Training in Clinical Radiology.* London: RCR, 1994:items 1.5 and 3.7.

5 Rickenbach M. Hospital vocational training. Local audits are helpful. *BMJ* 1994;**309**:196.

6 Lowry S. *Medical Education.* London: BMJ Publishing, 1993.

SUBMITTED BY

Dr G de Lacey and Dr D Remedios, Northwick Park and St Mark's Hospitals, Harrow.

104 Trainees and Audit

- Structure
- Process
- ☐ Outcome

THE AUDIT

Trainees' perceptions of audit and local audit arrangements.

(See Appendix, pages 288–289).

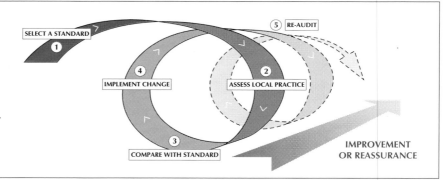

BACKGROUND

- **Why this audit is worth doing**

Postgraduate deans are under an obligation to ensure that an understanding of the principles of clinical audit is part of postgraduate medical education (Ref. 1). The Standing Committee on Postgraduate Medical Education (SCOPME) has recommended that a high priority be given to identifying training needs in clinical audit (Ref. 2). Research defines best practice, education introduces best practice into everyday practice, and audit is fundamental to determining whether best practice is occuring locally (Ref. 3). A clear lead from the *trainers* is necessary if specialist registrars are to acquire and develop an understanding as to why the audit process is crucial to good and successful medical practice (Ref. 4).

THE CYCLE

1 THE STANDARD

- **A locally agreed standard with two parts**

90% of specialist registrars will score *yes* to all of questions 5, 6 and 7 of Part A of the questionnaire (Appendix, page 288).

90% of specialist registars should give a score of *good* to *very good* to all of the questions in Part B of the questionnaire (Appendix, page 289).

2 ASSESS LOCAL PRACTICE

- **The indicators**

% of specialist registrars answering *yes* to all of questions 5, 6 and 7 of Part A of the questionnaire.

% of specialist registrars who give a score of *good* to *very good* (i.e. 4–6) to all questions in Part B of the questionnaire.

- **Data items to be collected**

Responses of specialist registrars to the questionnaire (Appendix, pages 288–289).

- **Suggested number**

All specialist registrars.

THE CYCLE (continued)

3 COMPARE FINDINGS WITH THE STANDARD

4 CHANGE

● **Some suggestions**

Make clear to all training staff within the department that audit is fundamentally an educational activity and is essential to seeing that the findings from research are being translated into everyday practice (Refs 3, 5 and 6).

The Head of Training should take a radical look at the local training arrangements in clinical audit and introduce the appropriate changes (Ref. 6).

A new lead consultant in clinical audit should be identified and his or her responsibilities and precise duties should be clearly defined.

Protected time should be set aside for audit activities (Ref. 6).

The annual forward programme of clinical audit should be carefully planned (Ref. 6).

5 RE-AUDIT Every 6 months.

RESOURCES

FIRST CYCLE £

● **Data collection**

Questionnaire (Appendix, pages 288–289).

● **Assistance required**

Secretarial.

● **Estimated radiologists' and radiographers' time to complete stages 1–3 of the first cycle**

Radiologist: 4 hours.

● **Other estimated costs**

None.

REFERENCES

1 Department of Health. *The Quality of Medical Care. Report of the Standing Medical Advisory Committee for the Secretaries of State for England and Wales.* London: HMSO, 1990.

2 Standing Committee on Postgraduate Medical Education. *Medical Audit: the Educational Implications.* London: SCOPME, 1989.

3 Jacyna MR. Pros and cons of medical audit: a conversation with a sceptic. *Hospital Update* 1992;**18**:512–18.

4 de Lacey G. Clincial Audit: don't look a gift horse in the mouth. *Clin Radiol* 1995;**50**:815–17.

5 Firth-Cozens J, Storer D. Registrars' and Senior Registrars' perceptions of their audit activities. *Quality in Health Care* 1992;**1**:161–4.

6 de Lacey G *et al*. Setting up hospital audit – one model. *Hospital Update* 1992;**18**:670–76.

SUBMITTED BY

Dr D Johnson, Northwick Park and St Mark's Hospitals, Harrow.

<table>
<tr><td><h1>105</h1></td><td><h1>Trainees and Research</h1></td><td>■ Structure
■ Process
□ Outcome</td></tr>
</table>

Trainees' perceptions of the local organisation of their research activities.

(See Appendix, page 290)

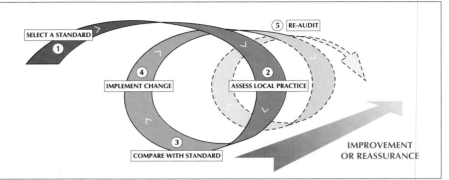

SELECT A STANDARD ①

④ IMPLEMENT CHANGE

③ COMPARE WITH STANDARD

② ASSESS LOCAL PRACTICE

⑤ RE-AUDIT

IMPROVEMENT OR REASSURANCE

BACKGROUND

Although inappropriate demands on trainees to carry out research should be resisted, it is of concern that many doctors after graduation do no research and those who do often do it badly (Ref. 1). Proper training and experience in research is valuable for those who will eventually be responsible for organising clinical services. It also enables individuals critically to appraise published findings which suggest that specific changes in practice and diagnosis need to be absorbed into routine practice (Refs 2–6).

All training programmes need to include experience in clinical research and in research techniques in order to meet the requirements of the Royal College of Radiologists (Ref. 7). Attendance at well organised research meetings can lead to improvements in the quality of the research undertaken by trainees (Ref. 8).

Funding for research within the NHS is becoming increasingly scarce, and thus there is a need for structures which lead to good quality research (Ref. 9).

For all these reasons a regular assessment of the local research organisation is essential.

THE CYCLE

1 THE STANDARD

● **A locally agreed standard**

Based on an 11 point questionnaire (Appendix, page 290), 90% of specialist registrars should respond *Yes* to all the points in Part A and *Good* or *Very Good* (4–6) to all the points in part B.

2 ASSESS LOCAL PRACTICE

● **The indicators**

% of trainees answering *Yes* in Part A and *Good* or *Very Good* (4–6) to all the points in Part B.

● **Data items to be collected**

For each specialist registrar, responses from the questionnaire (Appendix, page 290).

● **Suggested number**

All specialist registrars.

THE CYCLE (continued)

3 COMPARE FINDINGS WITH THE STANDARD

4 CHANGE

● **Suggested change**

The necessary changes will become apparent from the completed questionnaires. All areas where the standard has not been met will need to be addressed. Action may be required from: the Head of Training (organisation), the consultant responsible for the organisation of research (organisation), and the Clinical Director (resources).

5 RE-AUDIT 6–12 months depending on the result of the audit.

RESOURCES
FIRST CYCLE £

● **Data collection**

Questionnaire.

● **Assistance required**

Clinical Audit Office to distribute, collect and analyse the questionnaires.

● **Estimated radiologists' and radiographers' time to complete stages 1–3 of the first cycle**

Radiologist: 1–2 hours.

● **Other estimated costs**

None.

REFERENCES

1 Smith R. Their lordships on medical research: too backward looking. *BMJ* 1995;**310**:1552.

2 Smith R. Towards a knowledge based health service. *BMJ* 1994;**309**:217–18.

3 Tallis RC. Researchers forced to do boring research. *BMJ* 1994;**308**:591.

4 Does research make for better doctors? Editorial. *The Lancet*. 1993;**342**:1063–4.

5 Why clinical research needs medical audit. Editorial. *Quality in Health Care* 1993;**2**:1–2.

6 Bull A. Audit and research. *BMJ* 1993;**306**:67.

7 Royal College of Radiologists. *Structured Training in Clinical Radiology*. London: RCR, 1996.

8 Masterson GR, Ashcroft GS. Better libraries and more journal clubs would help. *BMJ* 1994;**308**:592–3.

9 James JH. Purchasing research in the NHS. *J R Coll Physicians, Lond* 1994;**28**:390–1.

10 Davies HTO, Crombie IK. Assessing the quality of care: measuring well supported processes may be more enlightening than monitoring outcomes. *BMJ* 1995;**311**:766.

SUBMITTED BY

Dr G de Lacey, Dr D Remedios and Dr N Ridley, Northwick Park and St. Mark's Hospitals, Harrow.

THE AUDIT

Transvaginal ultrasound (US) in the investigation of ectopic pregnancy.

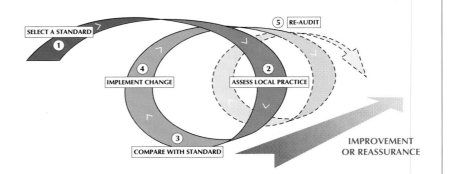

BACKGROUND

● **Why this audit is worth doing**

Transvaginal US is more effective than transabdominal US in the investigation of ectopic pregnancy (Ref. 1). This audit can help to ensure that the more effective technique is used in all cases.

THE CYCLE

1 THE STANDARD

● **A locally agreed standard**

All patients referred to the US Department with pelvic pain and/or vaginal bleeding and a positive pregnancy test should be investigated with transvaginal US.

2 ASSESS LOCAL PRACTICE

● **The indicator**

% of patients referred for US with pelvic pain and/or vaginal bleeding and a positive pregnancy test who have a transvaginal US examination.

● **Data items to be collected**

The number of patients referred with pelvic pain and/or vaginal bleeding and a positive pregnancy test. The number of these patients who are examined with transvaginal ultrasound.

● **Suggested number**

All patients over a 3-month period.

THE CYCLE (continued)

3 COMPARE FINDINGS WITH THE STANDARD

4 CHANGE

● **Some suggestions**

The results of the audit will indicate where changes need to be made. The Clinical Director will need to address the reasons why the departmental/Hospital policy is not being followed.

Ensure all sonographers involved are trained in transvaginal US.

Provide an adequate number of transvaginal transducers.

Identify sonographers who do not perform transvaginal US and discuss reasons for their not doing so.

5 RE-AUDIT Every 3–6 months.

RESOURCES   FIRST CYCLE £

● **Data collection**

Review of request cards.

Review of US reports and images.

● **Assistance required**

Film Library Clerks to pull request cards and reports.

● **Estimated radiologists' and radiographers' time to complete stages 1–3 of the first cycle**

Radiologist: 1 hour per week for 12 weeks = 12 hours.

● **Other estimated costs**

None.

REFERENCES

1 Barnhart-K et al. Prompt diagnosis of ectopic pregnancy in an emergency department setting. *Obstet-Gynecol* 1994;**84**:1010–15.

2 O'Brien MC, Rutherford T. Misdiagnosis of bilareral ectopic pregnancies: a caveat about operator expertise in the use of transvaginal ultrasound. *J Emerg Med* 1993; **11**:275-8.

3 Hunter O et al. Diagnosis of extrauterine pregnancy with transvaginal ultrasound. *Gynecol Obstet Invest* 1990;**30**:204-6.

SUBMITTED BY

Dr M Gowland, Bolton General Hospital.

THE AUDIT

Risk management in the ultrasound department.

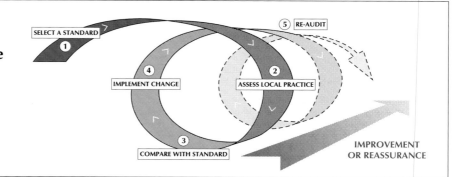

BACKGROUND

● **Why this audit is worth doing**

Medical litigation is rising and departments need to take steps to reduce the risk of accusations of malpractice (Refs 1–7). Doctors and radiographers working in ultrasound will often have been trained in different hospitals. Departmental guidelines are needed in order to standardise some aspects of practice. A written organisational protocol can assist in reducing the risk of litigation (Ref. 1). These aspects of ultrasound organisation need to be periodically assessed in order to see if the arrangements are effective.

THE CYCLE

1 THE STANDARD

● **A locally agreed standard**

All patients attending the ultrasound department will:

- have a written request which indicates the examination to be performed, states why the examination is being requested, is signed by the referring clinician and will be retained and available for inspection if the need arises;

- be assigned to a particular examination, defined in terms of a specific protocol which indicates the organs to be assessed as part of the examination;

- have sample hard copy images recorded which are correctly labelled with patient identification and the examination date;

- have their scan reported by the individual who carried out the examination, with an explicit statement that the scan was difficult, or sub-optimal, when either of these problems had occurred.

This is a modification of the recommendations made in Ref. 1.

2 ASSESS LOCAL PRACTICE

● **The indicator**

% of patients for whom all four of the elements within the standard are met.

● **Data items to be collected**

For each patient, record whether each of the four elements within the standard were met fully. Record any aspect in which the standard was not achieved.

● **Suggested number**

50 randomly selected patients attending for ultrasound examination.

THE CYCLE (continued)

3 COMPARE FINDINGS WITH THE STANDARD

4 CHANGE

● **Suggested change**

The precise changes will be indicated following analysis of the results of the audit. The Clinical Director should encourage all those working in the Ultrasound Department to become familiar with the four elements of the standard. Implement specific examination protocols. An opinion leader (Ref. 1) should be asked to speak to the consultant members of the department in order to reinforce sensible risk management (Refs 2–5).

5 RE-AUDIT Every 3 months if the standard is not met, otherwise every 12 months.

RESOURCES   FIRST CYCLE   £

● **Data collection**

Review request forms.

Review hard copy images.

Review reports.

Review log books in ultrasound rooms, to confirm that the name on the report represents the individual who performed the examination.

● **Assistance required**

Clerk (film pulling).

● **Estimated radiologists' and radiographers' time to complete stages 1–3 of the first cycle**

Radiologist or radiographer: 12 hours.

● **Other estimated costs**

None.

REFERENCES

1 Meire HB. Defensive ultrasound scanning. *RAD Magazine* 1995;**21**:15.

3 Trainor J, Appleby J. Medical negligence. *Health Service Journ* 1990;**100**:959.

2 Appleby J, Trainor J. Clinical negligence : who pays? *Health Service Journ* 1995;**105**:32–3.

4 Mant J and Gatherer A. Managing clinical risk. *BMJ* 1994;**308**:1522–3.

5 Orr CJB. How to minimise litigation. *Br J Hosp Med* 1989;**42**:439.

6 NHS Management Executive. *Risk Management in the NHS.* London: Department of Health, 1993.

7 Royal College of Radiologists. *Risk Management in Clinical Radiology.* London: RCR, 1995.

SUBMITTED BY

Dr T Johnson-Smith, Dr G Kaplan and Dr G de Lacey, Northwick Park and St. Mark's Hospitals, Harrow.

THE AUDIT

Evaluating the accuracy of abdominal ultrasound (US) in patients with obstructive jaundice.

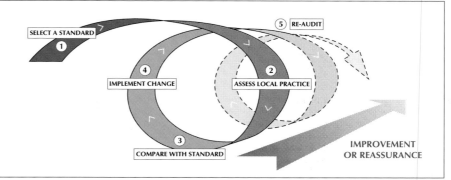

BACKGROUND

● **Why this audit is worth doing**

US is considered an accurate method of assessing the patient with obstructive jaundice, and should be able to distinguish between neoplastic causes and cholelithiasis. Endoscopic retrograde cholangiopancreatography (ERCP) carries a significant morbidity and mortality, and should be limited to those patients who require it.

THE CYCLE

1 THE STANDARD

● **A locally agreed standard**

Abdominal US in obstructive jaundice should be accurate in more than 80% of cases, defining both the site and cause of obstruction (e.g. calculus, tumour, etc.).

2 ASSESS LOCAL PRACTICE

● **The indicator**

% of cases in which US gives an accurate result.

● **Data items to be collected**

For each patient, record whether the final clinical diagnosis matches the US report, plus any other relevant clinical information.

● **Suggested number**

50 consecutive patients with jaundice referred for ultrasound.

THE CYCLE (continued)

3 COMPARE FINDINGS WITH THE STANDARD

4 CHANGE

● **Some suggestions**

Discuss and analyse the results to determine what lesions are being incorrectly interpreted.

Training and additional subspecialisation may be required to reach the required standard.

Consider the adequacy and quality of the US images, and review machine purchasing plans.

5 RE-AUDIT Every 12–24 months.

RESOURCES   FIRST CYCLE £

● **Data collection**
Retrospective.

● **Assistance required**
Audit officer.

● **Estimated radiologists' and radiographers' time to complete stages 1–3 of the first cycle**
Radiologist: 6 hours.

● **Other estimated costs**
None.

REFERENCES

1 Laing FC et al. Biliary dilatation: defining the level and cause by real-time ultrasound. *Radiology* 1986;**160**:39–42.

2 Freeny PC (ed.). Radiology of the Pancreas. *RCNA* 1989;**27**.

3 Malghow Moller A et al. A decision tree for early differentiation between obstructive and non-obstructive jaundice. *Scand J Gastroenterol* 1988;**23**:391–401.

SUBMITTED BY

Dr S Jones, Royal Bournemouth Hospital.

THE AUDIT

Lumbar puncture (LP) following requests for urgent CT brain scans.

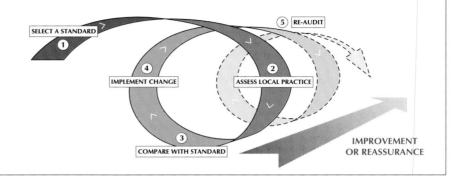

BACKGROUND

● **Why this audit is worth doing**

A significant number of urgent, or out-of-hours, requests for a CT brain scan are made because proceeding to a lumbar puncture (LP) is dependent on a normal CT scan. These urgent examinations should actually be followed by an LP with a similar degree of urgency.

This audit will confirm that this aspect of clinical care conforms to agreed guidelines and that urgent or out-of-hours services are being used properly.

THE CYCLE

1 THE STANDARD

● **A locally agreed standard**

In all cases where patients undergo urgent out-of-hours CT as a prerequisite for proceeding to a LP, if CT does not reveal either a contraindication to LP, or any finding rendering LP unnecessary, then an LP should be performed and the result known within 3 hours of completion of the CT examination.

2 ASSESS LOCAL PRACTICE

● **The indicator**

Of cases in which patients undergo urgent out-of-hours CT as a prerequisite for proceeding to an LP, and the CT does not reveal either a contraindication to LP, or any finding rendering LP unnecessary, % who actually undergo the LP and have the LP results available within 3 hours of completion of the CT examination.

● **Data items to be collected**

For each patient:

• the time of the CT examination;

• whether the CT report precludes LP;

• whether the CT reveals any finding that renders LP unnecessary;

• if and when the LP was performed;

• the result and time of the report on the LP.

● **Suggested number**

20 consecutive requests.

THE CYCLE (continued)

3 COMPARE FINDINGS WITH THE STANDARD

4 CHANGE

● **Some suggestions**

Discuss the audit results with radiologists and clinical referring teams.

Reinforce the local guidelines for CT urgent requests.

Agree with clinicians that only a consultant or a specialist registrar at year 3 or higher can request an urgent CT scan in these circumstances.

5 RE-AUDIT Every 6 months.

RESOURCES   FIRST CYCLE   £

● **Data collection**

Review of request forms.

Review of patients' notes.

Review of laboratory log books.

Duty radiologist to record all cases of urgent CT examinations performed prior to LP.

● **Assistance required**

Clerk (film pulling and case note pulling).

● **Estimated radiologists' and radiographers' time to complete stages 1–3 of the first cycle**

Radiologist: 8 hours.

● **Other estimated costs**

None.

REFERENCES

1 Walton J. *Brain's Diseases of the Nervous System*. Ninth edition. Oxford: Oxford University Press, 1985:66.

2 Fisherman RA. Brain oedema and disorders of intracranial pressure. In: Roland EP, ed. *Merritt's Textbook of Neurology*. Eighth edition. Rowland (LP) Ed. Philadelphia: Lea and Febiger, 1989.

3 Moss JG, Murchison JT. Is Radiology a nine to five specialty? *Clin Radiol* 1992;**46**:124–7.

SUBMITTED BY

Dr G Dodge, Dr R Warwick, The Royal Free Hospital, London; Dr M de Jude, Dr A Newman-Saunders, St Mary's Hospital, London; Dr G O'Sullivan, St George's Hospital, London; Dr MI Shaikh, Northwick Park and St Mark's Hospitals, Harrow.

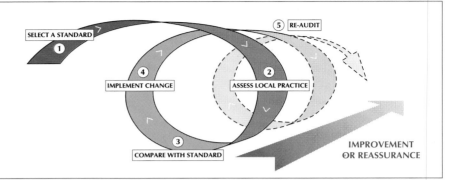

Adherence to an agreed protocol for intravenous urography (IVU) in acute renal colic.

(See Appendix, page 291)

BACKGROUND

● **Why this audit is worth doing**

Suspected acute renal colic is a common reason for IVU referral from the Accident and Emergency Department.

A limited urographic examination (sometimes only two films) is all that is required.

Adherence to a set protocol reduces radiation dose, is cost effective, and utilises radiographers' and radiologists' time efficiently.

THE CYCLE

1 THE STANDARD

● **A locally agreed standard**

In all cases of limited IVUs carried out on patients with suspected renal colic, all elements of the local protocol (Appendix, page 291) should be followed.

2 ASSESS LOCAL PRACTICE

● **The indicator**

% of limited IVUs in which all elements of the protocol are followed.

● **Data items to be collected**

For each patient record:

• whether the preliminary radiograph is technically adequate;

• whether there is renal or ureteric calcification on the preliminary radiograph;

• the number and timing of post injection radiographs;

• whether each of the stages described in the protocol (Appendix, page 291) has been adhered to.

● **Suggested number**

20 consecutive patients referred for urography because of suspected acute renal colic.

THE CYCLE (continued)

3   COMPARE FINDINGS WITH THE STANDARD

4   CHANGE

● **Suggested change**

Present the results of the audit to all the radiologists and to all the radiographers, with full and frank discussion, in order to identify the reasons for any variation. The Clinical Director should make appropriate organisational changes (these will be clear from an analysis of the results) to ensure that the protocol is adhered to.

Display the protocol as an algorithm in the IVU room to ensure that all are aware of it (Ref. 1).

5   RE-AUDIT   Every 6–12 months.

RESOURCES   FIRST CYCLE   £

● **Data collection**

Computer records to identify the patients.

Review request forms.

Review films.

● **Assistance required**

Clerk (film pulling).

● **Estimated radiologists' and radiographers' time to complete stages 1–3 of the first cycle**

Radiologist: 3 hours.

● **Other estimated costs**

None.

REFERENCES

1 McNally E *et al.* Posters for accident departments: simple method of sustaining reduction in x ray examinations. *BMJ* 1995;**310**:640–42.

2 Grainger RG, Allison DJ eds. Diagnostic Radiology. Second Edition. Volume 2. Edinburgh: Churchill Livingstone, 1992, 1253–67.

3 Haddad MC, *et al.* Renal colic: diagnosis and outcome. *Radiology* 1992;**184**:83–8.

4 Raby N, Berman L, de Lacey G. *Accident and Emergency Radiology. A Survival Guide.* London: WB Saunders, 1995: 206.

5 National Radiological Protection Board. *Patient Dose Reduction in Diagnostic Radiology.* Didcot: NRPB, 1990.

SUBMITTED BY

Dr B Shah and Dr MI Shaikh, Northwick Park & St. Mark's Hospitals, Harrow.

THE AUDIT

Effect of ventilation and perfusion scintigraphy findings on patient management.

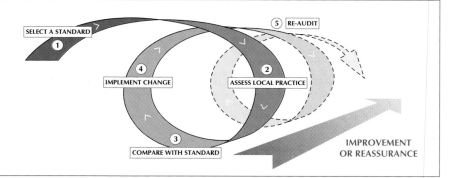

BACKGROUND

● **Why this audit is worth doing**

The findings from radiological examinations should result in appropriate decisions on patient management if the radiation dose and use of resources is to be justified (Refs 1 and 2).

THE CYCLE

1 THE STANDARD

● **A locally agreed standard**

In at least 90% of V/Q scans, there should be evidence in the clinical notes that the radiological diagnosis is accepted, and a subsequent appropriate clinical decision has been taken.

2 ASSESS LOCAL PRACTICE

● **The indicator**

% of V/Q scans in which there is evidence in the clinical notes that the radiological diagnosis has been accepted, and a subsequent appropriate clinical decision taken.

● **Data items to be collected**

For each V/Q scan, record:

• the clinical diagnosis before examination;

• the clinical diagnosis after radiological diagnosis;

• whether there is evidence in the clinical notes that the radiological diagnosis has been accepted;

• whether the subsequent management is appropriate to the radiological diagnosis;

• the physician requesting the scan.

● **Suggested number**

20 consecutive V/Q scans.

THE CYCLE (continued)

3 COMPARE FINDINGS WITH THE STANDARD

4 CHANGE

● **Some suggestions**

If tests are being performed, and the results are not being acted upon, then the usefulness of these tests should be discussed with the physicians concerned. The results of the V/Q scan should be written in the patient's notes so as to assist with management decisions.

5 RE-AUDIT Every 6 months.

RESOURCES   FIRST CYCLE £

● **Data collection**

Notes search.

● **Assistance required**

Note pulling by audit staff (18 hours).

● **Estimated radiologists' and radiographers' time to complete stages 1–3 of the first cycle**

Radiologist: 4 hours.

● **Other estimated costs**

None.

REFERENCES

1 Royal College of Radiologists. *Making the Best Use of a Department of Clinical Radiology. Guidelines for Doctors.* Third edition. London:RCR, 1995.

2 The Audit Commission. *Improving your Image. How to Manage Radiology Services More Effectively.* London: Audit Commission, 1995.

3 Royal College of Radiologists. *Clinical Radiology Quality Specification for Purchasers.* London: RCR, 1995.

SUBMITTED BY

Dr D Rose, Nottingham City Hospital.

R E C I P E S

THE AUDIT

An audit of the
appropriateness of
nuclear medicine (NM)
requests.

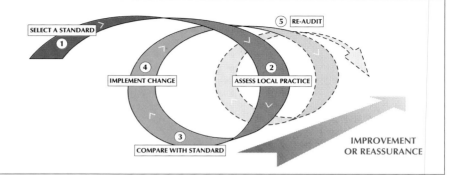

BACKGROUND

● **Why this audit is worth doing**

The indications and usefulness of NM investigations are often poorly understood. This audit will provide re-assurance that resources are being used appropriately and radiation doses are being minimised. A significant reduction in workload may be achievable by vetting all requests sent to the NM department.

THE CYCLE

1 THE STANDARD

● **A locally agreed standard**

All requests for NM investigations should be appropriate to the clinical problem.

2 ASSESS LOCAL PRACTICE

● **The indicator**

% of requests for NM investigations which are appropriate.

● **Data items to be collected**

For each request record:

• a patient identifier;

• the clinical problem;

• the test requested;

• whether the request was appropriate or inappropriate (if inadequate or no clinical information is present, classify under inappropriate).

● **Suggested number**

100 consecutive requests.

THE CYCLE (continued)

3 COMPARE FINDINGS WITH THE STANDARD

4 CHANGE

● **Suggested change**

Promulgate the Royal College of Radiologists' guidelines for NM investigations (Ref. 1). Include these guidelines in the specialist registrars' Induction Pack, and reinforce them at clinical meetings. Where requests are inappropriate according to the guidelines, then send (a relevant summary) or a reference to the guidelines back with the original request form for future guidance.

5 RE-AUDIT Every 6–12 months.

RESOURCES

● **Data collection**

Ongoing data recording.

● **Assistance required**

In some departments the NM Physician will carry out the data analysis.

● **Estimated radiologists' and radiographers' time to complete stages 1–3 of the first cycle**

Radiologist or NM Physician: 6 hours.

● **Other estimated costs**

None.

REFERENCES

1 Royal College of Radiologists. *Making the Best Use of a Department of Clinical Radiology*. Third edition. London: RCR, 1995.

SUBMITTED BY

Dr J Tawn, Royal Bournemouth Hospital.

THE AUDIT

Waiting time of patients prior to appointment.

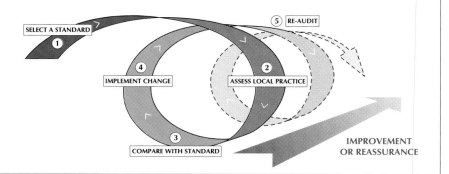

BACKGROUND

● **Why this audit is worth doing**

Patients find waiting for an examination distressing. Unnecessary waiting reduces departmental efficiency and increases departmental congestion (Ref. 1). This audit can help to reduce patients' waiting times.

THE CYCLE

1 THE STANDARD

● **A locally agreed standard**

90% of patients should be called into the examination room within 10 minutes of their allocated appointment time.

2 ASSESS LOCAL PRACTICE

● **The indicator**

% of patients who are called into the examination room within 10 minutes of their appointment time.

● **Data items to be collected**

For each patient record on a short proforma:

• the appointment time allocated;

• the actual time of the examination;

• the identifiable reason for any delay.

● **Suggested number**

All patients attending with appointments over a 1-week period.

THE CYCLE (continued)

3 COMPARE FINDINGS WITH THE STANDARD

4 CHANGE

● **Suggested change**

If waiting times are too long, then the allocation of the number of appointments in any one session should be reviewed. This may involve reorganisation of staff working hours. Avoid allocating multiple patients to the same appointment time. Review arrangements for patients changing their clothes prior to examination. Recruit x ray helpers.

5 RE-AUDIT Every 6–12 months.

RESOURCES   FIRST CYCLE £(££)

● **Data collection**

Ongoing data recording.

● **Assistance required**

Reception clerks to fill in the proforma.

● **Estimated radiologists' and radiographers' time to complete stages 1–3 of the first cycle**

Radiographer: 2 hours for recording of information.

● **Other estimated costs**

No other expense neccesary, but a Dymo time/date stamp (at £160.00) may be useful in some departments.

REFERENCES

1 The Audit Commission. *Improving your Image. How to Manage Radiology Services More Effectively.* London: Audit Commission, 1995.

2 *Patient's Charter* (1995). London: National Charter Standards, Department of Health, Richmond House, 79 Whitehall, London SW1A 2NS.

SUBMITTED BY

Dr D Wheatley and Mrs C Soar (Radiology Audit Officer), Nottingham City Hospital.

Ward Nurses and X Ray Procedures

THE AUDIT

The understanding of x ray procedures and related patient care by ward nurses.

(See Appendix, pages 292–293)

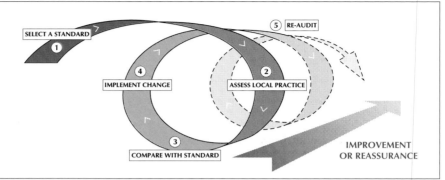

SELECT A STANDARD ①
② ASSESS LOCAL PRACTICE
③ COMPARE WITH STANDARD
④ IMPLEMENT CHANGE
⑤ RE-AUDIT
IMPROVEMENT OR REASSURANCE

BACKGROUND

● **Why this audit is worth doing**

A proper understanding of the need for correct pre- and post-procedure care will assist in reducing:
(a) the number of unsatisfactory or cancelled procedures; and (b) post-procedure complications.

THE CYCLE

1 THE STANDARD

● **A locally agreed standard**

All permanent trained nursing staff in the hospital should be able to demonstrate an understanding of x ray procedures.

2 ASSESS LOCAL PRACTICE

● **The indicators**

% of permanent trained nursing staff who demonstrate an understanding of current x ray procedures.

● **Data items to be collected**

Responses to the attached questionnaire (Appendix, pages 292–293). For each individual staff member, regard a score of eight correct answers as demonstrating an understanding of current x ray procedures.

● **Suggested number**

An agreed random sample of 100 nurses.

THE CYCLE (continued)

3   COMPARE FINDINGS WITH THE STANDARD

4   CHANGE

● **Suggested change**

Involve the Director of Nursing in any changes.

Organise formal and informal study sessions as needed.

There should be ready access at ward level to written information that relates to these procedures. Review written information and ensure that it is clear, current, and readily available.

Improve communicaiton between ward and Department of Clinical Radiology nursing staff.

5   RE-AUDIT   Every 6–12 months.

RESOURCES   FIRST CYCLE   £

● **Data collection**

Questionnaire (Appendix, pages 292–293).

● **Assistance required**

Secretarial.

Co-operation of ward staff.

● **Estimated radiologists' and radiographers' time to complete stages 1–3 of the first cycle**

Radiologist: 5 hours.

● **Other estimated costs**

None.

REFERENCES

1   Hjelm-Karlsson K. Effects of information to patients undergoing intravenous pyelography: an intervention study. *Journal of Advanced Nursing* 1989;**14**:853–62.

2   Clark CR, Gregor F. Developing a sensation of information message for femoral arteriography. *Journal of Advanced Nursing* 1988;**13**:237–44.

3   Royal College of Nursing. *Standards of Care – Radiology Nursing*. London: RCN, 1993.

SUBMITTED BY

Sister Celia Whelan, Department of Radiology, West Suffolk Hospital, Bury St Edmunds.

THE AUDIT

Your use of *Clinical Audit in Radiology: 100+ Recipes.*

(See also pages 302–303)

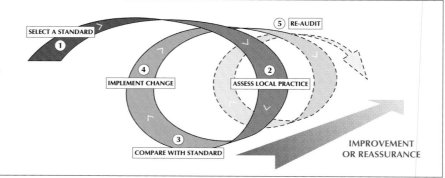

BACKGROUND

● **Why this audit is worth doing**

In excess of £200m has been allocated to support the introduction and organisation of clinical audit in the NHS (Ref. 1) and some of the cost of this book has come from those monies. This book is primarily an educational tool. Its use needs to be evaluated (Ref. 2).

THE CYCLE

1 THE STANDARD

The Editors' standard has five elements. Twelve months after publication:

- All UK Departments of Clinical Radiology should remember receiving one or more copies of the book;

- All UK Departments of Clinical Radiology should still have available for use a copy of this book in their library or Publication Department;

- All the designated audit leads in Departments of Clinical Radiology will have utilised some aspect of the book;

- 90% of clinical radiologists (consultants and specialist registrars) should be aware of the existence of the book;

- 70% of all hospital audit co-ordinators (i.e. the Senior Audit Officer) will be aware of the book and have used some aspect of it or concept within it when assisting with the audit programmes of non-radiological specialties.

2 ASSESS LOCAL PRACTICE

● **The indicators**

% of Departments of Clinical Radiology who state that they have received one or more copies of the book.

% of Departments of Clinical Radiology who state that they have available for use a copy of this book in their department library;

% of Departments of Clinical Radiology who state that the designated audit lead has utilised some aspect of the book.

% of clinical radiologists who state that they are aware of the existence of the book.

% of hospital audit co-ordinators who state that they are aware of the book, and have used some aspect/concept within it when assisting with the audit programmes of other non-radiological specialties.

THE CYCLE (continued)

● **Data items to be collected**

A questionnaire will be sent to each selected Department of Clinical Radiology. The responses will be used to measure the five indicators.

● **Suggested number**

100 randomly selected Departments of Clinical Radiology.

3 COMPARE FINDINGS WITH THE STANDARD

4 CHANGE

● **Possible changes**

Improved clarification (via the *Royal College of Radiologists' Newsletter*) of the objectives behind the production of this book.

Advertise the book more widely.

5 RE-AUDIT 12–24 months if the standard has not been met.

RESOURCES   FIRST CYCLE £

● **Data collection**

Audit leads will be asked to record episodes of local use of the book on pages 302–303 and to use this information to fill in the questionnaire which will be sent to them.

A questionnaire will be sent to the designated audit lead in 100 randomly selected Departments of Clinical Radiology.

● **Assistance required**

Clinical Audit Adviser of the RCR for data analysis.

● **Estimated radiologists' and radiographers' time to complete stages 1–3 of the first cycle**

Radiologist (the audit lead): 1 hour in each of 100 hospitals to complete the questionnaire.

● **Other estimated costs**

Postage and stationery.

REFERENCES

1 NHS Management Executive. Clinical Audit, meeting and improving standards in healthcare. *EL (93)* **59**:1993,6.

2 McKee M. Is money wasted on audit? Report of meeting of Forum on Quality in Healthcare. *Journal of the Royal Society of Medicine.* 1994;**87**:52–5.

SUBMITTED BY

The Clinical Radiology Audit Sub Committee (CRASC) of The Royal College of Radiologists.

Appendix

The Appendix on the following pages contains further information
and forms (e.g. questionnaires) relating to specific recipes.
The number at the top of each page is the recipe number.

Accepting Recommendations for Change

Departmental record (page 1)

CLINICAL RADIOLOGY

A RECORD OF THE RESULTS OF THE MONTHLY AUDIT MEETING

Date:	Duration of meeting
	Start: Finish:
Those present at meeting:	Members absent from meeting:
Subjects discussed: 1. 2. 3.	*Proposals arising and action required:* 1. 2. 3. The individual(s) designated to take the above action are: 1. 2. 3. *continued*

Appendix

Accepting Recommendations for Change

Departmental record (page 2)

Review of progress on action agreed at previous meetings:

☐ **No review today**

☐ **Action has been taken as follows:**

Specific issues to be communicated to (or requiring the assistance of) the Clinical Director or the Chairman of the Hospital Clinical Audit Committee:

Any other matters raised:

Name of chairman: Signature:

Adapted from a proforma designed by Brighton Health Authority, 1991

A P P E N D I X

Barium Meal Training

The local protocol for barium meal examinations

All positions as for overcouch tube

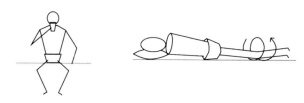

1	LPO		
2	AP		
3	RT LAT		
4	RPO		
5	LPO		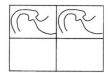
6	Prone RAO		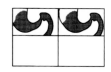
7	Erect LPO	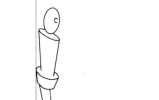	

Bone Scintigraphy Images

Checklist for assessing bone scan images

All bone scan images will be of high technical quality, as indicated by this checklist:

	Yes	No
FOR EACH CASE		
Name	☐	☐
X ray number or hospital number	☐	☐
Date	☐	☐
Anatomical Markers	☐	☐
If a 2 phase bone was required, was it performed?	☐	☐
If a 3 phase bone was required, was it performed?	☐	☐
Not applicable	☐	
FOR 2 OR 3 PHASE BONES		
All areas of interest included	☐	☐
Timings indicated (immediate, blood pool or 3 hour)	☐	☐
Not applicable	☐	
FOR FULL BONES CARRIED OUT AT 3 HOURS		
• Chest to include both shoulders	☐	☐
• Pelvis	☐	☐
• Femora to include both knees	☐	☐
• Left lateral Skull and C. Spine oblique	☐	☐
• Lumbar spine to include all of the SIJs	☐	☐
• Thoracic spine and both shoulders	☐	☐
COUNT DENSITY WAS CORRECT	☐	☐
(Not too dark nor too pale)		
TOTAL		
	YES	NO

Comments:

Courtesy

Questionnaire

The x ray helper will ask each of 100 consecutive patients to complete this questionnaire before they leave the department. The questionnaire will be analysed by the hospital's clinical audit department. The results will be anonymised.

Date: _____   Survey number: _____

Dear Patient

We are carrying out a survey with the full co-operation of our Radiology Department in order to see if we need to improve various aspects of our service. It would be very helpful to us if you would complete this form by ticking the appropriate boxes. Please complete the form before you leave the department and place it in the box provided. Your answers will be treated with complete confidence.

_____

Clinical Audit Co-ordinator

Q.1   What was your appointment time? _____

Q.2   Did your examination start on time?   ☐ Yes   ☐ No

Q.3   At what time (approximately) did your examination begin? _____

Q.4   If your answer to Question 2 was "Yes" then please move directly to Question 8.

Q.5   If your answer to Question 2 was "No" then please move on to Questions 6, 7 and 8.

Q.6   Did the Doctor (the Radiologist) apologise for the delay?   ☐ Yes   ☐ No

Q.7   Did you find the Doctor's explanation convincing?

☐ Yes   ☐ No   ☐ Sort of   ☐ No explanation given

Q.8   Do you have any other comments?

Thank you very much. Please put this sheet into the box.

Notes

1 The patient's (i.e. author's) view.

The purpose behind any audit of this type is to stimulate change. This audit has been submitted by a patient (a businessman) who had experienced a lack of simple courtesy when a doctor arrived late for an examination. This affected the attitude of the patient to the doctor. It is possible that those Departments of Clinical Radiology which may be experiencing a similar problem will seek to address this particular difficulty by conducting an audit along the lines of this recipe.

2 Confidentiality

The importance of producing and processing a questionnaire through an independent agency – this particular survey is carried out by the hospital's Clinical Audit Department and not by the Department of Clinical Radiology – is recognised (Refs 1–3). An arms-length approach provides the patient with a more substantial assurance of confidentiality and neutrality.

References

1 Bamford C, Jacoby A. Development of patient satisfaction questionnaires: I. Methodological issues. *Quality in Health Care* 1992;**1**:153–7.

2 Fitzpatrick R. Surveys of patient satisfaction. II. Designing a questionnaire and conducting a survey. *BMJ* 1991;**302**:1129–32.

3 Hughes J, Humphrey C. *Medical audit in general practice: a practical guide to the literature.* London: King's Fund Centre, 1990.

CT Scanner Suite – hospital staff questionnaire (page 1)

The aim of this survey is to ascertain how well CT scanning is known to hospital staff. The results will help us in the CT Scanner Suite to take steps to improve the level of understanding of the procedure, and this will help both the patients and staff.

All questionnaires will be treated confidentially.

Do not give your name. Please ring the correct answer and/or write in your answer where appropriate.

Male/Female

Job title _____

Specialty _____

1   Do you know what the initials CT stand for?   Yes   No

2   Do you know the location of the CT Scanner?   Yes   No

3   Have you ever visited the CT Scanner?   Yes   No

4   Is the test a:

Nuclear Medicine Scan	Doppler	VQ Scan
Ultrasound Scan	Magnetic Resonance Scan	X Ray Scan

or none of the above?

5   How are the pictures (images) produced?

Sound Waves	Isotope Drugs	X Rays
Radio Waves	Electro-magnetism	

6   Can you give one clinical indication for a CT Scan?   Yes   No

If yes, please give a clinical indication here:

_____

7   Is the Scanner used routinely to scan pregnant ladies?   Yes   No

8   Which of the following conditions should the Radiologist know about before proceeding with the scan?

Allergies	Asthma	Claustrophobia
Diabetes	Hay Fever	Heart Disease
Parkinson's Disease	Renal Disease	Pregnancy

continued

CT Scanner Suite – hospital staff questionnaire (page 2)

9   Will the patient have an injection during the scan?

                       Yes   No   Sometimes   Don't know

10   Will the patient have to starve for a:

    a) Brain Scan?   Yes   No   Don't know

    b) Abdomen Scan?   Yes   No   Don't know

    c) Chest Scan?   Yes   No   Don't know

11   Will the patient have to drink a contrast agent (dye) for a:

    a) Brain Scan?   Yes   No   Don't know

    b) Abdomen Scan?   Yes   No   Don't know

12   If the answer to either 11a) or 11b) is yes, what is the drink?

    Barium   Water   Radioactive isotope

    Water Soluble Iodine   None of these   Don't know

13   Will the patient have to lie along an enclosed tunnel for the Scan?

                       Yes   No   Don't know

14   Are any patients restricted from using the Scanner?

                       Yes   No   Don't know

    If yes, give an example:

    _____

15   How long will each of the following Scans take?

    a) Brain   _____

    b) Chest   _____

    c) Abdomen _____

    d) Spine   _____

continued

CT Scanner Suite – hospital staff questionnaire (page 3)

16 Do you know what happens to the patient in a CT procedure?   Yes   No

17 Do you tell your patients what to expect?   Yes   No

18 In general, are your patients worried about an appointment
for a CT examination?   Yes   No

    If yes, please give an indication of how worried they are: _____

19 In general, are you able to reassure them successfully?   Yes   No

20 When your patients return to the ward after the scan are they:

    Relieved?

    Upset?

    In pain?

    Surprised that it was not as bad as they expected?

    Surprised that it was worse than they expected?

    Or are you not sure how they feel?

21 Please make any comments here

_____

_____

_____

_____

_____

_____

_____

Thank you for taking the time to complete this form.

Please return this form to the CT Scanner Suite before _____

_____

Superintendent Radiographer

CT Scanner Suite

_____

Questionnaire

Questionnaire number: _____ Today's date: _____

This Radiology Department offers open access for GP patients between the hours of 9.00 am and 5.00 pm, Mondays to Fridays, when you can walk in and wait for your investigation. Alternatively, you will be given the opportunity to request an appointment time on another day; if you choose this second option then you will be given priority, and you should have your investigation within 30 minutes of your appointment time. We are conducting a survey of patient satisfaction with the opening hours of this Department of Clinical Radiology. Please help us by answering the following questions. Please ring the best answer, or write in your answer where appropriate.

Age: _____ Male/Female _____

Employment status:

Employed	Self-employed	Unemployed	Student	Retired

1 How satisfied are you with the current hours of opening?

Not satisfied   Completely Satisfied

0	1	2	3	4	5

2 If you are not satisfied, when would you prefer to attend?

a) Early evening (before 6.30 pm)

b) Saturday morning

c) Some other time (please specify)_____

3 Did you walk in and wait, or have an appointment?

a) Walk in and wait

b) Have an appointment

4 How long did you wait for your x ray investigation (from arrival for walk in and wait, or from appointment time for those patients with an appointment)?

a) less than 15 minutes

b) 15–30 minutes

c) 30–45 minutes

d) 45–60 minutes

e) more than 60 minutes

5 If you have any comments please write here.

_____

THANK YOU FOR YOUR HELP

Emergency Skull Radiography

Head injury discharge card A

NB This card is given to patients who *have* been referred for skull radiography.

INFORMATION FOR PATIENTS RETURNING HOME AFTER AN INJURY TO THE HEAD

Name: _____ Seen by Doctor:_____ Date: _____

Following your examination by the Doctor we do not find any evidence to suggest that you have a serious head injury.

BUT

It is important to look out for delayed after-effects.

Therefore, please ask a relative (or a close friend) to check whether any of the following affect you during the next 24 hours:

    a)   Feeling increasingly sick, or persistent vomiting.

    b)   Persistent or increasing headache.

    c)   Increasing drowsiness or excessive sleepiness.

    d)   Stiff neck.

    e)   Fainting or passing out.

    f)   Weakness of any limb, or double vision.

    g)   A fit.

If any of the above do happen **within the next 24 hours**, then please tell your doctor or return to the hospital, immediately.

                  Accident department tel no: _____

- copy given to patient   ☐
- copy given to relative/friend   ☐

Doctor's signature: _____

Head injury discharge card B

NB This card is given to patients who *have not* been referred for skull radiography.

INFORMATION FOR PATIENTS RETURNING HOME AFTER AN INJURY TO THE HEAD

Name: _____   Seen by Doctor:_____   Date: _____

Following your examination by the Doctor we do not find any evidence to suggest that you have a serious head injury.

Please note that...

For good medical reasons we do not x ray everyone who has an injury to the head ... *and it is much more important to look out for delayed after-effects than to have an x ray examination.* [Parents can be reassured that an x ray examination in children is rarely helpful, and our doctors are encouraged not to expose your child to unhelpful x rays].

Therefore, please ask a relative (or a close friend) to check whether any of the following affect you during the next 24 hours:

   a)   Feeling increasingly sick, or persistent vomiting.

   b)   Persistent or increasing headache.

   c)   Increasing drowsiness or excessive sleepiness.

   d)   Stiff neck.

   e)   Fainting or passing out.

   f)   Weakness of any limb, or double vision.

   g)   A fit.

If any of the above do happen **within the next 24 hours**, then please tell your doctor or return to the hospital, immediately.

Accident department tel no: _____

- copy given to patient   ☐
- copy given to relative/friend   ☐

Doctor's signature: _____

Employee satisfaction

Further information (page 1)

Several different approaches are available for recording staff sickness rates (Refs 1–3). The approach described here can be modified so as to meet local conditions/requirements. This model allows a local standard (the Absence Ratio) to be defined.

1.0 GROUPS

For the purposes of this audit the members of the Department of Clinical Radiology are divided into the following staff groups: Clerical, Helpers, Managers, Porters, Radiographers, Radiologists.

2.0 WORKING DAYS AVAILABLE

2.1 The number of working days available within each staff group is measured over (say) a six or twelve month period. Working days being five out of seven in each week with adjustments being made for part time staff and for holidays and rest days. The number of staff in any one grouping is expressed as Whole Time Equivalents (WTE).

2.2 **WTE Example:**

- Hours worked
- Standard hours for grade

$$\frac{25}{36} = 0.69 \text{ (wte)}$$

- Standard hours for grade equals the full time hours for a given staff group.

- Three part-time employees working (say) 0.69 and 0.25 and 0.45 would equal a WTE of 1.39.

3.0 THE ABSENCE RATIO

3.1 Staff days available = (staff WTE) × (working days in period being measured).

3.2 The Absence Ratio = $\dfrac{\text{Staff days available}}{\text{Days sick}}$

3.3 **Example:**

$$\frac{\text{Days available}}{\text{Days sick}} \quad \frac{4301}{84} = 51:1 = \text{The Absence Ratio}$$

i.e. For every 51 days worked, one day is lost in sickness.

4.0 THE LOCAL STANDARD (USING THE ABSENCE RATIO)

A local standard can be defined as follows:

The Absence Ratio within any staff group and for the department overall should not fall below 30:1.

continued

Further information (page 2)

5.0 NOTE

5.1 The Absence Ratio (30:1) can also be expressed as a percentage. It is equivalent to a rate of absenteeism of 3.3% and indicates that 3.3 working days are lost (per person, or per group) per 100 working days.

5.2 The average rate of absenteeism for all workers in the UK (1994) was 3.6% (Ref. 4).

5.3 Absenteeism rates within some government departments and agencies (1994) varied between 8% and 10%. Very few met the average of 3.6% for all UK workers (Ref. 3).

5.4 Defining categories of Sickness Absence. This can assist with an analysis/investigation.

    (a)   Frequent Short Term Absence:

    Three or more separate episodes (1 day to 2 weeks) in a 2 month period.

    (b)   Long Term Sickness Absence:

    Either: 3 weeks continuous absence; or 3 absences from work within a period of 6 months, each of which lasted for 2 weeks or more.

5.5 *Data items to be Collected*, page 52. Reason for Sickness. If these data items are to be stored on an electronic data retrieval system such as a computer, then they fall under the auspices of the Data Protection Act (Ref. 5). The DPA indicates that the reason for sickness should not be published where identifying the employee by such means would be possible, although aggregated data such as "...25% of all absences in June/July were caused by asthma" is acceptable.

5.6 *Data items to be Collected*, page 52. Certification. There are three categories: ***Uncertified*** this obtains from day 1 to day 3; ***Self-certified*** runs from day 4 to day 7; ***Medically certified*** runs from day 8 onwards. This subdivision of data should only be collected **where it is of value** – for example where the percentage of uncertified or self-certified absences is significant. Unless analysis of this subdivision will provide valuable intelligence it appears to be irrelevant.

6.0 THE LOCAL APPROACH TO THE ABSENCE RATIO

The Clinical Director will investigate the cause of any Absence Ratio within any staff group which is found to be 30:1 or less.

REFERENCES

1 North F et al. Explaining Socioeconomic Differences in Sickness Absence: The Whitehall II Study. *BMJ* 1993;**306**:361–6

2 Pines A et al. Rates of Sickness Absenteeism among Employess in a Modern Hospital: the Role of Demographic and Occupational Factors. *Br J Ind Med* 1985;**42**:326–35

3 Absenteeism in Government: A Catalogue of Failure (1995). From: The Office of David Chidgey MP, House of Commons, London, SW1A 0AA.

4 From: Industrial Society report in Managing Best Practice, Nov/Dec 1994. The Industrial Society, Quadrant Court, 49 Calthorp Road, Birmingham.

5 Data Protection Act 1984.

Gall Bladder Ultrasound

Further information

Determining the adherence to an ultrasound protocol during routine examination of the gall bladder by trainees.

The hard copy images of 50 consecutive ultrasound examinations of the gall bladder carried out by trainees will be reviewed to determine whether the agreed protocol had been followed. The protocol is a modification of that described by Cosgrove *et al.* (Ref. 1) – as follows:

1) Longitudinal sections through the gall bladder to include the neck, body and fundus.

2) Evidence of medial and lateral angulation in the long axis.

3) Transverse scans obtained at 90° to the long axis.

4) Evidence of intercostal and oblique subcostal scans.

5) Scanning performed in the supine and lateral oblique positions.

6) 3.5 mHz and 5.0 mHz probes utilised.

7) Scanning technique indicated (written or graphic) on each recorded image.

NOTE: The design of this audit is an example of the use of an efficient process (the way the scans are performed) being used as a proxy for a good clinical outcome (finding or excluding gall stones). This design has been adopted because of the difficulty (in the case of gall stones) of obtaining accurate data on false negative and false positive rates – without the use of a very detailed and prolonged survey.

     A word of caution is necessary. As has been described elsewhere (Ref. 2), it is sometimes assumed that efficient structures and processes correlate with good clinical outcomes – but this link is not proven. Nevertheless there are times when a process audit (Ref. 3) such as this one is the only one which is a practical audit. This does have the added bonus of being a stimulus/reinforcement to the acquisition of good techniques by those in training.

REFERENCES

1 Cosgrove D, Meire H, Dewbury K. *Clinical Ultrasound. Abdominal and General Ultrasound.* Vol. 1. Edinburgh: Churchill Livingstone, 1993:178–80.

2 Robinson R. Accrediting hospitals: accreditation should move from structure and process to outcome. *Brit Med J* 1995;**310**:755–6.

3 Davies HTO, Crombie IK. Assessing the quality of care: measuring well supported processes may be more enlightening than monitoring outcomes. *BMJ* 1995:**311**:766.

GP Chest Radiography

Guidelines

These guidelines are taken from Ref. 1:

The following reasons for requesting chest radiographs are considered to be inappropriate:

1) Upper respiratory tract infection.

2) Chest wall pain of costochondritis origin – wait 6 weeks.

3) Mild chest trauma, e.g. fracture of lower ribs.

4) Routine x rays – except at-risk immigrants, occupational, e.g. divers; emigration.

5) Pre-operation – except before cardio-pulmonary bypass surgery, suspected malignancy, possible TB. If the patient is dyspnoeic or is elderly or has known cardiac disease, a chest radiograph may be reasonable. If a recent film is available, there my be no need for a repeat film.

6) Heart disease, hypertension, COAD, asthma – reasonable at initial presentation and thereafter only if signs and symptoms change.

NOTE

If the guidelines are not being followed, then a new request form can be issued with the objective of (a) assisting the referring GPs by providing an improved request form, and (b) making any repeat audit easier to carry out. An example of a form that could be used is given on page 250.

REFERENCE

1 Royal College of Radiologists. *Making the Best Use of a Department of Clinical Radiology. Guidelines for Doctors*. Third edition. London: RCR, 1995.

GP Chest Radiography

Example of appropriate (bespoke) request form

Request for chest x ray only ... GP referral

		Hosp or x ray No:
Surname	Mr Mrs Miss	Date of Birth
First Name		

Patient's Address

Tel No:

GP Name and Address

Tel No: Fax No:

Date of previous radiography at this hospital: _____

Is there any possibility of pregnancy?

☐ No/not applicable

☐ Yes, but examination essential

Radiographer's signature

Number of films taken

CLINICAL INFORMATION

Specific symptoms

Pain
  ☐ Ischaemic
  ☐ Pleuritic
  ☐ Traumatic

Cough
  ☐ Non-productive
  ☐ Productive
  ☐ Haemoptysis

Duration
  ☐ Days
  ☐ Weeks
  ☐ Months

Provisional Diagnosis

Signed: Date:

Interventional Radiology Patient Care

Pre-procedure questionnaire (page 1)

Example of a day case surgery checklist that has been adapted for use in an interventional radiology unit.

To be completed by the patient.

PLEASE BRING THIS FORM WITH YOU WHEN ATTENDING FOR THE EXAMINATION

Your doctor has asked us to carry out an interventional radiology procedure. (See accompanying explanation.) Before the examination we would be grateful if you would complete the questionnaire below. This questionnaire is desiged to help the doctors who will be looking after you. If any question is difficult to answer please consult your doctor or telephone the Department of Clinical Radiology: telephone number _____

Surname: _____

First name: _____

Date of Birth: _____

1 How would you rate your general health? (Please circle)

   Excellent   Good   Fair   Poor

2 Has there been a recent change in your health? (Please circle)

   Yes   No   Comment _____

3 Do you have or have ever had any of these problems? (Please circle)

   a) Heart attack or heart failure

   b) Stroke

   c) Lung problems (e.g. asthma, pneumonia, emphysema)

   d) Liver problems or hepatitis

   e) High blood pressure

   f) Diabetes

   g) Bleeding problems

   h) Seizures or epilepsy

   i) Rheumatic fever

   j) Other (please specify) _____

continued

Pre-procedure questionnaire (page 2)

4   Please list any medicines you are taking (including ALL prescription and non-prescription drugs, even aspirin and "the pill").

Name of Medicine	Dosage (amount)	How many times per day
(a) _____	_____	_____
(b) _____	_____	_____
(c) _____	_____	_____
(d) _____	_____	_____

5   Are you allergic or sensitive to anything, for example: medicines or adhesive tape? (Please circle)

     Yes   No

     If "yes", please list and describe what happened:

     _____

     _____

6   Have you, or any of your close relatives, had problems with anaesthetics or sedation? (Please circle)

     Yes   No

     If "yes", what problem?

     _____

7   Have you had a recent problem with (please circle):

     Cold   Flu   Bronchitis   Laryngitis   Sore throat   Fever

8   Do you have any other health problem at present? (Please circle)   Yes   No

     If "Yes", what problem? _____

Adapted from GD Bell *et al*. Recommendations for standards of sedation and patient monitoring during gastrointestinal endoscopy. *Gut* 1991;**32**:823–7.

A: Audit form for each patient

PART (1)

THE RADIOGRAPHER (who took the film) WILL COMPLETE:

Patient Name _____   Hospital Number _____

Patient (Audit) number _____   Date of Examination _____

Please put a **BLUE** dot with the patient's audit number on each of the following; tick each box when you have done this.

Request Form	
Film	
Audit Form	

Diamentor reading / TLD reading _____

Was the film quality acceptable to you? | Yes | No |

If the answer is no, give reasons

_____

_____

_____

Radiographer's signature / project number _____

PART (2)

THE ITU/CCU CLINICIAN WILL COMPLETE:

NOTE: *The standard for this audit is that 100% of all radiographs (whether normal or abnormal) should be of a quality which is helpful to you in addressing the clinical problem.*

Please indicate if this radiograph complies with this standard:

Y	N

If your answer is no, please give reasons

_____

_____

_____

Clinician's name _____   Signature _____

Please place this completed audit form in the box provided. Thank you for your co-operation.

B: Radiologist assessment form

PATIENT'S AUDIT NUMBER

RADIOLOGIST'S SIGNATURE / PROJECT NUMBER _____

Please put appropriate
number in the box

a) Patient Location

    CCU   =   1

    ITU   =   2

b) Is adequate diagnostic area demonstrated (i.e. sufficient to address the clinical question)?

    Yes   =   1

    No   =   2

c) For diagnosis – How good is the technical quality of the radiograph?

    Excellent   =   1

    Very good   =   2

    Adequate   =   3

    Not adequate   =   4

Please place this completed audit form in the audit box in the Instant Reporting Room.

C: Independent radiographer's evaluation

Patient (Audit) Number

FILM	MAXIMUM MARKS	MARKS AWARDED
IDENTIFICATION		
ALL DETAILS INCLUDED	2	
LEGIBLE	1	
AWAY FROM AREA UNDER EXAMINATION	1	
MARKERS		
CORRECT	1	
IN COLLIMATED AREA	1	
AWAY FROM EXAMINATION AREA	1	
EXAMINATION AREA		
CORRECT CENTERING	4	
COLLIMATION VISIBLE	4	
ALL AREAS INCLUDED	4	
EXPOSURE		
DENSITY	4	
CONTRAST	4	
SHARPNESS	4	
DETAILS RECORDED ON FILM		
DISTANCE	1	
MOBILE	1	
POSITION	1	
DATE	1	
TIME	1	
RESPIRATORY PHASE	1	
DETAILS RECORDED ON REQUEST FORM		
RADIOGRAPHER'S INITIALS	1	
NO. OF FILMS	1	
TIME OF EXAMINATION	1	
TOTAL MARKS	40	

Any comments:

IVU Examination Times

Protocol for radiographers/nurses injecting IVUs

1 An IVU can be injected only by a radiographer or by a nurse who has attended the IV course, and has been assessed as competent to perform IV injections.

2 Radiographers or nurses may inject IVUs only when there is a radiologist in the department. This radiologist **must** be informed that an IVU injection is scheduled.

3 Radiographers or nurses may inject IVUs only within normal working hours and only in the main department.

4 If venepuncture is unsuccessful after **three** attempts, the radiologist should be informed.

5 Only non-ionic contrast media may be used. The strength and volume will be decided by the radiologist.

6 In the event of the patient having a reaction to the contrast medium, the supervising radiologist must be informed immediately. Any treatment will be given by the radiologist. In the event of anaphylaxis, **CALL THE CRASH TEAM** immediately.

7 The following categories of patient must be discussed with the radiologist prior to injection:

   a) Patients under 16 years.
   b) Patients with known allergies.
   c) Patients with known cardiac problems.
   d) If the patient is a member of hospital staff.
   e) If the radiographer or nurse scheduled to carry out the injection has any doubts or anxieties about any patient.

8 Standard IV cannulation practice should involve the injector wearing surgical gloves.

Design of the audit

1 Identify eight radiology journals which will be available within the department/hospital library every month. These journals may include some or all of the following:

- American Journal of Radiology.

- British Journal of Radiology.

- Clinical Radiology.

- Journal of Interventional Radiology.

- Journal of Nuclear Medicine.

- Radiologic Clinics of North America.

- Radiology.

- Seminars in Roentgenology.

2 A minimum of four of these eight journals will be scrutinised each month by all specialist registrars (this is the locally defined standard).

3 Design a plastic cover for the journals and a front sheet for the specialist registrars' signatures (see examples on page 258).

4 All of the journals should be:

(i) Available within the department/hospital in a predetermined, accessible location.

(ii) Read within the department/hospital (i.e. not removed from the department)

(iii) Kept in plastic covers to prevent wear and tear to the journals. These covers are also used to contain a front sheet for each journal which allows for trainees' signatures.

(iv) Changed on the same date every month by a secretary. The front sheets will be collected for the previous month when the journals are changed. Front sheets to be scrutinised three monthly at the Journal Club.

5 Journal Club to be held at a specified time and day, each month (e.g. first Thursday of every month at 3.30 pm).

- the club should be consultant lead, with the departmental consultants being rostered in turn to supervise the club. The rostered consultant will need to be familiar with the contents of all of the issues of the journals published during the previous three months.

- trainees are questioned randomly on the contents of at least four journals (with use of the front sheet to see what journals the trainee has read in the previous month) by the consultant.

- a total is summated as a % every month of those trainees who have read a minimum of four journals each month.

- percentages are then recorded in a Journal Club Audit book each month (by the Journal Club Registrar).

- this is a relatively unobtrusive way of ensuring that each trainee is meeting the standard (i.e. reading at least four radiology journals each month).

continued

Covers

DOUBLE LEAVED PLASTIC COVER FOR JOURNALS

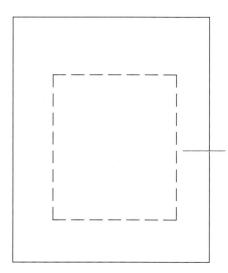

Plastic pocket on front of cover
for front sheet. Trainees remove
front sheet for signing and then
replace.

FRONT SHEET

JOURNAL: *CLINICAL RADIOLOGY*

Please sign your name
when you have read this journal.

                                    Signature

DR

LW

MOD

AB

IS

GK

Front sheet for April 1996

The initials of all
of the specialist
registrars are
included on this
front sheet.

Elements of the standard

The elements of the standard are derived from Royal College of Radiologists and NRPB guidelines.

LUMBAR SPINE X-RAYS ARE *NOT ROUTINELY* INDICATED IN THE FOLLOWING CIRCUMSTANCES:

Acute pain without trauma – *Wait 6 weeks except in older patients with possible osteoporotic vertebral collapse.*

Chronic pain with no clinical evidence of infection or trauma – *persistent, progressive, unremitting pain or neurological signs are exceptions.*

Before physiotherapy.

(Derived from Ref. 1)

A SINGLE, WELL CENTRED, LONG LATERAL RADIOGRAPH *ONLY*:

In patients aged 20–55 years with persistent backache, and:

- No surgery is planned;
- No history of trauma;
- No systemic symptoms;
- ESR less than 25 mm/hour;
- Lumbar flexion more than 3cm.

(Derived from Ref. 2)

REFERENCES

1   Royal College of Radiologists. *Making the Best Use of a Department of Clinical Radiology. Guidelines for Doctors*. Third edition. London: RCR, 1995.

2   National Radiological Protection Board. *Patient Dose Reduction in Diagnostic Radiology*. Didcot: NRPB, 1990.

Questionnaire

- Patient project number _____   Date _____

For the attention of the clinician who requested a VQ scan on:

Patient Name: _____   Date _____

Hospital Number: _____

Clinician's Name: _____

We wish to assess how well we are communicating the findings on VQ scans to the doctors who request the lung scans. We would be most grateful if you would take a few minutes to complete this questionnaire.

	Yes	No	Sort of
1) Are you familiar with the PIOPED study?			
2) In general, do you understand our use of language (based on PIOPED) which indicates the probability of a pulmonary embolus being present?			
3) Did you understand our report on this VQ scan (i.e. how well did we indicate the probability of a pulmonary embolus)?			

4) Please indicate if you are happy with the terms that we use (see 4.1 to 4.4 below) and indicate this as yes/no. If you are not happy then please select an alternate wording from the menu opposite and insert the corresponding letter in Table 4.

Table 4

	I am happy with this phrase	I would prefer these phrases
4.1 A normal lung scan		
4.2 Low probability for embolus		
4.3 Indeterminate for embolus		
4.4 High probability for embolus		

5) Would you like us to explain to you in more detail our current use of language in lung scan reports?

     Yes   ☐

     No   ☐

Many thanks

_____

Clinical Director.

continued

Alternative phrases for lung scan reports

This menu of alternative phrases should be used in conjunction with question 4 of the questionnaire.

a = PE ruled out	l = No definite evidence of PE
b = PE excluded	m = PE not confirmed
c = PE highly unlikely	n = Suspicious for PE
d = PE doubtful	o = PE highly likely
e = PE improbable	p = PE probable
f = PE unlikely	q = PE unequivocal
g = PE likely	r = normal
h = PE equivocal	s = low probability of PE
i = PE not excluded	t = Intermediate for PE
j = PE possible	u = High probability of PE
k = Diagnosis uncertain	

MRI Patients and Metal

Questionnaire

METAL CHECK LIST

Lister No.	Name	
Date		
Time	DoB	

PLEASE CHECK THE FOLLOWING

	Yes	No	Details
Cardiac Pacemaker			
Mechanical heart valve			
History of foreign body in eye			
Occupation as metal worker, grinder, welder			
Metallic implant, metal prosthesis, orthopaedic plates, screws			
Shrapnel			
Aneurysm clip/haemostatic clip			
Ear implants			
Artificial eye			
Coloured contact lenses			
Interventional radiological devices			
Pregnancy			
IUCD			
Implantable pumps/neurostimulators			
Allergies			

If the answer to any of these questions is "YES" please give details.

The high magnetic fields used within our MRI scanner can cause considerable internal body damage if scanning takes place near internal metal objects. It is essential for your safety that we know about such items before any scanning takes place.

This is to confirm that the above checklist has been completed.

Patient signature	MRI Unit Signature	Date

City Hospital and Lister Bestcare MRI Centre, Nottingham

Protocol

This protocol is taken from Refs 1 and 2.

- The patient is placed under the care of the specialist pediatric or orthopaedic team.

- On admission to the Accident and Emergency Department some local anaesthetic cream is placed on the hip skin crease.

- A plain radiograph is obtained.

  – Obvious Perthes' Disease or slipped femoral epiphysis – **stop.**

  – The film apears normal – **proceed to:**

  Immediate hip ultrasound for confirmation or exclusion of a joint effusion.

In every case of effusion the joint fluid is aspirated under ultrasound control. Immediate gram stains are performed. If positive start therapy. If negative the child may be safely discharged home whilst awaiting the result of culture – *provided that the family is within easy reach by telephone.*

All children are reviewed one week later in the pediatric or orthopaedic clinic. If the pain still persists then an isotope bone scan is obtained in order to exclude early Perthes' disease or other extremely rare causes of hip pain such as osteomyelitis or a bone tumour.

REFERENCES

1 Raby N, Berman L, de Lacey G. Accident and Emergency Radiology: a survival guide. London: W B Saunders, 1995.

2 Fink A M *et al.* The irritable hip: immediate ultrasound guided aspiration and prevention of hospital admission. *Arch Dis Child* 1995;**72**:110–14.

A
P
P
E
N
D
I
X

Questionnaire (page 1)

Department of Clinical Radiology

Thank you for taking the time to complete this questionnaire which we hope will enable us to improve our facilities and service in the Department of Clinical Radiology.

After your examination is completed and before you leave the department we would be grateful if you would complete the short questionnaire below.

Confidentiality – It will not be possible to identify you from your questionnaire nor from your answers. The information will be used solely to assess future needs and to help implement changes within the department.

Please circle the correct answer.

Your Age:

| 0–10 Yrs | 11–20Yrs | 21–40 Yrs | 41–60Yrs | over 60 |

For which type of examination did you attend?

X-ray	☐
Ultrasound	☐
CT Scanner	☐
Nuclear Medicine	☐

Are you an:

Out-patient	☐
Casualty Patient	☐
In Patient	☐
GP referral	☐
Other: (please specify)	☐

_____

_____

Patient Privacy: We are interested in knowing if you felt that your privacy (when talking to staff, changing, waiting to be seen, being examined or using changing or toilet facilities) was respected and appropriate.

Using the scale below please indicate your opinion on each of the questions which follow on page 265.

Excellent	☐ 6
Good	☐ 5
Acceptable	☐ 4
Poor	☐ 3
Very poor	☐ 2
No privacy	☐ 1

continued

Questionnaire (page2)

1 Reception Desk Area:

Excellent   No Privacy

☐ 6   ☐ 5   ☐ 4   ☐ 3   ☐ 2   ☐ 1

If 2 or 1 please indicate the problems you experienced

_____

_____

2 Waiting Room:

☐ 6   ☐ 5   ☐ 4   ☐ 3   ☐ 2   ☐ 1

If 2 or 1 please indicate the problems you experienced

_____

_____

3 Changing areas:

☐ 6   ☐ 5   ☐ 4   ☐ 3   ☐ 2   ☐ 1

If 2 or 1 please indicate the problems you experienced

_____

_____

4 Examination room:

☐ 6   ☐ 5   ☐ 4   ☐ 3   ☐ 2   ☐ 1

If 2 or 1 please indicate the problems you experienced

_____

_____

5 Toilets:

☐ 6   ☐ 5   ☐ 4   ☐ 3   ☐ 2   ☐ 1

If 2 or 1 please indicate the problems you experienced

_____

_____

6 In corridors:

☐ 6   ☐ 5   ☐ 4   ☐ 3   ☐ 2   ☐ 1

If 2 or 1 please indicate the problems you experienced

_____

_____

Finally, have you experienced any problems (not related to privacy) whilst you
were in the department and which you would wish to draw to our attention?

_____

_____   Thank you for your time
                                                          and attention

_____

_____   Consultant Radiologist

Patient Satisfaction I

Questionnaire (page 1)

Objective:
To determine how patients' viewed their recent (i.e. during the last 1–2 weeks) attendance at the Department of Clinical Radiology. Primarily, but not exclusively, to determine how they viewed the way they were treated by the doctors.

INTRODUCTION

We are carrying out a survey, with the full co-operation of the doctors in the Department of Clinical Radiology, to see if we need to improve our x ray services. It would be very helpful if you would complete the enclosed form by ticking the appropriate boxes. Please return it to me in the enclosed SAE.

Your reply will be treated with complete confidence. Many thanks for your co-operation.

_____

Clinical Audit Co-ordinator

_____

_____

1 AT YOUR <u>MOST RECENT VISIT</u> TO THE X-RAY DEPARTMENT – WHAT TEST DID YOU HAVE?

 ☐ X Ray   ☐ Ultrasound scan   ☐ Isotope scan

 ☐ MRI scan   ☐ CT scan   ☐ Mammogram

 Other _____ (Please specify the test)

2 BEFORE YOUR TEST:

Did you receive any instructions to follow (e.g. to drink a pint of water, not to eat for a number of hours)?

 ☐ yes   ☐ no   ☐ can't remember

...if yes, how easy were the instructions to follow?

Very confusing   Slightly confusing   Easy to follow

 1 _____ 2 _____ 3 _____ 4 _____ 5 _____ 6

continued

Questionnaire (page 2)

3 PLEASE THINK ABOUT THE TEST ITSELF

a) Who carried out the test?

☐ a doctor (radiologist)   ☐ a technician (radiographer)

☐ both a doctor and a technician   ☐ not sure

b) Were you asked to sign a consent form before the test?

☐ yes   ☐ no

... if yes, do you feel that you were given enough information about the test before you signed the consent form?

Inadequate information   Very good information

1 _____ 2 _____ 3 _____ 4 _____ 5 _____ 6

c) Did the doctor introduce himself/herself?

☐ yes   ☐ no   ☐ can't remember

d) Was the doctor pleasant and polite to you?

Impolite   Very polite

1 _____ 2 _____ 3 _____ 4 _____ 5 _____ 6

e) Did the doctor explain the test to you?

No explanation   Poor explanation   Clear explanation

1 _____ 2 _____ 3 _____ 4 _____ 5 _____ 6

f) Did you feel able to ask the doctor questions?

I felt completely   I felt very free
unable to ask questions   to ask questions

1 _____ 2 _____ 3 _____ 4 _____ 5 _____ 6

g) What is your *overall feeling* about the way you were treated by the doctor during your most recent visit to the Department of Clinical Radiology?

Very dissatisfied   Very satisfied

1 _____ 2 _____ 3 _____ 4 _____ 5 _____ 6

Please add any comments here:

_____

_____

_____

APPENDIX

Patient Satisfaction II

Questionnaire (page 1)

Objective:
To determine how patients' (GP referrals) viewed their recent (i.e. during the last 1–2 weeks) attendance at the Department of Clinical Radiology. Primarily to find out how they viewed the organisational aspects.

INTRODUCTION:
We are carrying out a survey, with the full co-operation of our Department of Clinical Radiology, to see if we need to improve our x ray services. It would be very helpful if you would complete the enclosed form by ticking the appropriate boxes. Please return it to me in the enclosed SAE.

Your reply will be treated with complete confidence.

Many thanks for your co-operation.

_____

Clinical Audit Co-ordinator

_____

_____

1 **During the last six months how often have you attended the Department of Clinical Radiology (or the Scanning Department) at this hospital?**

    ☐ once   ☐ 2–4 times   ☐ more than 4 times

2 **PLEASE THINK ABOUT YOUR <u>MOST RECENT VISIT</u>. PLEASE INDICATE WHAT TEST YOU HAD**

    ☐ X ray   ☐ Ultrasound scan   ☐ Isotope scan

    ☐ MRI scan   ☐ CT scan   ☐ Mammogram

    Other _____ (Please specify the test)

continued

Questionnaire (page 2)

3 WHEN YOU CAME FOR YOUR TEST:

a) On arrival at the department were you treated politely by the reception staff?

Very impolitely   Very politely

1 _____ 2 _____ 3 _____ 4 _____ 5 _____ 6

b) How long after your scheduled appointment time did you have to wait for the test to start?

1 _____ 2 _____ 3 _____ 4 _____ 5 _____ 6

60 minutes   30 minutes   15 minutes   On time

4 PLEASE THINK ABOUT THE WAITING AREA

a) Were there enough seats?

Too few   Barely adequate   Perfectly adequate

1 _____ 2 _____ 3 _____ 4 _____ 5 _____ 6

b) Was the area well decorated?

Very scruffy   Somewhat scruffy   Well decorated

1 _____ 2 _____ 3 _____ 4 _____ 5 _____ 6

c) Was the waiting area clean?

Very dirty   Very clean

1 _____ 2 _____ 3 _____ 4 _____ 5 _____ 6

5 What is your overall feeling about the way your visit to the Department was organised by the hospital?

Very poor organisation   Very good organisation

1 _____ 2 _____ 3 _____ 4 _____ 5 _____ 6

6 Please add any comments here:

_____

_____

_____

_____

Questionnaire (page 1)

PATIENT SATISFACTION SURVEY

Questionnaire number: _____ Today's date: _____

We are conducting a survey into patient satisfaction with the Radiology Department, with special reference to those patients over 60 years of age. Please help us by answering the following questions.

Your age: _____   Male/Female   (please circle)

Which investigation did you have?

☐ Chest x ray

☐ Lumbar spine x ray

☐ Intravenous urography (IVP)

☐ Barium meal

☐ Barium enema

Reception

1 Were the staff at reception polite?

Not polite   0   1   2   3   4   5   Very polite

2 Was the member of staff wearing a name badge?

No: 0   Yes: 5

3 Did the members of staff who spoke to you introduce themselves?

No: 0   Yes: 5

Waiting areas

4 Was the waiting area a pleasant place to wait?

Unpleasant   0   1   2   3   4   5   Very pleasant

5 Were there enough seats?

No: 0   Yes: 5

6 Were there enough magazines?

No: 0   Yes: 5

Changing cubicles

7 Were you satisfied with the privacy of the cubicle when you were getting changed for your investigation?

Not satisfied   0   1   2   3   4   5   Very satisfied

8 Were you embarrassed whilst getting changed?

Very embarrassed   0   1   2   3   4   5   Not embarrassed

continued

Patient Satisfaction in the Over 60s

Questionnaire (page 2)

9 Was there a clean white examination gown in the cubicle?

No: 0   Yes: 5

10 Was there a dressing gown in the cubicle?

No: 0   Yes: 5

Examination room

11 Were you satisfied with the explanation of what was about to happen to you?

Not satisfied   0   1   2   3   4   5   Very satisfied

12 Were all the staff wearing name badges?

No: 0   Yes: 5   If no, who was not?

---

13 Did all the staff introduce themselves to you?

No: 0   Yes: 5

14 Were you reasonably comfortable during your examination?

Very uncomfortable   0   1   2   3   4   5   Comfortable

If not, what did you find uncomfortable?

---

15 Were you anxious during your examination?

Very anxious   0   1   2   3   4   5   Not anxious

If you were anxious, what was the main reason for this?

After the examination

16 Were you told how you would obtain the results of your examination?

No: 0   Yes: 5

17 On the whole, what was your *overall impression* of the Radiology Department?

Not favourable   0   1   2   3   4   5   Very favourable

18 Have you any comments that you would like to make?

Thank you for your help.

Pre-Op Chest X Rays for Elective Surgery

Further information

This audit is based on work carried out at the Royal Bournemouth Hospital, from 12 to 26 June 1992 (Ref. 1). There is no *hot seat* reporting system, so pre-operative chest radiographs are performed during the patient's admission and returned to the ward unreported, with the patient.

Method

During the review period, we audited all admissions in all specialties of all patients due to have elective surgery. The pre-operative chest radiographs were returned to the ward in film envelopes labelled with the patients' details and sealed with staples. The packets were returned to the radiology department after the patients had been discharged from hospital. If the staples on the film envelopes had been removed, we concluded that the radiographs had been viewed. If the staples were still present, the radiograph could not have been viewed.

Result

75% of the film envelopes were returned with the staples intact.

Guidelines

The following guidelines are currently in use at the Royal Bournemouth Hospital:

Guidelines for pre-operative chest radiography in patients scheduled for elective surgery

The Royal College of Radiologists' guidelines for pre-operative chest radiography among patients admitted for elective non-cardiopulmonary surgery state that *routine* chest radiography is no longer justified. However, this investigation may be clinically desirable in certain patients in the following categories:

- Those with acute respiratory symptoms

- Those with possible metastases

- Those with suspected or established cardio-respiratory disease, who have not had a chest radiograph during the past 12 months

- Recent immigrants from countries where tuberculosis is still endemic, and who have not had a chest radiograph during the past 12 months.

Pre-operative chest radiography will also be performed in the following categories of patients:

- Those with a recent history of chest trauma

- Those whose operation may involve a thoracotomy

- Those undergoing a major abdominal operation, who run a high risk of respiratory complications

- Heavy smokers who have not had a chest radiograph during the past 12 months

- Patients not included in the above categories, if the request is made by the appropriate anaesthetist.

It should be noted that none of the above categories of request is routine, and therefore the reasons for chest radiography should always be stated on the request form.

Reference

1 Walker D, William P, Tawn J. Audit of requests for pre-operative chest radiography. *BMJ* 1994;**309**:772–3.

Notes and norms

• Carrying out any medical examination, and this includes all radiological examinations, is not like installing a car door on a factory production line. Each examination is individual. The competence and efficacy with which each examination (procedural or reporting) is carried out is dependent not only upon the skill and knowledge of the radiologist but also on the individual characteristics of each clinical case. All of these features affect the throughput of patient examinations. Consequently, throughput will vary between individual radiologists, and will also vary between superficially similar procedural or reporting sessions because of differences in the type and mix of cases (Refs 5 and 24).

• Quantity is often seen as being evidence of effective work and value for money. In clinical medicine, and this includes diagnostic radiology, it is possible to carry out large amounts of poor quality work. The individual who spends least time with the patient, carries out a procedure very quickly, and reports most films in the shortest period of time may not be producing high quality work (indeed it may be the very opposite). A rapid and large throughput of examinations may not produce the most beneficial effect upon subsequent patient care and clinical outcome.

• There has been a rapid increase in both hands on practice and in the proportion of complex radiological investigations during the last few years. Consequently the simplistic application of a general and imprecise formula (Ref. 5) to a hospital, to a group of consultants, or to a teaching Department, may draw misleading and unhelpful conclusions. *A more accurate and informative approach is to determine the number of examinations which it is reasonable to expect a particular consultant to perform during his or her allotted clinical sessions and this number should be tailored to the type of work carried out by that individual.* The number of examinations to be expected per annum will necessarily take into account the other NHS duties and roles performed by that individual both within the hospital and elsewhere in the NHS. Where innovative changes (utilising skill mix) have been introduced into a department (Ref. 6) it is also necessary to determine the number of examinations which can be properly supervised and/or checked and/or performed each year by matching them to the specific areas of responsibility of each individual consultant; the precise responsibilities will vary between hospitals and between consultants.

• The specimen examples shown in the Table will in some instances be an underestimate of the number of examinations (column 2) that will be performed by an individual because he or she may choose to increase the number of sessions devoted to reporting and procedural work from six NHDs (District General Hospital) to seven or eight NHDs per week (Ref. 5). This may be entirely proper. However, these consultants and their clinical director will be aware of the other contractual responsibilities which need to be met (additional to reporting and procedural work) since sessional time needs to be apportioned to on call, research, teaching, management, clinical conferences, and clinical audit (Ref. 25). It needs to be emphasised that time for contemplative study and keeping up to date (Ref. 26) is essential but is often not catered for (Ref. 27). This time, which is separate from reporting, procedural work and the other contractual duties, is necessary in order to address the need for professional and personal development (Ref. 27), which includes the acquisition of new skills in a systematic way. Consultants need to make time available for these personal development needs since they are often quite different to those addressed by CME which frequently focuses mainly, and sometimes solely, on clinical skills already acquired (Ref. 27).

• All health care tasks are demanding and these demands are compounded when rapid and radical changes affect the work and responsibilities of doctors. Each new task requires new time (Ref. 30). Maintaining the balance between competing commitments requires not only constant attention but also the introduction of appropriate and effective adjustments which will ensure that the best use is made of scarce personal resources – including the crucial asset of professional enthusiasm (Ref. 30). Health Service managers need to be aware that performance indicators per se may be of limited use in determining value for money (Refs 23 and 31). Vaughan and Higgs (Ref. 30) emphasise that the simplistic application of such indicators does not place any value on the richness and variety of the skills that doctors and other professionals provide, and it is therefore essential that the profession maintains its confidence in respecting, and also in defending, its tradition of setting the proper boundaries for the job (Ref. 30). Energy and creativity are inherent to the practice of medicine, and these features must be recognised and a value placed upon them; if this does not happen then professional commitment will cease to flourish.

• For the illustrations in the Table on page 274, the number of working weeks per annum has been taken as approximating to 45 (allowing for holiday and study leave (Refs 28 and 29), but not for Bank Holidays and sickness). It has been advised that a consultant at a District General Hospital should carry out reporting and procedural work during the equivalent of six NHDs per week, and that the figure for a consultant at a teaching hospital should be equivalent to five NHDs per week (Ref. 24). One NHD is 3.5 hours.

continued

Radiology Workload

Table

These figures are provided as an example of how the number of examinations expected per annum can be estimated by a prospective and separate assessment of each consultant's actual clinical practice. *These figures relate to these particular consultants only. In all other hospitals a prospective assessment would be expected to produce different numbers for each individual consultant.*

Seven of the Consultants working in a DGH[1]	Expected examinations per year *(Approximate range)*[6,7]
Dr A • Barium enemas @ 1 NHD @ 6–8 patients per NHD • IVUs and small bowel barium examinations @ 2 NHDs @ 6–8 patients per NHD • Plain film reporting (and mammography) @ 3 NHDs @ 20–25 cases per hour[2]	10,300————12,900
Dr B • CT @ 2 NHDs @ 10 patients per NHD • Ultrasound @ 2 NHDs @ 10–15 patients per NHD[3] • Plain film reporting @ 2 NHDs @ 25–30 cases per hour	9,700————11,700
Dr C • Vascular and interventional radiology @ 4 NHDs @ 3 patients per NHD • Plain film reporting @ 2 NHDs @ 25–30 cases per hour	8,500————10,000
Dr D • CT @ 2 NHDs @ 6 patients per NHD[3] • Ultrasound @ 1 NHD @ 10–15 patients per NHD[3] • Barium meals @ 1 NHD @ 10 patients per NHD • Plain film reporting @ 2 NHDs @ 20–25 cases per hour[2]	7,700————9,500
Dr E • Technique based and working mainly in Ultrasound • Ultrasound examinations @ 5 NHDs @ 15–20 patients per NHD • Plain film reporting at 1 NHD @ 25–30 cases per hour	7,300————9,200
Dr F • CT @ 2 NHDs @ 10 patients per NHD • Ultrasound @ 2 NHDs @ 15–20 patients per NHD • Barium enemas @ 1 NHD @ 6–8 patients per NHD • Plain film reporting @ 1 NHD @ 25–30 cases per hour	6,500————7,800
Dr G • Technique based and working mainly in CT • Supervises and reports Helical CT (Body) @ 5 NHDs @ 10 patients per NHD • Plain film reporting at 1 NHD @ 25–30 cases per hour	6,200————7,000[4]
Total Examinations expected [5, 7, 8, 9]	56,200————68,100

continued

Notes on Table

These notes relate to the superscript numbers in the Table opposite.

(1) The details in the Table are not intended to represent the precise work pattern in a typical DGH Dpartment of Clinical Radiology; the casemix will vary between hospitals.

(2) Drs A and D report plain films at a different rate to the other doctors because the cases that are seen by them are more time consuming.

(3) Drs B and D examine fewer patients during their ultrasound sessions compared with Doctors E and F because some of their cases are more complex. The same applies to Dr D's CT sessions, as compared with Drs B, F and G.

(4) If Dr G worked solely in CT and *did not cover any plain film reporting sessions* then Dr G could perform as few as 2,700 examinations per year and this would represent a proper number of examinations consistent with the maintenance of high clinical standards.

(5) Should one of these Drs be the Clinical Director then the overall number of examinations expected during the year will be reduced by the one NHD (often, more properly, two NHDs) which will need to be allocated to these managerial duties.

(6) The *range* of the expected number of examinations per year is arrived at by taking the lowest agreed number of patients examined in all sessions and expressing this as the lowest total to be expected during the year. The highest total to be expected takes the highest agreed number of patients to be examined in all sessions. The lowest and highest number of examinations expected during a particular session are indicated in the left hand column of the Table.

(7) The range of the expected number of examinations for an individual consultant will move to the right (i.e. the upper limit will be increased) if that individual organises his or her job plan so that more than six NHDs per week are devoted to reporting or procedural work.

(8) Other examinations will need to be carried out which are not included in this Table (e.g. nuclear medicine studies, MRI examinations).

(9) Locums:

– The figures shown under Total do not include any activity by employed locum consultants.

– It cannot be assumed that a locum will possess skills which precisely duplicate those of the consultant(s) whom he or she is temporarily replacing.

continued

Radiology Workload

Resources

● **Data collection**

Departmental computer data, collected retrospectively.

● **Assistance required**

Clinical Audit Officer, to carry out the analysis.

● **Estimated radiologists' and radiographers' time to complete stages 1–3 of the first cycle**

Radiologist: 2 hours per consultant radiologist – for standard setting.

● **Other estimated costs**

None.

continued

References

1   Doctors in trouble. *The Independent Magazine*. London. 8 July 1995: 8–16.

2   Yates J. *Private Eye, Heart and Hip: Surgical Consultants, The National Health Service and Private Medicine*. Edinburgh: Churchill Livingstone, 1995.

3   Spiers J. John Yates has a powerful case, both morally and practically. *Health Service Journal* 1995;**105**:18.

4   McKee M. Medicine and Books. (Reviewing Ref. 2 above). *BMJ* 1995;**311**:637.

5   Royal College of Radiologists. *Medical Staffing and Workload in Clinical Radiology in the United Kingdom National Health Service*. London: RCR, 1993.

6   Irving H. No change is no option. *Radiology Now* 1995;**12**:17–18.

7   Witcombe B. Emotional Iteration. *RCR Newsletter* 1995;**43**:15.

8   Holl-Allen R. Cap hours and lift morale of seniors. *Hospital Doctor*, 21 September 1995. Page 11.

9   Moore W. Is the 56 hour week good for you, your family, or the NHS? *Health Service Journal* 1995;**105**:24–7.

10 O'Kelly L. Lonely life on the British treadmill. *The Observer*. London. 31 July 1994: 21.

11 Thackray J. Overworked over there. *The Observer*. London. 27 August 1995. Page 7.

12 Handy C. *Understanding Organisations*. Fourth edition. Harmondsworth: Penguin Books, 1993:chapter 3.

13 Austin Knight Ltd. *The Family Friendly Workplace*. London: Austin Knight Ltd.,1995.

14 Handy C. *Empty Raincoat: Making Sense of the Future*. London: Hutchinson, 1994.

15 Saxton, HM. Should radiologists report on every film? *Clin Rad* 1992;**45**:1–3.

16 Loughran CF. Diagnostic performance of radiographers can be improved. *BMJ* 1995;**310**:1003.

17 Robertson, M. Technicians could be trained to interpret screening mammograms. *BMJ* 1995;**310**:1003.

18 Mannion RAJ *et al*. A Barium Enema Training Programme for Radiographers: A pilot study. *Clin. Radiol*. 1995;**50**:715–9.

19 Salvage, J. What's happening to nursing? The traditional division of labour between nurses and doctors is changing. *BMJ* 1995;**311**:274–5.

20 Maynard A. Continuous Tory Revolution, *Health Service Journal* 1995;**105**:19.

21 Wilson-Barnet J, Beech S. Evaluating the Clinical Nurse Specialist: A review. *Int J Nurs Stud* 1994;**31**:561–71.

22 Walmsley, J, Reynolds J, Shakespeare P, Woolfe, R, eds. *Health, Welfare and Practice: Reflecting on roles and relationships*. London: Sage, 1993.

23 Pollock AM, Vickers N. Measuring NHS activity. *BMJ* 1995;**311**:454.

24 Royal College of Radiologists. Guidelines for a model job description for a Consultant post in Clinical Radiology. *RCR Newsletter* 1990;**24**:34–38.

25 Royal College of Radiologists. Guide to Job Descriptions, Job Plans and Work Programmes. *Clinical Radiology*. RCR: London, 1990.

26 Lilley R. Editorial. Aim to give dodgy doctors the bullet. *Hospital Doctor*. 7 September 1995, page 10.

27 Easmon C. Refocusing the training. The IHSM Network 1995;**2**:4–5.

continued

References (continued)

28 Hospital Medical and Dental staff: Study leave. HC (79) 10. April 1979.

29 NHS Hospital Medical and Dental Staff (England and Wales). Terms and conditions of service. April 1986. HMSO.

30 Vaughan C, Higgs R. Doctors and Commitment: nice work – shame about the job. *BMJ* 1995;**311**:1654–5

31 Radical Statistics Health Group. NHS indicators of success: what do they tell us? *BMJ* 1995;**310**:1045–9.

Proforma

Ten randomly selected reports made by each specialist registrar in years 1–3 of training will be analysed as follows. The examinations will be selected from:

- IVUs
- Barium examinations
- Non Obstetric Ultrasound
- CT

The results of the analysis will be anonymised.

FOR EACH REPORT THE FOLLOWING IS RECORDED

Trainee code # _____ Examination: _____

Patient name and x-ray number: _____ Date: _____

THE RADIOLOGY REPORT MET THE FOLLOWING REQUIREMENTS:	YES	NO	N/A
1 Precise imaging examination stated.			
2 Drugs/intravenous contrast media recorded, including the dose. Note: paediatric gastrointestinal examinations – the type and volume of alimentary medium was recorded.			
3 The description: 3.1 was brief and succinct 3.2 recorded relevant positive and negative findings 3.3 provided relevant differential diagnosis 3.4 made appropriate suggestion regarding useful further imaging.			
4 A Conclusion/Impression/Summary: 4.1 was included 4.2 included only the significant diagnostic possibilities 4.3 avoided any repetition of the description 4.4 addressed any question posed on the request form.			
TOTAL NUMBER OF (YES AND N/A) POINTS			
MAXIMUM POSSIBLE NUMBER OF (YES AND N/A) POINTS	10		

Resuscitation Skills

Levels of competence

LEVEL 1   ALL STAFF, INCLUDING CLERKS AND SECRETARIES.

BASIC LIFE SUPPORT (BLS). AS DEFINED BY REF. 1

SUMMARY:

- Recognition of unconsciousness.
- Manual clearance of airway.
- Maintenance of airway.
- Look, listen and feel for respiration and pulse.
- Perform mouth-mouth ventilation, if required.
- Perform cardiac massage, if required.
- Location of "panic buttons".
- Knowledge of crash call number.
- Location of resuscitation equipment in the department.

LEVEL 2   NURSES AND RADIOGRAPHERS

LEVEL 1 PLUS THE FOLLOWING:

BLS WITH AIRWAY ADJUNCTS

- Use of airways, face masks, suction equipment and oxygen.
- Knowledge of site of storage of equipment for treatment of a pneumothorax.

RCR/RCA WORKING PARTY REPORT (Ref. 2) recommendations:

- Monitoring of sedated patients.
- Detection of adverse reactions to both contrast media and sedative drugs.

LEVEL 3   DOCTORS

LEVEL 2 PLUS THE FOLLOWING:

- Defibrillation techniques.
- Management of pneumothorax.

  i.e. Adopt British Thoracic Society Guidelines (Ref. 3).

- Recognition and management of adverse reactions to contrast media and sedative drugs.

REFERENCES

1. The European Resuscitation Council Basic Life Support Working Group. Guidelines for basic life support. *BMJ* 1993;**306**:1587–9.

2. Royal College of Anaesthetists and Royal College of Radiologists. *Sedation and Anaesthesia in Radiology. Report of a Joint Working Party.* London: RCR, 1992.

3. Miller AC *et al.* Guidelines for the Management of Spontaneous Pneumothorax. *BMJ* 1993;**307**:114–16.

Further information (page 1)

The standard has six separate elements:

I SLIDES – TEXT

All slides will meet the following criteria (Ref. 1):

- Maximum content for a landscape slide
  - five words in title, five lines, five words per line

- Text will be legible from the back of the hall
  - bold and bright lettering
  - space between lines is *at least* the height of a capital letter

- No (apologies for) out of date text

- No faded slides – faded as a result of frequent use

II SLIDES – TABLES/DIAGRAMS

- All slides will meet the following criteria (Refs 1–3):

MAXIMUM CONTENT		
Tables	–	five vertical columns, five horizontal lines (including the title)
Graphs	–	five different lines or curves.
Bar charts	–	10 bars per cluster or five segments per bar
Pie charts	–	five wedges

- Essential information will be presented so as to achieve:
  - simplicity, brevity, lucidity

(If the data cannot be kept simple *then the speaker will have broken it down into a series of slides*.)

- All tables will have been specially prepared – not photographed from a book or journal.

- A maximum of three colours per slide.

- Apologetic expressions. **None of the following will be used by the speaker**: "there are a lot of data on this slide but I only want you to look at the two left hand columns ...", "I know you probably can't read this slide" or "this slide is a bit difficult but bear with me".

continued

Speaker's Technique

Further information (page 2)

III DOUBLE PROJECTION

All slides will meet the following criteria (Refs 2 and 4):

- The standard will be the same as for single projection (*vide supra*).

- The other half of a pair of slides will contain only a simple diagram/radiograph or a maximum of eight words.

- Apologetic expressions. **None of the following will be used by the speaker**: "Keep the slide on the left until I tell you, and change the one on the right" or "no, change the one on the right … Can we go back on the right … sorry, no the left".

- The number of slides – single projection – or number of slide pairs for double projection will not exceed a ratio of one slide (or pair) per minute of lecture time.

IV LASER USE

- The laser pointer will be used with maximum simplicity – either to point directly at a word, to point at a graph, or to trace an outline on a radiograph.

- The pointer will not be used erratically, i.e. rapid and disjointed circular, or back and forth, movements.

V THE SPEAKER'S VISIBILITY/APPROACH

- the speaker will not become disembodied but will remain in contact with the audience. He/she should be visible for all or most of the time (Ref. 3). This requires:
  - adequate lighting
  - bold, legible, and bright slides so that it is not necessary to extinguish the lights completely

- the speaker will speak to (i.e. face) the audience. The presentation will not be delivered whilst the speaker stares at the slides for 40–100% of the time.

VI THE RADIOGRAPHS

- Neither too pale nor too dark.

REFERENCES

1 Kodak Ltd. *Let's Stamp out Awful Lecture Slides. Kodak Publication No. S-22 (H)*. Hemel Hempstead: Kodak, 1982.

2 Heyderman E et al. Down with double projection. *The Lancet* 1991;**338**:1463.

3 Cull P. Making and using medical slides. *BJ Hosp Med* 1992;**47**:132–5.

4 Harden RM. Twelve tips on using double slide projection. *Med Teach* 1991;**13**:267–71.

Evaluation sheet

The appointed assessor will complete this evaluation sheet.

(NB Some course organisers may choose to audit only one or two of the six separate elements indicated below.)

Code number for speaker or lecture: _____

THE FOLLOWING CRITERIA WERE MET:	YES	NO	N/A*
1 Slides – text 1.1 The majority of slides had no more than five words in the title and no more than five words per line with a maximum of five lines. 1.2 Text legible from back of the hall. 1.3 All slides were bright (ie. no faded slides).			
2 Slides – tables/diagrams 2.1 Tables: no more than five vertical columns and five horizontal lines. 2.2 Graphs: no more than five different lines or curves. 2.3 Bar charts: no more than 10 bars per cluster. 2.4 Pie charts: no more than five wedges. 2.5 Data did not require breaking down further so as to achieve simplicity, brevity, lucidity. 2.6 All tables specially prepared (i.e. no photographs from books/journals). 2.7 No more than three colours per slide. 2.8 None of the apologetic expressions (see standard) were used.			
3 Double projection 3.1 Content for each pair did not exceed the standard (see 2.1–2.7 above) 3.2 None of the apologetic/critical instructions to the projectionist (see standard) were used.			
4 Laser use 4.1 No waving or chaotic movements. 4.2 Brightness of laser dot was adequate.			
5 The speaker's visibility/approach 5.1 The speaker was visible for most of the time. 5.2 Lighting of hall was adequate. 5.3 Speaker faced the audience for 80% or more of the presentation.			
6 Radiographs 6.1 Not too pale. 6.2 Not too dark.			
TOTAL YES AND N/A POINTS [MAXIMUM 20]			
(*n/a = not applicable)	YES	NO	N/A*

Questionnaire (page 1)

THE EFFECTIVENESS OF A RADIOLOGY TEACHING COURSE

Example : A Course in Accident and Emergency Radiology.

The questionnaire is given to all registrants for completion at the end of the course.

EVALUATION QUESTIONNAIRE

- This questionnaire is designed to be anonymous and to elicit your feelings toward various aspects of the course.

- Please circle or mark the appropriate figure to indicate your opinion of each item.

- Your feedback will help us to develop a more effective course for future participants.

1 Present post (no need to name your hospital) ⎯⎯⎯⎯⎯⎯⎯⎯⎯⎯⎯⎯⎯⎯⎯⎯⎯

2 How did you rate the course overall?

Very poor   *Very good*

1 ⎯⎯⎯⎯⎯ 2 ⎯⎯⎯⎯⎯ 3 ⎯⎯⎯⎯⎯ 4 ⎯⎯⎯⎯⎯ 5 ⎯⎯⎯⎯⎯ 6

3 How far did the programme fulfil your expectations?

Complete failure   *Fully*

1 ⎯⎯⎯⎯⎯ 2 ⎯⎯⎯⎯⎯ 3 ⎯⎯⎯⎯⎯ 4 ⎯⎯⎯⎯⎯ 5 ⎯⎯⎯⎯⎯ 6

4 Quality of the pre-course information?

Very poor   *Very good*

1 ⎯⎯⎯⎯⎯ 2 ⎯⎯⎯⎯⎯ 3 ⎯⎯⎯⎯⎯ 4 ⎯⎯⎯⎯⎯ 5 ⎯⎯⎯⎯⎯ 6

5 Quality of the lectures?

Very poor   *Very good*

1 ⎯⎯⎯⎯⎯ 2 ⎯⎯⎯⎯⎯ 3 ⎯⎯⎯⎯⎯ 4 ⎯⎯⎯⎯⎯ 5 ⎯⎯⎯⎯⎯ 6

6 How useful was the small group work?

Not useful   *Very useful*

1 ⎯⎯⎯⎯⎯ 2 ⎯⎯⎯⎯⎯ 3 ⎯⎯⎯⎯⎯ 4 ⎯⎯⎯⎯⎯ 5 ⎯⎯⎯⎯⎯ 6

continued

Questionnaire (page 2)

7 Which **TWO** aspects of the teaching programme did you find **MOST** helpful?

   7.1 _____

   7.2 _____

8 Which **TWO** aspects of the teaching programme did you find **LEAST** helpful?

   8.1 _____

   8.2 _____

9 Quality of the handouts/notes?

Very poor   *Very good*

1 _____ 2 _____ 3 _____ 4 _____ 5 _____ 6

10 What is your opinion of the venue and the facilities?

Very poor   *Very good*

1 _____ 2 _____ 3 _____ 4 _____ 5 _____ 6

11 How did you rate the catering?

Very poor   *Very good*

1 _____ 2 _____ 3 _____ 4 _____ 5 _____ 6

12 How did you hear about this course?

13 Any additional comments?

(use reverse if necessary)

Thank you!

Information

Recommendations from the Royal College of Radiologists.

See: Curriculum Framework for Training in Clinical Radiology. The Royal College of Radiologists, 1994.

Item 1.5 All trainees will have regular assessments and career guidance. Responsibilities for overseeing these will rest with the Head of Training, who will collaborate with the Regional Post-Graduate Education Adviser and Post-Graduate Dean. College Tutors should also be involved in the process. The College also strongly encourages the inclusion of an external assessor (such as a consultant radiologist from another training programme) in the annual assessment of trainees.

Item 3.7 The (annual) assessments will aim to:

- document experience gained during the preceding year.

- ensure that targets set during the previous year have been met.

- review clinical and technical skills as well as success in acquiring the general professional development skills.

- identify any deficiencies in expected knowledge/experience so that these may be remedied in the ensuing year.

- set targets for the forthcoming year.

- offer career guidance/counselling as appropriate.

Questionnaire

NOTE:
- This questionnaire will be circulated by, returned to, and analysed by the hospital's Clinical Audit Department.
- The results will be anonymised.

Number of years/months since commencing training in Clinical Radiology.

_____ Years _____ Months

	YES	NO	NOT SURE
1 My local assessment took place during the last 12 months.			
2 The Head of Training was present.			
3 The RCR Tutor was present.			
4 An outside Consultant was present.			
5 The purpose and method of this assessment had been explained and discussed with me individually and/or with all the trainees as a group.			
6 I understand that the assessment has been documented and is available for inspection by me – if I wish to see it.			
7 The changes agreed at the time of the assessment (affecting my personal education plan) have subsequently been addressed.			
TOTAL			

Any Comments:

_____

_____

_____

_____

_____

_____

_____

Thank you

_____

Clinical Audit Co-ordinator

Questionnaire (page 1)

Trainees' perceptions of the local training arrangements in clinical audit.

Note: (1) Part of this questionnaire is based on some of the concepts outlined in: Firth-Cozens J, Storer D. Registrars' and Senior Registrars' perceptions of their audit activities. Quality in Health Care 1992;**1**:161–4.

(2) The questionnaire will be circulated by, returned to, and analysed by the hospital's Clinical Audit Department.

(3) The results will be anonymised.

PART (A)

1 Number of years/months since commencing training in clinical radiology.

_____ Years _____ Months

	Yes	No	Sort of
2 I fully understand the meaning of clinical audit; I can explain it and define it.			
3 Clinical audit is educationally valuable.			
4 Clinical audit is beneficial to patient care.			
5 There is enough time within my timetable to carry out the clinical audit tasks assigned to me.			
6 There has been adequate support from the hospital Clinical Audit Department to help with the audit projects assigned to me.			
7 There is regular feedback on the results of audits carried out by members of the Department of Clinical Radiology.			
8 Clinical audit is carried out within our department for reasons other than solely meeting the requirements made by the Royal College of Radiologists and/or our local managers and/or the local purchasers of health care.			

continued

Questionnaire (page 2)

PART (B)

very poor   very good

9   The arrangements for the involvement
of all clinical professionals in the
department's audit activity is: 1 ___ 2 ___ 3 ___ 4 ___ 5 ___ 6

10 The leadership provided by the lead
consultant in clinical audit is: 1 ___ 2 ___ 3 ___ 4 ___ 5 ___ 6

11 The organisation of the annual forward
programme in clinical audit is: 1 ___ 2 ___ 3 ___ 4 ___ 5 ___ 6

12 Attendance by the radiology trainees at
the regular clinical audit meetings is: 1 ___ 2 ___ 3 ___ 4 ___ 5 ___ 6

13 Attendance by the radiology consultants
at the regular clinical audit meetings is: 1 ___ 2 ___ 3 ___ 4 ___ 5 ___ 6

14 Please add any comments here:

_____

_____

_____

_____

_____

_____

_____

Thank you for your help.

Project code number

APPENDIX

Questionnaire

NOTE:
- All trainees will be sent a questionnaire.
- The questionnaire will be circulated by, returned to, and analysed by the hospital's Clinical Audit Department.
- The results will be anonymised.

PART A

1.0 Number of years / months since commencing training in the Department of Clinical Radiology.

_____ Years _____ Months

	YES	NO	NOT SURE
2.1 A named consultant is in charge of the overall organisation of research within the training programme.			
2.2 There is protected time within my timetable which represents time to be allocated to research.			
2.3 There is a regular meeting dedicated to research.			
2.4 Adequate facilities and funds are available for preparing posters, slides and prints in order to present or publish research studies.			
2.5 Statistical help / advice is available.			
2.6 The selection of journals related to diagnostic imaging and held in the department or in the hospital library is satisfactory.			
2.7 The selection of diagnostic imaging text books held in the department or in the hospital library is satisfactory and up to date.			

PART B

	Very poor				Very good

2.8 The involvement of most of our trainers (i.e. the consultants) in the department's research activity (i.e. support, encouragement, advice, ideas) is: 1 __ 2 __ 3 __ 4 __ 5 __ 6

2.9 The leadership provided by the consultant in charge of the overall organisation of research is: 1 __ 2 __ 3 __ 4 __ 5 __ 6

2.10 The organisation of the annual forward programme of research which involves the trainees is: 1 __ 2 __ 3 __ 4 __ 5 __ 6

2.11 Attendance by the radiology trainees at the regular departmental research meetings is: 1 __ 2 __ 3 __ 4 __ 5 __ 6

3.0 Add any comments here:

_____

_____

_____

Please return this form to the Clinical Audit Office   **Project Code number** [   ]

Protocol

THE LOCAL PROTOCOL FOR CARRYING OUT AN IVU IN A PATIENT SUSPECTED OF ACUTE RENAL COLIC

1   Preliminary radiograph.

2   15 minutes full length film following 50 mls of IV contrast medium.

3   If normal excretion – **STOP**.

4   If abnormal excretion and a definite calculus in the renal pelvis or ureter on the preliminary film – **STOP**.

5   If abnormal excretion, but uncertainty whether there is a calculus on the preliminary film, then obtain additional images at 30 minutes and thereafter at 2, 4, 8, 12 and 24 hours until the level of obstruction is identified. When the level of obstruction is identified – **STOP**.

Ward Nurses and X Ray Procedures

X ray procedures questionnaire (page 1)

We would be grateful if you would complete this short questionnaire so that we can find out whether the information about radiological procedures for in-patients is available to you, known to you, and understood by you.

The questionnaire is anonymous and you will not be identifiable either by ward or name. This questionnaire is being used as part of a clinical audit process.

Please place a tick next to your chosen answer.

1 Do you know of a source of information (concerning Radiological Procedures) which is available to you on the ward?

       YES   NO

   i) If available, is this

     – On paper?   YES   NO

     – On computer?   YES   NO

   ii) If available is it easily accessible to you?

       YES   NO

4 Please consider some of the radiological procedures which may be carried out on in-patients:

   a) **For patients who are to undergo CT Scanning:**

     i)   What is the imaging system used in this procedure?

Choose one answer

       – Ultrasound

       – X rays

       – Nuclear Isotopes

       – Don't know

     ii)   Will an injection be given?

Choose one answer.

       – Always

       – Sometimes

       – Never

       – Don't know

continued

X ray procedures questionnaire (page 2)

b) **For patients who are to undergo an IVU**

(Intravenous Urogram – also known as an IV Pyelogram or IVP)

i) The contrast medium given to the patient is:

– Taken by mouth

– Put into the bladder

– Injected IV

– Don't know

ii) The contrast medium is:

– Colourless

– Blue

– Green

– Don't know

iii) The preparation prior to the examination is:

Choose one answer

– Nothing to drink for 6 hours prior to the examination

– Nothing to eat or drink for 4 hours

– Drink 2 litres of fluid in the 2 hours before the examination

– Don't know

c) **For patients booked for a Barium Meal examination**

i) The preparation procedure is:

Choose one answer

– Nothing to drink for 6 hours prior to the examination

– Nothing to eat or drink after midnight

– No fatty foods after midnight

– Don't know

ii) After the examination the patient is advised to:

Choose one answer

– Drink nothing for 4 hours

– Double their fluid intake for the next 24 hours

– Stay in bed for 6 hours

– Don't know

Thank you for your time and help.

Please send the completed questionnaire to:

The Audit Officer

_____

(A pre-addressed envelope is included with this questionnaire.)

Proformas

Planning a new audit project

● Refer to page xxv *How to Use this Book*

AN AUDIT OF ...

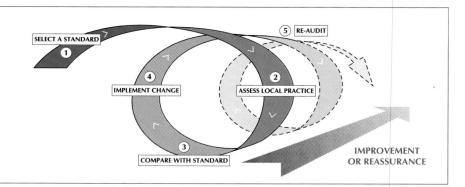

SELECT A STANDARD
1

5 RE-AUDIT

4
IMPLEMENT CHANGE

2
ASSESS LOCAL PRACTICE

3
COMPARE WITH STANDARD

IMPROVEMENT OR REASSURANCE

BACKGROUND

● Why this audit is worth doing

● Staff groups involved

THE CYCLE

1 **THE STANDARD** ☐ National ☐ Local

● The agreed standard is as follows

2 **ASSESSMENT OF LOCAL PRACTICE**

● The indicator(s)

● Data items to be collected

● Suggested number of patients / cases / episodes _____

3 **COMPARISON OF THE FINDINGS WITH THE STANDARD**

THE CYCLE (continued)

4 CHANGE

● Some suggestions as to what *might* be needed if the standard is not met

5 RE-AUDIT (a) If the standard is met: _____ months

(b) If the standard is not met: _____ months

RESOURCES NEEDED

THE DATA will be collected by ...

- ☐ Computer records
- ☐ Review of images
- ☐ Review of reports

- ☐ Review of requests
- ☐ Ongoing data recording
- ☐ Questionnaire

- ☐ Other (specify)
  _____
  _____

ASSISTANCE from ...

- ☐ None
- ☐ Secretarial
- ☐ Audit office
- ☐ Medical records

- ☐ Data analysis
- ☐ Software (off shelf)
- ☐ Software (customised)
- ☐ Clinical professionals

- ☐ Other (specify)
  _____
  _____
  _____

TIME to help complete stages 1–3 of the first cycle

RADIOLOGIST	RADIOGRAPHER	OTHER (specify)
Approx _____ hrs per week	Approx _____ hrs per week	Approx _____ hrs per week
for _____ weeks	for _____ weeks	for _____ weeks
= total _____ hours	= total _____ hours	= total _____ hours

COSTS (stages 1–3 of the cycle) apart from radiologists' / radiographers' time

- ☐ None/minimal
- ☐ Temporary staff
- ☐ Information technology

- ☐ Other (specify)
  _____
  _____

Stages 1–3 of the first cycle

£ _____

USEFUL REFERENCES

THE INDIVIDUAL(S) RESPONSIBLE FOR CARRYING OUT THIS AUDIT

● Lead individual _____ Tel. No _____

● Others

Recording the results of a completed audit (The *complete* cycle)

AN AUDIT OF ...

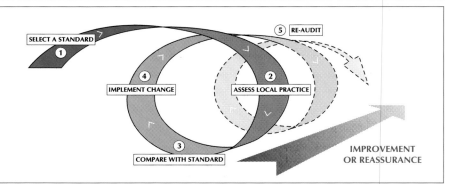

BACKGROUND

● **Why this audit is worth doing**

THE CYCLE

1 **THE STANDARD**   ☐ National   ☐ Local

2 **LOCAL PRACTICE WAS ASSESSED AS FOLLOWS**

● **The indicator(s)**

● **Data items collected**

● **Number of patients / cases / episodes** _____

3 COMPARISON OF THE FINDINGS WITH THE STANDARD FOUND THAT ...

4 THE CHANGES INTRODUCED ...

(a) were the responsibility of _____

(b) were as follows ...

5 RE-AUDIT occurred after _____ months

THE RESOURCES USED

THE DATA was collected by ...

☐ Computer records ☐ Review of requests ☐ Other (specify)

☐ Review of images ☐ Ongoing data recording _____

☐ Review of reports ☐ Questionnaire _____

ASSISTANCE

☐ None ☐ Data analysis ☐ Other (specify)

☐ Secretarial ☐ Software (off shelf) _____

☐ Audit office ☐ Software (customised) _____

☐ Medical records ☐ Clinical professionals _____

TIME to help complete stages 1–3 of the first cycle

RADIOLOGIST	RADIOGRAPHER	OTHER (specify)
Approx ____ hrs per week	Approx ____ hrs per week	Approx ____ hrs per week
for ____ weeks	for ____ weeks	for ____ weeks
= total ____ hours	= total ____ hours	= total ____ hours

COSTS (stages 1–3 of the cycle) apart from radiologists' / radiographers' time

☐ None / minimal ☐ Other (specify) Stages 1–3 of the first cycle

☐ Temporary staff _____

☐ Information technology _____ £ _____

DETAILS OF THE COMPLETED CYCLE are shown on the next page

RESULTS OF THE COMPLETED CYCLE

5 RE-ASSESS LOCAL PRACTICE

6 COMPARE WITH STANDARD

IMPROVEMENT OR REASSURANCE

● Local practice was re-assessed _____ months after the changes were introduced

● Date of re-assessment _____

● Data items collected

● Assistance obtained from

● Costs (stages 5–6) of the re-audit (not including the cost of the changes) £ _____

COMPARISON OF FINDINGS ...

(a) with the standard, shows that ...

(b) with the previous audit findings, shows that ...

(c) indicates that an improvement on the previous audit findings has occurred ☐ Yes ☐ No

A FURTHER AUDIT WILL OCCUR ...

in _____ months   to start (date) _____

USEFUL REFERENCES

THE AUDIT WAS CARRIED OUT BY ...

Stages 1–4 _____   Stages 5–6 _____

Hospital _____

Address _____   Telephone No: _____

_____   _____

_____   Fax No: _____

A COPY OF THIS FORM HAS BEEN ...

☐ placed in the Department's Audit File

☐ sent to the Hospital's Audit Office

☐ sent to the Clinical Audit Unit at the RCR

APPENDIX

Further information (audit design / questionnaire / analysis of results / introduction of change)
is included as follows ...

PROFORMAS

How and when this recipe book has been used

- Please record your use of this book.
- Your record will assist The Royal College of Radiologists when it carries out an audit (during 1996–1997) of the usefulness of this book.
- These two pages will enable you to collect some of the data necessary for this audit.

DATE	WHO USED THIS BOOK?	WHY WAS THE BOOK USED?

DATE	WHO USED THIS BOOK?	WHY WAS THE BOOK USED?

Index

Index by Topic

Topic	Audit Recipe Number
28 day rule	Pregnancy Questioning 76
A&E	Clinical Information from A&E 13
	Emergency Skull Radiography 25
	Foreign Body Radiography 32
	Majax Call-In 59
	Radiography Referral Rate from A&E 82
Abdomen	GP Abdominal Ultrasound 36
Absenteeism	Employee Satisfaction 26
Angioplasty	Iliac Angioplasty Outcome 39
Audit of audit	Accepting Recommendations for Change 1
	Attendance at Audit Meetings 4
	Radiological Errors 83
	Trainee Assessment 103
	Trainees and Audit 104
	Your Use of this Book 115
Audit organisation	Accepting Recommendations for Change 1
	How to Use this Book (page xxiii)
	Proforma for planning a new audit project (page 296)
	Proforma for recording the results of a completed audit project (page 298)
	Trainees and Audit 104
Barium	Barium Enema Fluoroscopy Times and Doses 5
	Barium Meal Reports 6
	Barium Meal Training 7
Biopsy	CT Guided Biopsies 18
	Percutaneous Biopsy Procedures 73
	Pneumothoraces Post Lung Biopsy 74
Bladder	Bladder Cancer CT 8
Brain	Head CT – Lens Exclusion 38
	Urgent CT Brain Scans and LPs 109
Cancer	Bladder Cancer CT 8
	Cancer Staging 10
Cardiac	Cardiac Catheterisation 11
	Coronary Angiography 16
Change	Accepting Recommendations for Change 1
Chest	Chest Radiographs: Skin Dose and Film Quality 12
	GP Chest Radiography 37
	ITU and CCU Chest Radiographs 48
	Pre-Op Chest X Rays for Elective Surgery 77
Children	Painful Hip 65
Clinical Director	Accepting Recommendations for Change 1
	Courtesy 17
	Employee Satisfaction 26
	Patient Privacy 67
	Patient Satisfaction I 68
	Patient Satisfaction II 69
	Patient Satisfaction in the Over 60s 70
	Patient's Charter 71
	Radiology Workload 87
	Security – Staff ID 95
	Your Use of this Book 115

Topic	Audit Recipe Number
Communications	Courtesy 17
	In-Patient Information Letters 41
	Radiologists' Availability 85
	Reporting Skills 90
	Speaker's Technique 96
	Teaching Course Assessment 102
Complications	Percutaneous Biopsy Procedures 73
	Pneumothoraces Post Lung Biopsy 74
	Resuscitation Skills 92
Consent	Consent for a Radiological Examination 14
Contrast media	IVU Radiograph Series 51
	Leg Venograms and Patient Management 53
	Low Osmolar Contrast Media 54
	Urography In Renal Colic 110
Courtesy	Courtesy 17
CT	Bladder Cancer CT 8
	Cancer Staging 10
	CT Guided Biopsies 18
	CT – Ward Staff Knowledge 19
	Head CT – Lens Exclusion 38
	Radiation Dose to Radiologists during CT Injections 80
	Urgent CT Brain Scans and LPs 109
Dark room	Dark Room Safety 20
Delegation	Radiology Reporting by Other Doctors 86
DVT	Doppler in DVT 23
	Leg Venograms and Patient Management 53
Education	Attendance at Audit Meetings 4
	Barium Meal Reports 6
	Barium Meal Training 7
	CT – Ward Staff Knowledge 19
	Fire Training 31
	Gall Bladder Ultrasound 33
	Journal Use 52
	Lung Scan Reports 57
	Radiological Errors 83
	Radiology Workload 87
	Radiology Reporting by Other Doctors 86
	RCR Guideline Distribution 88
	Reporting Skills 90
	Resuscitation Skills 92
	Speaker's Technique 96
	Study Leave for Consultants 99
	Study Time for Trainees 100
	Teaching Course Assessment 102
	Trainee Assessment 103
	Trainees and Audit 104
	Trainees and Research 105
	Ward Nurses and X Ray Procedures 114
Equipment	Adequate Completion of Radiology Request Forms 2
	Interventional Radiology Packs 46
	Resuscitation Equipment 91
Errors meeting	Radiological Errors 83
Eye	Head CT – Lens Exclusion 38
	Radiation Dose to Radiologists during CT Injections 80
Film processing	Air Quality in the Process Area 3

Topic	Audit Recipe Number	Topic	Audit Recipe Number
Film retrieval	Film Envelope Availability 29 Image Labelling and Identification 40 Missing Films 61 Return of ICU Radiographs 93		GP Chest Radiography 37 Image Labelling and Identification 40 ITU and CCU Chest Radiographs 48 Pre-Op Chest X Rays for Elective Surgery 77
Fire	Fire Training 31	Lung	Lung Scan Reports 57
Foreign bodies	Foreign Body Radiography 32		Lung Scintigraphy 58 Pneumothoraces Post Lung Biopsy 74
Gallbladder	Gall Bladder Ultrasound 33		see: Chest
Gonad	Gonad Protection I 34 Gonad Protection II 35	Major accident	Majax Call-In 59
GP issues	Barium Meal Reports 6 GP Abdominal Ultrasound 36 GP Chest Radiography 37	Mammography	Double Reading Of Mammograms 24 Mammography 60
Guidelines	Bladder Cancer CT 8 Emergency Skull Radiography 25 GP Chest Radiography 37 Lumbar Spine 55 Pre-Op Chest X Rays for Elective Surgery 77 Radiography in Acute Back Pain 81 Radiography Referral Rate from A&E 82 RCR Guideline Distribution 88 Urgent CT Brain Scans and LPs 109 Urography In Renal Colic 110	Meetings	Attendance at Audit Meetings 4 Speaker's Technique 96
		MRI	MRI Patients and Metal 62
		Neuroradiology	Emergency Skull Radiography 25 Head CT – Lens Exclusion 38 Lumbar Spine 55 Lumbar Spine Radiation Dose 56 Neural Tube Defect 63 Swimmer's Views 101 Urgent CT Brain Scans and LPs 109
Gynaecological	Transvaginal Ultrasound 106		
Health & safety	Air Quality in the Process Area 3 Dark Room Safety 20 Fire Training 31 Radiation Dose to Radiologists during CT Injections 80 Resuscitation Equipment 91 Resuscitation Skills 92 Staff Radiation Dose In Angiography 98	Nuclear medicine	Bone Scintigraphy Images 9 Finger Doses 30 Lung Scan Reports 57 Lung Scintigraphy 58 Radiologist Response Time 84 Ventilation and Perfusion Scintigraphy 111 Vetting Nuclear Medicine Requests 112
Hip	Painful Hip 65	Nursing	CT – Ward Staff Knowledge 19
In-patient	In-Patient Information Letters 41 In-Patient Reporting I 42 In-Patient Reporting II 43		Interventional Radiology Packs 46 Interventional Radiology – Care of the Patient 45 Patient Privacy 67 Resuscitation Skills 92 Ward Nurses and X Ray Procedures 114

Interventional	CT Guided Biopsies 18
	Iliac Angioplasty Outcome 39
	Insertion of Oesophageal Stents 44
	Interventional Radiology Packs 46
	Interventional Radiology – Care of the
	  Patient 45
	IVC Filter Outcome 49
	Percutaneous Biopsy Procedures 73
	Pneumothoraces Post Lung Biopsy 74
	Staff Radiation Dose in Angiography 98
		Obstetric	Fetal Abdominal Circumference
			  Measurements 27
			Fetal Anomaly Scan 28
			Neural Tube Defect 63
			Pelvimetry 72
			Second Trimester Screening 94

ITU	ITU and CCU Chest Radiographs 48 Return of ICU Radiographs 93	Organisation	Courtesy 17 Department Opening Hours 21 Film Envelope Availability 29 Image Labelling and Identification 40 In-Patient Information Letters 41 In-Patient Reporting I 42 In-Patient Reporting II 43 Missing Films 61 Patient Arrival Times 66 Portering 75 Private Hospital Examinations 78 Radiologist Response Time 84 Radiologists' Availability 85 Radiology Workload 87 RCR Guideline Distribution 88 Return of ICU Radiographs 93 Security – Staff ID 95 Ultrasound Organisation 107
IVU	IVU Examination Times 50 IVU Radiograph Series 51 Urography in Renal Colic 110		
Jaundice	Ultrasound Scanning in Obstructive Jaundice 108		
Kidney	IVU Examination Times 50 IVU Radiograph Series 51 Urography in Renal Colic 110		
Labelling	Bone Scintigraphy Images 9 Chest Radiographs: Skin Dose and Film Quality 12		

Index by Topic (continued)

Topic	Audit Recipe Number
Out-of-hours	Out-of-Hours Imaging 64
	Urgent CT Brain Scans and LPs 109
Outcome	Iliac Angioplasty Outcome 39
	IVC Filter Outcome 49
Over 60s	Patient Satisfaction in the Over 60s 70
Patients – how they are treated	
	Consent for a Radiological Examination 14
	Courtesy 17
	Department Opening Hours 21
	Fetal Anomaly Scan 28
	In-Patient Information Letters 41
	Interventional Radiology – Care of the Patient 45
	Patient Arrival Times 66
	Patient Privacy 67
	Patient Satisfaction I 68
	Patient Satisfaction II 69
	Patient Satisfaction in the Over 60s 70
	Patient's Charter 71
	Private Patient Satisfaction 79
	Waiting and Appointment Times 113
Porterage	Portering 75
Pregnancy	Pregnancy Questioning 76
Privacy	Patient Privacy 67
Private hospital	Private Hospital Examinations 78
	Private Patient Satisfaction 79
Prostate	Investigation of Prostatism 47
Purchaser issues	
	Patient's Charter 71
	Radiology Workload 87
Questionnaire	Bone Scintigraphy Images 9
	Courtesy 17
	GP Chest Radiography 37
	ITU and CCU Chest Radiographs 48
	Lung Scan Reports 57
	MRI Patients and Metal 62
	Patient Satisfaction I 68
	Patient Satisfaction II 69
	Patient Satisfaction in the Over 60s 70
	Pregnancy Questioning 76
	Reporting Skills 90
	Speaker's Technique 96
	Study Leave for Consultants 99
	Teaching Course Assessment 102
	Trainee Assessment 103
	Trainees and Audit 104
	Trainees and Research 105
	Your Use of this Book 115
Radiation dose	Barium Enema Fluoroscopy Times and Doses 5
	Cardiac Catheterisation 11
	Chest Radiographs: Skin Dose and Film Quality 12
	Coronary Angiography 16
	Finger Doses 30
	Gonad Protection I 34
	Gonad Protection II 35
	Head CT – Lens Exclusion 38
	Lumbar Spine Radiation Dose 56
	Missing Films 61
	Pelvimetry 72

Topic	Audit Recipe Number
	Radiation Dose to Radiologists during CT Injections 80
	Staff Dosimetry 97
	Staff Radiation Dose in Angiography 98
Radiation protection	
	Gonad Protection I 34
	Gonad Protection II 35
	Head CT – Lens Exclusion 38
Radiography	Foreign Body Radiography 32
	Image Labelling and Identification 40
	ITU and CCU Chest Radiographs 48
	Lumbar Spine 55
	Missing Films 61
	Reject Analysis of Radiographs 89
	Swimmer's Views 101
Records	Contrast and Drug Recording 15
Rejects	Reject Analysis of Radiographs 89
Renal	IVU Examination Times 50
	IVU Radiograph Series 51
	Urography In Renal Colic 110
Repeat films	Missing Films 61
	Reject Analysis of Radiographs 89
Reporting	Barium Meal Reports 6
	Do the Reports Address the Questions? 22
	In-Patient Reporting I 42
	In-Patient Reporting II 43
	Lung Scan Reports 57
	Reporting Skills 90
Requests	Adequate Completion of Radiology Request Forms 2
	Clinical Information from A&E 13
	Do the Reports Address the Questions? 22
	GP Chest Radiography 37
	Out-of-Hours Imaging 64
	Urgent CT Brain Scans and LPs 109
	Vetting Nuclear Medicine Requests 112
Research	Radiology Workload 87
	Trainees and Research 105
Research and Audit	
	See How to Use this Book (page xxiii)
Resuscitation	Resuscitation Equipment 91
	Resuscitation Skills 92
Risk and Risk Management	
	Consent for a Radiological Examination 14
	Contrast and Drug Recording 15
	Dark Room Safety 20
	Fire Training 31
	Pelvimetry 72
	Pneumothoraces Post Lung Biopsy 74
	Pregnancy Questioning 76
	Radiation Dose to Radiologists during CT Injections 80
	Resuscitation Equipment 91
	Resuscitation Skills 92
Satisfaction	Employee Satisfaction 26
	Patient Satisfaction I 68
	Patient Satisfaction II 69
	Patient Satisfaction in the Over 60s 70
	Private Patient Satisfaction 79

Topic	Audit Recipe Number
Security	Security – Staff ID 95
Service level	Department Opening Hours 21
	In-Patient Reporting I 42
	In-Patient Reporting II 43
	IVU Examination Times 50
	Lung Scintigraphy 58
	Patient Arrival Times 66
	Patient's Charter 71
	Private Hospital Examinations 78
	Radiologist Response Time 84
	Radiologists' Availability 85
	Radiology Workload 87
	Waiting and Appointment Times 113
Skill-mix	Radiologist Response Time 84
	Radiology Workload 87
	Radiology Reporting by Other Doctors 86
Skull	Emergency Skull Radiography 25
Specialist Registrars	
	Barium Meal Reports 6
	Barium Meal Training 7
	Gall Bladder Ultrasound 33
	Journal Use 52
	Reporting Skills 90
	Resuscitation Skills 92
	Speaker's Technique 96
	Study Time for Trainees 100
	Teaching Course Assessment 102
	Trainee Assessment 103
	Trainees and Audit 104
	Trainees and Research 105
Spine	Lumbar Spine 55
	Lumbar Spine Radiation Dose 56
	Radiography in Acute Back Pain 81
	Swimmer's Views 101
Staff protection	Air Quality in the Process Area 3
	Dark Room Safety 20
	Employee Satisfaction 26
	Fire Training 31
	Radiation Dose to Radiologists during CT Injections 80
	Radiology Workload 87
	Resuscitation Equipment 91
	Resuscitation Skills 92
	Security – Staff ID 95
	Staff Radiation Dose in Angiography 98
	Study Leave for Consultants 99
	Ultrasound Organisation 107
Staffing	Attendance at Audit Meetings 4
	Employee Satisfaction 26
	Out-of-Hours Imaging 64
	Radiologist Response Time 84
	Radiologists' Availability 85
	Radiology Workload 87
	Radiology Reporting by Other Doctors 86
	Staff Dosimetry 97
	Study Leave for Consultants 99
	Trainees and Audit 104
Staging	Bladder Cancer CT 8
	Cancer Staging 10
Thyroid	Radiation Dose to Radiologists during CT Injections 80

Topic	Audit Recipe Number
Training	Barium Meal Reports 6
	Barium Meal Training 7
	Gall Bladder Ultrasound 33
	Journal Use 52
	Reporting Skills 90
	Resuscitation Skills 92
	Speaker's Technique 96
	Study Time for Trainees 100
	Teaching Course Assessment 102
	Trainee Assessment 103
	Trainees and Audit 104
	Trainees and Research 105
U/S	Doppler in DVT 23
	Fetal Abdominal Circumference Measurements 27
	Fetal Anomaly Scan 28
	Gall Bladder Ultrasound 33
	GP Abdominal Ultrasound 36
	Investigation of Prostatism 47
	Neural Tube Defect 63
	Painful Hip 65
	Second Trimester Screening 94
	Transvaginal Ultrasound 106
	Ultrasound Organisation 107
	Ultrasound Scanning in Obstructive Jaundice 108
Uroradiology	Bladder Cancer CT 8
	Investigation of Prostatism 47
	IVU Examination Times 50
	IVU Radiograph Series 51
	Urography in Renal Colic 110
Venography	Doppler in DVT 23
	Leg Venograms and Patient Management 53
Workload	Employee Satisfaction 26
	GP Abdominal Ultrasound 36
	GP Chest Radiography 37
	In-Patient Reporting I 42
	In-Patient Reporting II 43
	Lung Scintigraphy 58
	Out-of-Hours Imaging 64
	Portering 75
	Pre-Op Chest X Rays for Elective Surgery 77
	Private Hospital Examinations 78
	Radiography Referral Rate from A&E 82
	Radiology Workload 87
	Radiology Reporting by Other Doctors 86
	Study Time for Trainees 100
	Trainee Assessment 103
	Urgent CT Brain Scans and LPs 109

INDEX

Index by Author and Hospital or Address

All numbers quoted are Recipe numbers.

Addenbrooke's Hospital, Cambridge CB2 2QQ

Dr L Berman   Barium Meal Training 7
Painful Hip 65

Dr A Fink   Painful Hip 65

c/o A Alagappa & Co., 4 Kingsend, Ruislip, Middlesex

Mr R Glanville-Brown
Courtesy 17

Bolton General Hospital, Bolton BL1 4QS

Dr M Gowland   Fetal Abdominal Circumference
Measurements 27
Fetal Anomaly Scan 28
Neural Tube Defect 63
Second Trimester Screening 94
Transvaginal Ultrasound 106

6 Carmalt Gardens, London SW15

Mr R Knowles   Teaching Course Assessment 102

Clementine Churchill Hospital, Harrow-on-the-Hill HA1 3RX

Mr K Tyrrell   Private Hospital Examinations 78
Private Patient Satisfaction 79

Dundee Royal Infirmary, Dundee DD1 9ND

Dr A Cook   Foreign Body Radiography 32
Iliac Angioplasty Outcome 39
Investigation of Prostatism 47
IVC Filter Outcome 49
IVU Radiograph Series 51
Low Osmolar Contrast Media 54
Mammography 60
Radiography in Acute Back Pain 81
RCR Guideline Distribution 88
Return of ICU Radiographs 93

Glenfield Hospital, Leicester LE3 9QP

Dr R Keal   Cardiac Catheterisation 11

Dr C Reek   Cardiac Catheterisation 11

Guy's & St Thomas' Hospital, London SE1 9RT

Dr P Scott-Mackie
Study Time for Trainees 100

Dr L Apthorp   Barium Meal Reports 6

Hull Royal Infirmary, Hull HU3 2KZ

Dr J Dyet   Iliac Angioplasty Outcome 39
IVC Filter Outcome 49

Mrs V Benneson
Foreign Body Radiography 32

Ms C Lowley   Foreign Body Radiography 32

Dr A Nicholson   Iliac Angioplasty Outcome 39
IVC Filter Outcome 49

Dr M O'Sullivan
Foreign Body Radiography 32

Inverclyde Royal Hospital, Greenock PA16 0XL

Dr R Shaw   Pelvimetry 72

Northwick Park & St Mark's Hospitals, Harrow HA1 3UJ

Dr A Brown   Employee Satisfaction 26

Mrs J Brown   Coronary Angiography 16
Staff Radiation Dose in Angiography 98

Mrs J Chapman   Patient Satisfaction I 68
Patient Satisfaction II 69

Dr G de Lacey   Employee Satisfaction 26
Missing Films 61
Patient Satisfaction I 68
Patient Satisfaction II 69
Radiology Workload 87
Reporting Skills 90
Speaker's Technique 96
Study Leave for Consultants 99
Teaching Course Assessment 102
Trainee Assessment 103
Trainees and Research 105
Ultrasound Organisation 107

Mr R Douglas-Law
Dark Room Safety 20

Dr E Elson   Journal Use 52
Resuscitation Equipment 91
Resuscitation Skills 92

Dr C Green   Finger Doses 30
Lumbar Spine Radiation Dose 56

Dr P Gibson   Barium Meal Training 7
Bladder Cancer CT 8
Gall Bladder Ultrasound 33

Dr D Johnson   Attendance at Audit Meetings 4
Trainees and Audit 104

Dr T Johnson-Smith
Painful Hip 65
Staff Dosimetry 97
Ultrasound Organisation 107

Dr G Kaplan   Clinical Information from A&E 13
Coronary Angiography 16
GP Chest Radiography 37
ITU and CCU Chest Radiographs 48
Lumbar Spine Radiation Dose 56
Staff Dosimetry 97
Ultrasound Organisation 107

Ms A McQueen   Employee Satisfaction 26
Missing Films 61
Patient Satisfaction I 68
Patient Satisfaction II 69
Patient's Charter 71

Dr M O'Driscoll   Resuscitation Equipment 91
Resuscitation Skills 92

Ms A Paris   Patient's Charter 71

Dr D Remedios Bone Scintigraphy Images 9
Clinical Information from A&E 13
CT Guided Biopsies 18
Emergency Skull Radiography 25
Journal Use 52
Lung Scintigraphy 58
Radiological Errors 83
Reporting Skills 90
Resuscitation Equipment 91
Resuscitation Skills 92
Trainee Assessment 103
Trainees and Research 105

Dr N Ridley Barium Meal Reports 6
Doppler in DVT 23
Speaker's Technique 96
Trainees and Research 105

Ms J Ryder Bone Scintigraphy Images 9
Finger Doses 30
Lung Scan Reports 57
Lung Scintigraphy 58
Radiologist Response Time 84

Mrs K Rose Employee Satisfaction 26

Dr B Shah Study Time for Trainees 100
Urography in Renal Colic 110

Dr M Shaikh Bladder Cancer CT 8
Gall Bladder Ultrasound 33
Urgent CT Brain Scans and LPs 109
Urography In Renal Colic 110

Miss M Saint Leger
Dark Room Safety 20

Mr L Taylor Lumbar Spine Radiation Dose 56

Mrs S Taylor ITU and CCU Chest Radiographs 48

Dr L S Wilkinson
Barium Meal Reports 6
Doppler in DVT 23
Interventional Radiology – Care of the Patient 45
Lung Scan Reports 57
Radiologist Response Time 84
Speaker's Technique 96

Mr M West Staff Radiation Dose in Angiography 98

Nottingham City Hospital, Nottingham NG5 1PB

Dr B Barry Chest Radiographs: Skin Dose and Film Quality 12

Dr N Broderick Chest Radiographs: Skin Dose and Film Quality 12

Mrs H Brooks Interventional Radiology Packs 46

Dr A Ceccherini Out-of-Hours Imaging 64

Mr A Cooper MRI Patients and Metal 62

Mr P Davis Reject Analysis of Radiographs 89

Dr M de Nunzio
In-Patient Information Letters 41

Dr K Dunn Contrast and Drug Recording 15

Dr A Manhire Adequate Completion of Radiology Request 2
Air Quality in the Process Area 3
In-Patient Information Letters 41
Insertion Of Oesophageal Stents 44
Interventional Radiology Packs 46

Leg Venograms and Patient Management 53
MRI Patients and Metal 62
Out-of-Hours Imaging 64
Pneumothoraces Post Lung Biopsy 74

Dr A Nair Pneumothoraces Post Lung Biopsy 74

Dr D Rose Leg Venograms and Patient Management 53
Ventilation and Perfusion Scintigraphy 111

Mr A Rogers Chest Radiographs: Skin Dose and Film Quality 12

Mr G Ramsey Air Quality in the Process Area 3
Reject Analysis of Radiographs 89

Mrs C Simons Interventional Radiology Packs 46

Mrs C Soar Adequate Completion of Radiology Request Forms 2
Contrast and Drug Recording 15
Patient Arrival Times 66
Waiting and Appointment Times 113

Dr K Stevens Insertion of Oesophageal Stents 44

Dr D Wheatley Patient Arrival Times 66
Waiting and Appointment Times 113

Nuffield Orthopaedic Centre, Oxford OX3 7LD

Dr E McNally Emergency Skull Radiography 25

The Queen Elizabeth Hospital, King's Lynn PE30 4ET

Dr M Brindle In-Patient Reporting I 42
Radiology Reporting by Other Doctors 86

Royal Bournemouth Hospital, Bournemouth BH7 7DW

Miss D Bratcher IVU Examination Times 50
Dr M Creagh-Barry
Double Reading of Mammograms 24

Miss A Forbes Patient Satisfaction in the Over 60s 70

Miss S Grundy CT – Ward Staff Knowledge 19

Mr G Horne Department Opening Hours 21

Dr S Jones Ultrasound Scanning in Obstructive Jaundice 108

Dr J Tawn Barium Enema Fluoroscopy Times and Doses 5
CT – Ward Staff Knowledge 19
Department Opening Hours 21
Double Reading of Mammograms 24
IVU Examination Times 50
Patient Satisfaction in the Over 60s 70
Percutaneous Biopsy Procedures 73
Pre-Op Chest X Rays for Elective Surgery 77
Radiography Referral Rate from A&E 82
Vetting Nuclear Medicine Requests 112

The Royal College of Radiologists, London W1N 4JQ

Clinical Radiology Audit Sub-Committee
Accepting Recommendations for Change 1
Your Use of this Book 115

Royal Free Hospital, London NW3 2QG

Dr G Dodge Urgent CT Brain Scans and LPs 109

Dr R Warwick Urgent CT Brain Scans and LPs 109

I N D E X

Index by Author and Hospital or Address (continued)

St Bartholomew's Hospital, London EC1A 7BE

Dr L Jelly   Study Time for Trainees 100

Dr L King   Study Time for Trainees 100

Dr S Sohaib   Study Time for Trainees 100

St George's Hospital, London SW17 0QT

Dr A Joseph   Radiology Workload 87

Dr G O'Sullivan Urgent CT Brain Scans and LPs 109

St Mary's Hospital, London W2 1NY

Dr M de Jude   Urgent CT Brain Scans and LPs 109

Dr A Newman-Saunders
          Urgent CT Brain Scans and LPs 109

Southampton General Hospital, Southampton SO9 4XY

Dr M Sampson   GP Abdominal Ultrasound 36

University of Wales College of Medicine, Cardiff CF4 4XW

Professor G Roberts
          Reporting Skills 90

West Suffolk Hospital, Bury St Edmunds IP33 2QZ

Mr N Beeton   Image Labelling and Identification 40

Dr R Godwin   Cancer Staging 10
          Consent for a Radiological Examination 14
          Do the Reports Address the Questions? 22
          Film Envelope Availability 29
          Head CT – Lens Exclusion 38
          Image Labelling and Identification 40
          In-Patient Reporting II 43
          Majax Call-In 59
          Patient Privacy 67
          Pregnancy Questioning 76
          Radiologists' Availability 85
          Security – Staff ID 95

Mr B Hall   Portering 75

Mrs C Hepburn Gonad Protection I 34

Mr W King   Portering 75

Mrs S Peagram Gonad Protection II 35

Mr P Smith   Portering 75

Ms D Spencer   Head CT – Lens Exclusion 38

Miss J Wright   Fire Training 31
          Security – Staff ID 95

Sister C Whelan Patient Privacy 67
          Ward Nurses and X Ray Procedures 114

Wycombe General Hospital, High Wycombe HP11 2TT

Dr C Charlesworth
          GP Abdominal Ultrasound 36
          Lumbar Spine 55
          Pelvimetry 72
          Radiation Dose to Radiologists during CT
          Injections 80
          Swimmer's Views 101

Index by Type of Audit

Outcome Audits

Department Opening Hours 21
Iliac Angioplasty Outcome 39
Insertion of Oesophageal Stents 44
IVC Filter Outcome 49
Missing Films 61
Neural Tube Defect 63
Patient Privacy 67
Patient Satisfaction I 68
Patient Satisfaction II 69
Patient Satisfaction in the Over 60s 70
Pneumothoraces Post Lung Biopsy 74
Private Patient Satisfaction 79
Ultrasound Scanning in Obstructive Jaundice 108

Structure Audits

CT – Ward Staff Knowledge 19
Dark Room Safety 20
Film Envelope Availability 29
Gonad Protection I 34
Interventional Radiology – Care of the Patient 45
Interventional Radiology Packs 46
Majax Call-In 59
Resuscitation Equipment 91
Study Leave for Consultants 99
Study Time for Trainees 100
Teaching Course Assessment 102
Trainee Assessment 103
Trainees and Audit 104
Trainees and Research 105
Ward Nurses and X Ray Procedures 114
Your Use of this Book 115

Process Audits

All the other Recipes in this book are Process Audits. (See Glossary page xv for a discussion of the use of the terms Structure, Process and Outcome to classify audits.)